PRA[illegible]

A Short His[illegible]

"Thrilling . . . a bracing [illegible] rned [from] 'archaeogenetics'—the study [illegible] . . . Krause and Trappe capture the excitement of this young field." —*The Wall Street Journal*

"Krause and Trappe make complicated scientific processes accessible to lay leaders and offer hope that the ongoing study of ancient genetics and the development of new technologies will help to fight pathogens including Covid-19. The result is a captivating and informative look at the origins and future of humanity." —*Publishers Weekly*

"A splendid account of human origins, migrations, and pathogens from the perspective of DNA evidence. Unique among other world histories . . . provides new avenues of understanding the human past." —*Library Journal*

"*A Short History of Humanity* is an eloquent and timely reminder that viruses and other pathogens of infectious disease are merely fellow-travelers in an epic journey that began when the first human migrants left Africa around 200,000 years ago. The solution to pandemics is not to close borders in the hope of keeping viruses out but to recognize that we are a fundamentally peripatetic species united in our shared genetic inheritance and common humanity."
—Mark Honigsbaum, author of *The Pandemic Century*

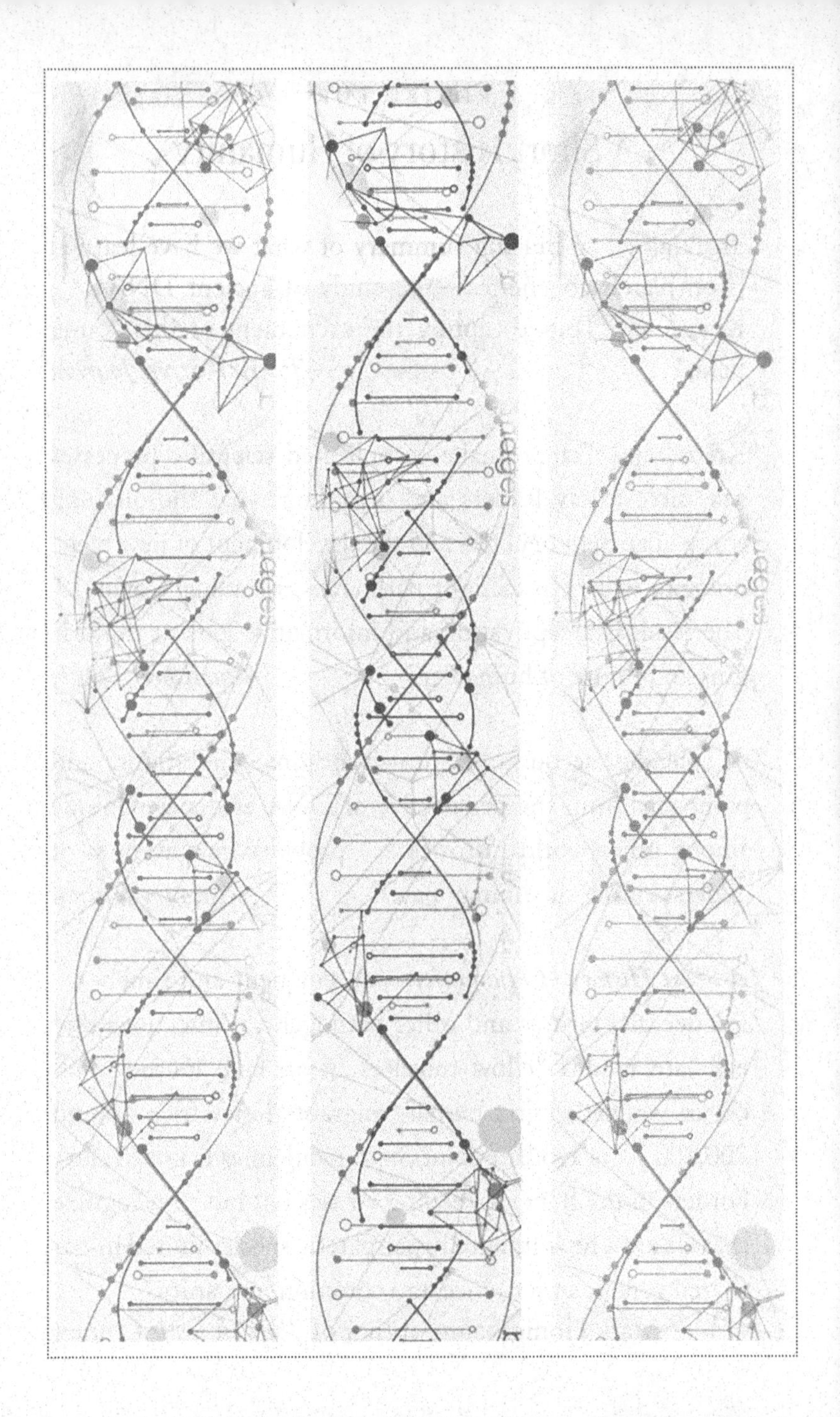

A SHORT HISTORY OF HUMANITY

A NEW HISTORY OF OLD EUROPE

Johannes Krause and
Thomas Trappe

TRANSLATED BY CAROLINE WAIGHT

RANDOM HOUSE • NEW YORK

2022 Random House Trade Paperback Edition

Published in the United States by Random House,
an imprint and division of
Penguin Random House LLC, New York.

RANDOM HOUSE and the HOUSE colophon are registered
trademarks of Penguin Random House LLC.

Originally published in German as *Die Reise Unserer Gene*
by Propyläen Verlag in 2019, copyright © 2019
by Ullstein Buchverlage GmbH, Berlin.
English translation first published in 2021 by WH Allen,
an imprint of Ebury. Ebury is part of the
Penguin Random House group of companies.

ISBN 978-0-593-22943-9
Ebook ISBN 978-0-593-22944-6

Printed in the United States of America
on acid-free paper

randomhousebooks.com

Frontispiece art from istock

Book design by Barbara M. Bachman

CONTENTS

INTRODUCTION

AFTER THE PANDEMIC, NOTHING WILL BE AS IT was. A previously unknown illness has swept across Europe like a storm, and wherever it has raged, entire social systems have been utterly changed. Humanity has known the brutal power of pathogens before. Four thousand eight hundred years ago, a sickness that began in the East almost wholly transformed the genetic structure of people living in Europe; Eastern Europeans took control of the continent, ultimately ushering in the Bronze Age. This sickness was the plague. It ravaged Europe probably for the first time during the Stone Age, then repeatedly devastated the continent throughout its subsequent history, each attack worse than the last. Even then, people tried to curb the disease by closing borders, implementing quarantines, and reducing trade. Though they did not understand what caused it, they were able to observe its spread at close quarters. In Venice during the Middle Ages, for instance, which was in those days an economic powerhouse, trade almost ground to a halt. Countless people died in the streets, their numbers now revealed only by mass graves. Until recently, we had hoped the story would never be repeated. But in 2020, images were broadcast of trucks carrying the bodies of deceased COVID-19 victims to crematoriums and mass graves all over the world—in Bergamo, New York, and other cities and towns.

It would take nearly 5,000 years for us simply to discover the existence of the Stone Age plague. Armed with revolutionary technology, we ground ancient bones to dust and distilled from their DNA the stories told in this book. Archaeogenetics, a young branch of science, uses methods developed in the field of medicine to decode ancient genomes, some of which are hundreds of thousands of years old. The field is still only just taking off, yet already its contribution to our store of knowledge is vast. Using human bones from the distant past, we can uncover not only the genetic profiles of the dead but also how their genes spread across Europe—in other words, when our ancestors arrived and where they came from. Today we are also able to sift out DNA from bacteria that cause deadly diseases—not just the plague—from blood dried in teeth hundreds and thousands of years old. Thanks to archaeogenetics, history and the story of disease in Europe can be told in an entirely new way. And it turns out that two of the biggest issues the world is currently facing are constants in human history: deadly pandemics and constant migration.

When this book was first published in February 2019, the political discussion in Germany was still very much shaped by the "refugee crisis" of 2015. Readers and the press focused mainly on the passages that dealt with the archaeogenetic evidence of countless waves of past migration across the globe and constant genetic intermingling among our ancestors. A little more than a year later, as the entire planet reels from the ruthless SARS-CoV-2 virus, that particular crisis has fallen somewhat out of the spotlight despite the countless precarious journeys made by migrants every day. And although there's no real comparison between the far more lethal plague and the novel coronavirus, there is one parallel: invisible pathogens have always been capable of stopping a society in its tracks from one day to the next, jolting us out of our sense of unassailability into a paralyzing helplessness. What the consequences of the current pandemic will be for humankind, no one is currently in a position to say. In this book, however, we will show what impact such events had on the earliest denizens of Europe. It would be presumptuous to draw political conclusions from this and apply them to the present day—that is not the task of archaeogenetics—but we can help to clarify a few things. We can try to understand the world for what it undoubtedly is: a site of progress that has spanned millennia, progress that without migration and human mobility would have been impossible. Time and time again populations have been ultimately strengthened by adversity, even after catastrophic pandemics. In this sense, at least, we should make no secret of hoping that history will repeat itself.

The initial pages of this book explore the great waves of migration that have shaped Europe since its earliest times, as well as those that began there and founded the Western world. We are concerned, among other things, with the ever-present route through the Balkans and the conflicts that have accompanied migration since time immemorial. We will explain why the first Europeans had dark skin, and why we can use DNA analyses to pinpoint individual Europeans on a map but not to draw sharp genetic lines around ethnic groups—and certainly not nationalities. We trace an arc from the Ice Age, when Europeans' genetic journey began, to the present day, where we are on the verge of taking evolution into our own hands. Our book seeks to address not only political controversies but also the contributions of archaeogenetics to our understanding of the history of Europe.

This new information does not provide black-and-white answers. It's clear that migrants shaped Europe, and there's no question the resulting upheavals caused a good deal of suffering—for hunter-gatherers, for instance, who were displaced by Anatolian farmers. It's also true that the history of migration has always also been the history of deadly diseases. We know that people open to migration will find arguments in this book to support their beliefs, as will those in favor of stricter border control. Instead, our hope is that after reading our book no reader will dispute mobility's integral part of human nature. Ideally, you will be persuaded that a global approach to society—an approach that has been field-tested for thousands of years—will also be the key to progress in the future. The times we are living in have placed human mobility—with all its complications and side effects—under a powerful magnifying glass. On the one hand, the spread of COVID-19 would be unthinkable without it. On the other, placing large-scale limitations on migration for only a few weeks led to social upheaval and economic collapse, the worldwide effects of which will be felt in our everyday lives for years to come.

Two authors have contributed to this book. The first is Johannes Krause, who assumes the role of first-person narrator from the next chapter onward. He is one of the most established international experts in the field of archaeogenetics (for reasons of modesty this passage was written by the second author) and is director of the Max Planck Institute for Evolutionary Anthropology in Leipzig, Germany. His coauthor, Thomas Trappe, was tasked not only with compressing Krause's knowledge into a compact narrative but also with placing it in a contemporary context and framing it within ongoing political debates. Trappe has previously collaborated with Krause several times; he has also reported on nationalism and contemporary populist ideas. Over the course of many conversations, both authors realized they wanted to write a book that would bring together science and up-to-the-minute debates.

We would like to start with a whistle-stop tour of the field of archaeogenetics—and with a finger bone that altered the course of scientific understanding as well as Krause's own scientific career. Quite unexpectedly, the bone revealed a new type of hominin, indirectly revealing the affinity between early Europeans and Neanderthals. This unlikely discovery is where we choose to begin our short history of humanity.

A SHORT HISTORY OF HUMANITY

CHAPTER

I

A New Science Is Born

A SIBERIAN FINGER POINTS US TO *a new archaic human. Archaeogenetics comes alive. Geneticists are feeling the gold rush with their shiny new toys.* Jurassic Park *makes everybody go nuts. Yes, we're all related to Charlemagne. Adam and Eve didn't live together. The Neanderthal reveals an error.*

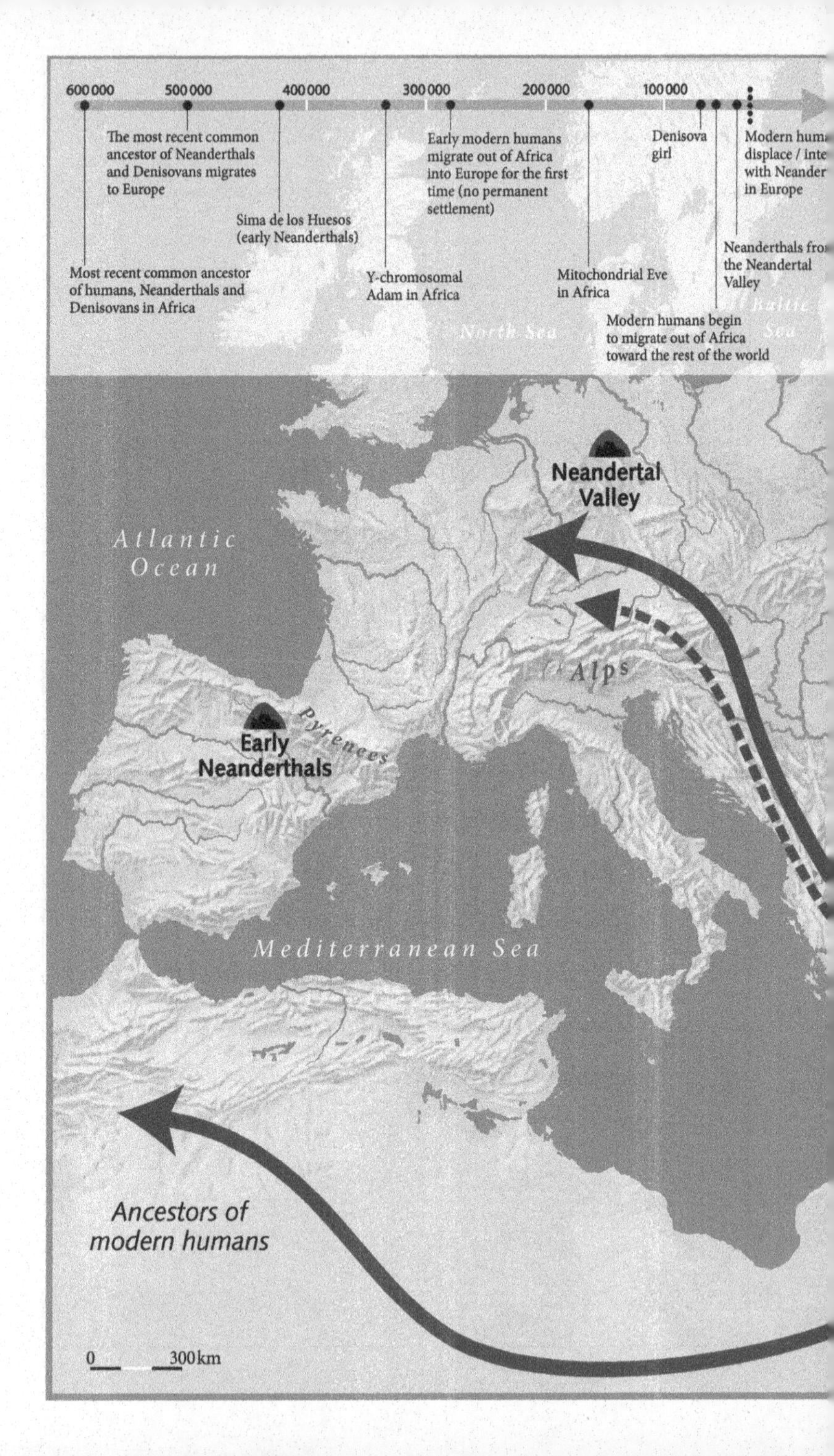

600 000
500 000
400 000
300 000
200 000
100 000
The most recent common ancestor of Neanderthals and Denisovans migrates to Europe
Early modern humans migrate out of Africa into Europe for the first time (no permanent settlement)
Denisova girl
Sima de los Huesos (early Neanderthals)
Most recent common ancestor of humans, Neanderthals and Denisovans in Africa
Y-chromosomal Adam in Africa
Mitochondrial Eve in Africa
Modern humans begin to migrate out of Africa toward the rest of the world
North Sea
Neandertal Valley
Atlantic Ocean
Alps
Pyrenees
Early Neanderthals
Mediterranean Sea
Ancestors of modern humans
0
300km

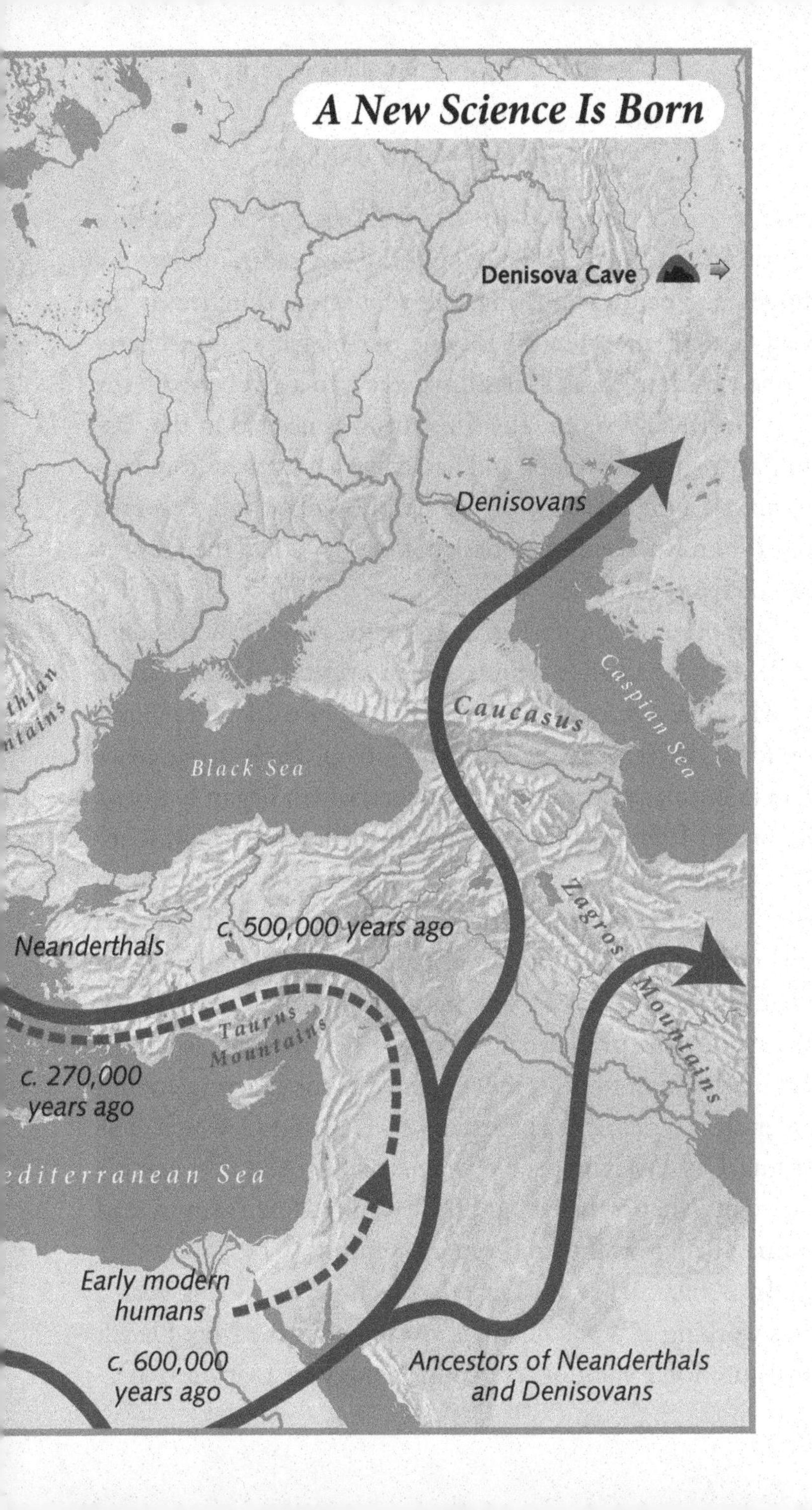
A New Science Is Born
Denisova Cave
Denisovans
Caspian Sea
Caucasus
Black Sea
Zagros Mountains
c. 500,000 years ago
Neanderthals
Taurus Mountains
c. 270,000 years ago
Mediterranean Sea
Early modern humans
c. 600,000 years ago
Ancestors of Neanderthals and Denisovans

A BONE ON MY DESK

THE FINGERTIP I FOUND ON MY DESK ONE WINTER'S morning in 2009 was really only the last sad remnant of a finger. The nail was missing, and so was the skin; it was the very end of the outermost bone, no bigger than a cherry stone. It belonged, as I later discovered, to a girl between the ages of five and seven. The fingertip was nestled in the customary padded envelope and had come a long way, from Novosibirsk. Not everyone would be pleased to find a severed digit from Russia on their desk before they'd had their morning coffee—but I was.

Almost a decade earlier, in 2000, the American president Bill Clinton had given a press conference at the White House in which he announced that, after years of work and billions of dollars invested in the Human Genome Project, our genes had at last been decoded. The project, which began ten years before, in 1990, was the first-ever international scientific research attempt to sequence all of the genes of our own species—otherwise known as the human genome. It remains one of the most ambitious and groundbreaking moments in scientific history. DNA was instantly headline news across the world: one of Germany's biggest newspapers cleared its features section to print the sequence of the human genome, an endless series of the base pairs A, T, C, and G, which constitute DNA. Many people were struck by the new significance of genetics, believing DNA would allow them to read human beings as though from a blueprint.

In 2009, science was already much closer to this goal. I was working as a postdoctoral researcher at the Max Planck Institute for Evolutionary Anthropology in Leipzig (MPI-

EVA). The institute was the world's most important research hub for scientists wanting to sequence DNA from old bones, providing them with cutting-edge technology. More than a decade of laborious genetic research had already been conducted there, research without which the finger bone on my desk could never have been used to alter our understanding of the history of human evolution. The bone, discovered in Siberia, represented the 70,000-year-old remains of a girl who belonged to a previously unknown kind of archaic hominin. It took only a few milligrams of bone powder—and a highly complex sequencing machine—to reveal this fact. Just a few years earlier it would have been technologically inconceivable to determine from such a tiny fragment whom it belonged to. Yet the bone had more to tell us. Not only did we learn what made the girl similar to human beings alive today, we learned how she was different.

ONE TRILLION A DAY

THE NOTION THAT DNA IS LIFE'S BLUEPRINT HAS BEEN around for more than a hundred years. In 1953, using pioneering work by British chemist Rosalind Franklin, American biologist James Watson and British physicist Francis Crick discovered the structure of DNA. Nine years later the two men were both awarded the Nobel Prize in Physiology or Medicine (by that point Franklin had died, passing away at the young age of thirty-seven). Ever since then, the medical community had put in the work on DNA that ultimately heralded the Human Genome Project.

In the 1980s, another milestone along the road toward decoding, or reading, DNA was reached with the development of the polymerase chain reaction.[1] This process allows us to determine the order of base pairs within a DNA molecule, and it is indispensable to sequencers today. Since the turn of the century, sequencing technology has been advancing apace. If you compare the old Commodore 64 computer with a smartphone today, you'll have an idea of how swiftly technology has progressed in the field of genetics.

Let me give you a few statistics to illustrate the scale of what we're discussing when we talk about decoding DNA. The human genome consists of 3.3 billion base pairs.[2] In 2003, when the Human Genome Project came to an end, it would have taken more than ten years to unravel the genetic code of a particular individual.[3] Today our laboratory can process a trillion base pairs every day. The throughput of these machines has increased by a factor of 100 million over the past fifteen years: currently, one sequencer can decode an extraordinary 300 human genomes in a single day. In ten years the genome of a billion people worldwide will have been decoded with some degree of certainty, and so far we've systematically underestimated the rate of technological development. DNA sequencing is becoming quicker and cheaper all the time and will soon be an option for almost everybody. Mapping out someone's DNA currently costs less than a full blood panel, so it will hardly be surprising if young parents start routinely requesting the decoded genome of their newborns. DNA sequencing offers undreamed-of possibilities—catching genetic predispositions to certain illnesses early, for example—and this potential continues to grow.[4]

While the medical community tries to improve their understanding of disease and develop new therapies and drugs

Johannes Krause extracts a DNA sample from the upper-arm bone of a Neanderthal from the Neandertal Valley, which gave the Neanderthals their name.

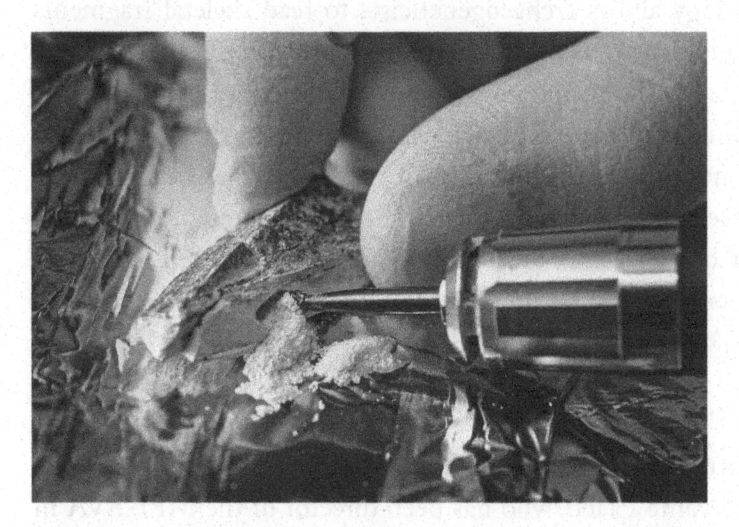

The biggest risk in DNA analysis is contamination. In order to prevent this, the bone samples are extracted while wearing protective clothing and in air-tight, isolated rooms.

by decoding the genomes of living people, archaeogeneticists are harnessing this technology to analyze archaeological finds. Old bones, teeth, or even soil samples can help archaeogeneticists to draw conclusions about the origins and genetic relationships of people long dead. This work has opened up entirely new avenues for the field of archaeology. We no longer have to rely solely on theories and interpretation; rather, genetic analyses allow us to pin down, say, migration patterns more precisely than ever before. The ability to decode ancient DNA has proved as momentous for archaeology as another technological revolution that dates back to the 1950s, when the radiocarbon method transformed the way archaeological finds were dated. Carbon dating was the first tool that enabled scientists to reliably date human remains, albeit not to the precise year.[5] DNA technology allows archaeogeneticists to read skeletal fragments and identify connections that would have been unknown even to the people to whom the bones once belonged. The remains of human beings who have lain in the earth, sometimes for tens of thousands of years, have thus become valuable messengers from the past. In these fragments the stories of our ancestors are written, stories we will tell—some of them for the first time—in this book.

HUMANS MUTANTS

ONE OF ARCHAEOGENETICS' MOST IMPORTANT PIONEERS is Svante Pääbo, who has been director of the MPI-EVA in Leipzig since 1999. Originally from a medical background, in 1984 Pääbo extracted DNA from an Egyptian mummy as part of his PhD research at Uppsala University in Sweden, working more or less secretly at night in the lab. In 2003, Pääbo accepted me as a graduate student in Leipzig. When, two years later, I was casting about for a topic for my doctoral thesis, he suggested I work with him to help decode the Neanderthal genome. Frankly, the idea sounded nuts: such an undertaking would have taken decades with the technology available at the time, not to mention that we'd have to grind to dust dozens of kilograms of precious Neanderthal bones. Still, I trusted Pääbo and his judgment; if he said the project was feasible, then I believed him. I took the offer. This turned out to be the right decision. Sequencing technology developed at breakneck speed, and we were able to conclude our work in five years—and with minimal destruction to the bones. It was during this period that, examining the piece of finger from the Altai Mountains, I discovered a new relative of modern humans—the Denisovans—which fundamentally revised our story of human history (you can read more about my discovery in the box at the end of this chapter, "Working Our Fingers to the Bone"). Bones like these are the storage media of archaeogenetics, and they can tell us all sorts of things. Was the archaic human to whom this bone belonged one of our ancestors, or did their line die out? How is their genetic makeup different from ours?

In archaeogenetics, we use the genome of archaic humans as a kind of template and compare it to our own, contemporary DNA. As researchers, we're interested in the places where the DNA doesn't line up, because these are the places where it has changed, or mutated. The word "mutation" holds unpleasant connotations for many people, but mutations are the engine of evolution; they're the reason human beings and chimpanzees stand on different sides of the fence at the zoo. Mutations are the milestones of human history.

In the time it takes you to read this chapter, the DNA in millions of your cells will undergo chemical changes—in your skin, in your gut, everywhere. Usually these changes are immediately corrected by the body, but not always. When this process goes awry, it's called a mutation. If mutations appear during the formation of germ cells—that is, in sperm or egg cells—they can be passed on to the next generation. The body has mechanisms to prevent this; as a result, fertilized germ cells with mutations that cause serious illnesses usually die. But smaller mutations often slip through the net, and a genetic change can thus, under certain circumstances, become hereditary.[6]

Genetic changes that result in more offspring tend to spread more rapidly through a population, because they're more frequently passed on. There were probably several mutations, for instance, that led to our relative hairlessness compared to apes, our distant cousins. We developed sweat glands, a more effective cooling system that allowed less hairy archaic hominins to run farther, hunt better, and escape from predators more effectively, meaning they lived longer and had better odds of reproducing. Archaic humans with genes predisposing them to hairiness, on the other hand, less able to compete for resources and outrun prey, died out.

Of course, most mutations aren't adapted to any particular purpose. Either they have no effect on the organism at all or they damage it and are therefore negatively selected, or weeded out. In the rare cases where they prove useful to survival and reproduction, they're positively selected and propagate throughout the gene pool, driving evolution permanently forward. We can thus describe evolution as interplay of random accidents during an ongoing field trial, the field trial that is humanity's life on earth.

HALF JUNK, HALF BLUEPRINT

Anyone keen to understand their genetic blueprint should remember that of the 3.3 billion base pairs in our genome, most are considered junk—only 2 percent are genes. That 2 percent codes for proteins, the building blocks of our bodies, representing the blueprint for roughly 30 trillion cells.[7] A human being has only around 19,000 genes in total, a remarkably small number. An amoeba, a tiny single-celled organism, has 30,000 genes, while some ordinary beetles have more than 50,000. By itself, the number of genes in an organism does, therefore, not dictate its complexity. In an organism with cell nuclei, information from a single gene can be combined into a wide variety of building blocks; the gene is not necessarily responsible for only one function in the body. In more primitive organisms—bacteria, for instance—one gene can usually be turned into only one building block, which usually undertakes only one task. Another way of putting this is that human genes, and the genes of most animals, are a very small team that shows outstanding teamwork.

Fifty percent of the human genome is littered with junk, much like a computer hard drive that's far too big. By "junk" I mean DNA sequences that serve no discernible purpose. Besides genes, molecular "switches" play an important role, constituting approximately 10 percent of our immensely complex genetic structure. These switches are activated and deactivated by transcription factors, ensuring that every part of the body is producing the right protein—that the cells in your fingertip, for example, don't suddenly decide they're stomach cells and start producing acids. Fundamentally, all cells in the human body contain the same information; it's a question of discerning what information is relevant.

For archaeogeneticists, the useless parts of the genome are worth their weight in gold, because they allow us to establish what we call the molecular clock. Scientists measure mutations throughout the genome, drawing conclusions about, say, when two populations diverged—the further back this happened, the more new variants will have accumulated in the DNA or altered their frequency. If the entire genome consisted of genes, the number of variants—that is, mutations—would depend not on how long ago the split occurred but on how widely the two populations' environments differed. For example, sub-Saharan Africans have fewer changes in several of their genes than the descendants of people who migrated out of Africa. This is because the migrants' genes had to adapt to new conditions, while those of the people who remained in

Africa did not, or only to a lesser degree. Yet today the genome of sub-Saharan Africans contain even more mutations compared to people outside Africa. The reason? Mutations take place in the genome's junkyard, just as they do in genes, but are not as much subject to positive or negative selection. The same number of mutations has accumulated in all of us since our most recent common ancestor, so the molecular clock still works—no matter how far the actual genes of two comparable populations have diverged. Sub-Saharan African groups separated from each other much further back in time and therefore had more time to accumulate neutral mutations.

For archaeogeneticists, looking at the genetic material of old bones is like going back in time: using the DNA of ancestors who lived many thousands of years ago, we can learn which mutations have persisted till the present day and which have disappeared. But very few bones are suitable for sequencing, because the DNA must be well preserved. Radiation, heat, and moisture are among DNA's enemies, but its greatest enemy is time. The older the bone, the less likely it is that we can extract usable DNA. And then there is the problem of contamination. Modern DNA is as easily scattered as sand in a seaside vacation home: ceaselessly and into every nook and cranny. The DNA that Svante Pääbo extracted from his mummy in the eighties, for example, almost certainly came not from Egypt but from contemporary Sweden—in other words, from him.

Nonetheless, the nineties saw an explosion in DNA sequencing. The topic, which seemed a highly promising area of research, was a crowd-pleaser, especially since broad swaths of the public believed that dinosaurs could be brought to life from ancient mosquitos trapped in amber, as depicted in Steven Spielberg's *Jurassic Park*. Many of the sequencing studies carried out on ancient DNA weren't worth the paper they were printed on. Contamination of the fossils was a perpetual problem, and even the most careful testing couldn't exclude the possibility that the fossils had come into accidental contact with bacterial and researcher-related DNA. By the end of the 1980s, there were scientific criteria regarding the authenticity of ancient DNA, yet many researchers simply ignored them.

The Denisova Cave in the Siberian Altai Mountains, where the finger bone of the Denisova girl were found. Early modern humans and Neanderthals both lived in this cave.

The revolution in sequencing technology that began in the mid-2000s made it much easier to exclude contamination, thanks to the significantly higher throughput of data. Another breakthrough occurred in 2009 during a study that I led at MPI-EVA. For the first time, we decoded the complete mitochondrial DNA (mtDNA) of an Ice Age early modern human from western Russia. The most important thing about the work from today's perspective, however, was its method. Earlier we developed a process to analyze damage in human DNA that is now standard in archaeogenetics. It involves checking for specific patterns of damage that reliably occur as DNA steadily decays over time—the more advanced the decay, the older the DNA. From this we can

Reconstruction of a Neanderthal at the Neanderthal Museum in Mettmann, Germany. Most people alive today carry some of this archaic human's DNA, although mostly it only makes up about 2 percent of our genetic material.

derive a standard. If the patterns of damage indicate we're dealing with young DNA, then the sample is contaminated and should no longer be used. With the Russian Ice Age human, we were able to use this method for the first time to prove that its DNA could not be recent human contamination but had to be old and real, producing the oldest modern human DNA sequence to date and opening the possibility of studying our ancestors directly.

THE MYTH OF TRUE ORIGINS

THE DAMAGE WROUGHT BY YEARS-OLD PSEUDOSCIENtific publications is still felt today. For an archaeogeneticist it's hair-raising to see how many misunderstandings about genetic heredity remain in circulation, and how brazenly they're touted. There are some companies enticing customers interested in genealogy with the promise that they can trace their specific "personal origins." One of these outfits even claims to have discovered the "Napoleon gene."

These genetic tests aren't cheap—some even demand four-figure sums. Unfortunately, they are absolutely not trustworthy. These companies simply compare their customers' mtDNA and Y chromosomes with the DNA of people from the past. One popular showpiece is the Celts. If a customer's mtDNA matches DNA samples from Celtic burial sites, a direct line of descent is assumed. Yet Celtic mtDNA was also around during the Stone and Bronze Ages, as well as in medieval Europe, when there was no Celtic culture anymore. Moreover, mtDNA is totally inappropriate as a means of proving a close relationship with anybody. As I discuss later in further detail, it's merely the genetic information of a single female ancestor, one among millions. The notion of Celtic "ancestry" is no more than a fairy tale. Nor will anybody keen to establish a kinship with Napoleon learn much from these tests. Napoleon shared mtDNA not only with his mother but probably with thousands of other people alive at the same time.

If you still fancy the idea of having a famous ancestor, rest assured you do: I can tell you that for free. Charlemagne, who fathered at least fourteen children more than a thousand years ago, is probably directly related to almost everyone in Europe today. It's just mathematics. From a purely arithmetical perspective, every contemporary European had many more ancestors a thousand years ago than the number of people actually alive at the time. Or, to put it another way, nearly every line of descent spanning from the age of Charlemagne to the present day leads to each and every European. The probability that this includes at least one of Charlemagne's children borders on certainty.[8] You could just as easily say that all Europeans have had common ancestors at some point in the last thousand years. At the same time, with each generation the DNA shared with an ancestor is just halved, so the genetic makeup of a particular forebear ten generations back will most probably no longer be discernible in a contemporary genome.

Of course, there are also serious companies out there that will examine the whole nuclear genome (the differences between nuclear and mtDNA will be explained at the end of this chapter) and provide valid results on genetic ancestry. This involves tracing genetic characteristics to particular regions. The principle behind it is simple: the closer the geographical proximity between two people, the more closely they are likely related, because less time has passed between their most recent common ancestor. The genetic distance between the British and the Greeks is thus the same as between the Spanish and people from the Baltics, while Central Europeans sit somewhere in between. If you plot the genetic distance between Europeans on *x*- and *y*-axes, the resulting coordinates are nearly identical to a geographical map of Europe.

This has nothing to do with our "true origins." Take the migration period, for example, a time in European history that certainly witnesses a lot of genetic exchange between various European populations, but no fundamental genetic shift. You have to go back almost 5,000 years into the past to find the last major migration movement that altered the DNA of all Europeans. The DNA of people who came from the Eastern European steppes 5,000 years ago is still one of the three dominant genetic components on the continent today. The other two originate from early hunter-gatherers and from farmers who migrated there from Anatolia. The genetic ratio of these three archaic populations can be quantified through DNA testing in every person who has European roots. By now, there are numerous companies offering this type of service.

It's doubtless interesting to discover whether you have more in common genetically with hunter-gatherers, early farmers, or steppe populations. But most commercial testing companies can offer little more than folklore, because these different components tell us solely about our genetic ancestry; they often tell us nothing about our predispositions. Even if you tested the two most genetically different people on Earth, they would still share 99.8 percent of their DNA. In fact, we differ from Neanderthals in less than half a percent of our genome. So when we talk about genetic shifts, we're really only talking about changes to a tiny fraction of DNA. Populations that lived in close geographical and genetic proximity, such as the French and the Portuguese, are thus only distinguishable through genome-wide analysis.

The genetic foundations of Europeans were laid approximately 4,500 years ago, but this doesn't mean that archaeogenetics has nothing to contribute to what happened after. The discipline is still in its early years. Until now it has focused primarily on prehistory and early history, but its next step will probably be to focus on the Sumerians, Egyptians, Greeks, and Romans. So far there has been less interest in these populations because so many written sources already offer us a wealth of historical detail, right down to what the Roman emperors ate for dinner. Most archaeogeneticists have therefore prioritized eras that lack a written record, so that we can, through our genetic research, build a picture of events that happened before anybody wrote them down.

DNA testing of ancient skeletons can also expand our knowledge of mobility during the migration period after the collapse of the Roman Empire. However, those iconic migrations of Longobards, Anglo-Saxons, or Goths were not major migration events; it was, rather, the big prehistoric migrations during the Stone and Bronze Ages that shaped European genetics. During the migration period in the sixth century CE, migrants coming to Europe would have left very few genetic fingerprints. There were simply too many people living there already for the genetic pool to be affected or remodeled by the small number of new arrivals. Even DNA from several tens of thousands of migrants would have not changed the genetic landscape of Europe. This says nothing, however, about their social, political, and cultural impact.

THE JOURNEY OF PLAGUE AND CHOLERA

ARCHAEOGENETIC RESEARCH IS NOT MERELY CONCERNED with decoding the DNA of long-dead humans. Another branch of the field has drawn considerable attention in recent years, as scientists work to decode the DNA of ancient pathogens. Migration and the interaction between populations has made modern human beings what we are today, allowing us to build a highly developed and globally interconnected civilization. Yet this mobility has come at a significant price: the spread of infectious diseases.

Countless millions have died over the millennia as a result of bacteria and viruses, fostered by two interrelated megatrends. As the world has become ever more densely settled, it is now easier and easier for pathogens to spread. And greater interaction between populations—especially through trade—was very likely to be the reason pathogens were able to reach new regions of the world.

This effect has continued well into the modern era—for instance, when indigenous North American peoples died in mass numbers from smallpox and measles after the Europeans arrived on their continent. In return, they probably gifted the Europeans with syphilis, which was then brought back home, creating immense suffering and countless victims well into the twentieth century. When Ebola broke out a few years ago in West Africa, there was worldwide fear that the virus might travel to other regions. When COVID-19 spread throughout the world in 2020, fears of a global pandemic were realized.

There is increasing evidence that early waves of migrants globally were connected to the spread of infectious disease around the world. We know that plague bacteria existed in the south of what is now Russia at least 5,000 years ago, a region that later saw a mass exodus to Central Europe, where around the same time there was a sharp decline in the size of the local population. Could it be that a recently introduced pathogen killed these people, and that they were replaced by a group who was already adapted to it? There is plenty of evidence to suggest this was the case.

The Europeans' genetic journey largely concluded around 3,000 years ago, but pathogens continued to ravage the continent well into the last century, and continue to wreak havoc today. Understanding the evolution of these tiny critters is and will continue to be a major challenge facing archaeogeneticists and the medical community. Humans may be the most successful and mobile species in world history, but in terms of genetic development, bacteria and viruses have been hot on our heels for millennia. What we know about the race between humans and these two antagonists—and what this knowledge tells us about how we can withstand them—will be described in detail in this book as we strive to understand how our shared genetic histories, and our diseases, have made us into the complex, intertwined, and resilient human beings that we are today.

WORKING OUR FINGERS TO THE BONE

The bone that appeared on my desk at the beginning of this chapter was discovered by Anatoly Derevyanko, one of Russia's most renowned archaeologists. His team found the 70,000-year-old bone in the Denisova Cave, roughly 700 meters above sea level in the Altai Mountains. The range is situated more than 3,500 kilometers east of Moscow, on the border with China, Kazakhstan, and Mongolia, in the heart of Central Asia. The Denisova Cave is not only a popular spot for day-trippers but a treasure trove for scientists, who regularly find bones and various human-made objects dating from the Stone Age there. The Siberian climate in the Altai Mountains is a huge advantage, because the cold preserves the finds exceptionally well. When I visited the region to meet Derevyanko with Svante Pääbo and a few colleagues in 2010, I learned quickly that minus forty-two degrees Celsius is when ice crystals start to form on human skin.

BACK AT THE LAB in Leipzig, the finger bone was run through processes we've conducted umpteen times. We drilled a tiny hole into the bone, mixing the resulting bone powder with a special fluid that allows us to extract the molecules of DNA. We didn't have much room for error, because we could only extract ten milligrams of bone powder—roughly one breadcrumb's worth. We assumed we were dealing with the bone of a modern human being, or perhaps with a Neanderthal's. But then the sequencer spat out the results. At first I couldn't make head or tail of them: the DNA didn't belong to either a modern human being or a Neanderthal. I assembled our team hurriedly to present the puzzling results. "Where was my mistake?" I asked. Together we examined the data, combing through it again and again, until at last we realized there was no mistake. When, later, I called my boss, I asked him to sit down: "Svante, I think we have found *Homo erectus.*" *Homo erectus* is the common ancestor shared by modern human beings and Neanderthals, and none of its DNA had ever been decoded before. We were the first researchers to do so—or so I thought at the time.

WHAT HAD WE SEEN in the finger bone DNA? It differed from the contemporary human mitochondrial DNA in twice as many positions as the Neanderthal mtDNA does from ours. This could only mean that the individual from the Denisova Cave had been on a separate evolutionary path from the Neanderthals for longer than Neanderthals and modern humans. Our current calculations suggested that two separate lines had developed from *Homo erectus* approximately 1 million years ago in Africa. One led to Neanderthals and modern human beings; the other developed into the Denisova hominin in Asia. This overturned much of the established wisdom in the field of evolutionary research, including the "fact" that no other forms of archaic hominin had lived on the planet besides early modern humans and Neanderthals 70,000 years ago.

THE DATA HAD LED us to make an error, however, one we didn't realize at the time. When we first made our results public in *Nature*, the holy grail of scientific publications, in March 2010, the world instantly came crashing down on my head. I can still remember several camera teams following us around in the lab at the same time. For a week I gave nonstop telephone interviews on the discovery of the "Denisovan," as we had called our archaic human. After only a couple of weeks, however, we began to have misgivings, wondering whether the data we'd just published was entirely correct. Or, more accurately, whether our interpretation of the data was wrong.

OUR DOUBTS ABOUT HOW we'd interpreted the Denisova DNA proved justified. The way we later uncovered the real and no less astonishing story behind the data is an example of how rapidly archaeogenetics has developed in recent years—and how many supposed certainties of the field were toppled, even those that had seemed unassailable for decades. As it turned out, our incorrect interpretation of the data enabled us to uncover an even bigger false assumption. The Denisova hominin's DNA offered us—indirectly but unambiguously—an entirely new glimpse into the settlement of Europe by modern humans. We learned that early modern humans had encountered Neanderthals there hundreds of thousands of years ago and had sex with them.

TO RECONSTRUCT THE LINEAGE of the Denisova girl for the initial publication, we used mtDNA. Mitochondrial DNA comes from an organelle that is often referred to as a cell's "powerhouse," and its mtDNA represents only a tiny fraction of our genome. Whereas today it's standard to sequence the much more extensive and relevant nuclear DNA, until 2010 it was common to use mtDNA, because it was vastly more time- and cost-efficient.[9] The downside, however, is that while mtDNA is well suited to establishing a lineage, it may not provide the full story. For one thing, all human beings inherit their mtDNA exclusively from their mother; for another, a mutation reliably appears in mtDNA only every 3,000 years on average, and is passed down to subsequent generations. This means that for 3,000 years the mtDNA passed down along a female line is identical.

IF WE COMPARE THE mtDNA of two individuals, we can figure out when their most recent matrilineal common ancestor lived—using the molecular clock. The mtDNA of all living modern human beings can be traced back to a single female ancestor, a prehistoric mother. She lived around 160,000 years ago, and in the genetics literature she's referred to as "mitochondrial Eve." She has a male counterpart, "Y-chromosomal Adam," to whom the Y chromosomes passed from father to son can be traced. This Adam lived almost 200,000 years before mitochondrial Eve, however, so we can say with certainty that they weren't a couple.[10]

THERE WAS A SIMPLE reason we didn't want to wait for the results of the nuclear DNA sequencing before publishing the first Denisova paper. Anatoly Derevyanko had sent a piece of the same finger bone to another lab besides ours, and we were afraid our colleagues would scoop us. Under normal circumstances only presenting the mtDNA shouldn't be a problem, because both mtDNA and nuclear DNA can be used to reconstruct genetic history and mostly tell the same story.[11] Nuclear DNA, however, affords significantly deeper knowledge than mtDNA but doesn't ordinarily contradict it. In the case of the Denisova girl, however, it did. The nuclear DNA revealed an entirely different story. The Denisovans branched off not from the common ancestors of modern humans and Neanderthals—that is, *Homo erectus*—but much later, from the Neanderthal line. In other words, the nuclear DNA data implied that one line initially diverged from the ancestors of modern humans, then afterward split into the Neanderthals and the Denisovans. The ancestors of Neanderthals moved to Europe, the others to Asia. This accords closely with our current knowledge. But there was still another surprise ahead, one we had to wait another six years for.

THIS CONTRADICTION BETWEEN THE nuclear and mtDNA was resolved after remains of an archaic human were found at a site in northern Spain called Sima de los Huesos (literally, "pit of bones"). A genetic examination conducted by Svante Pääbo's team in 2016 revealed that the bones were approximately 420,000 years old, and their nuclear DNA showed they had belonged to a Neanderthal. The punch line? Until then, it had been assumed that there were no Neanderthals in Europe at that time. All previous examinations of Neanderthal bones had concluded, based on mtDNA, that this type of hominin branched off from our ancestors in Africa 400,000 years ago at most. The Spanish find revealed that they had actually arrived in Europe much earlier. Clearly, somewhere along the line, a mistake had been made in the calculations.[12] The publication also observed that the Spanish Neanderthal's mtDNA did not match that extracted from other, much later Neanderthals. In fact, it most resembled the mtDNA of the Denisova girl. And that was our decisive proof that the mtDNA of late Neanderthals must come from a different source and that early Neanderthals looked like the Denisova girl.

THE ERRONEOUS INTERPRETATION IN our first Denisova publication had arisen because we used the mtDNA of late Neanderthals as a reference, which was profoundly different from mtDNA of early Neanderthals—the DNA that rather looked like the Denisovans'. Our hypothesis is now that early Neanderthals had incorporated different mtDNA into their genetic makeup at some point after the Spanish Neanderthal had died—mtDNA from an early modern human woman from Africa. An early Neanderthal in Europe or the Near East had mated with this woman, resulting in a closer relationship between late Neanderthals and modern humans. The Denisovans in Asia, however, did not mix and thus preserved a relatively close resemblance to early Neanderthals in their nuclear and mtDNA. With this new information, we could now make sense of the discrepancy between the nuclear and mtDNA. All we needed to do was revise the established timeline of human ancestry by pushing all the dates back 100,000–200,000 years. The Neanderthals and Denisovans must have parted genetic ways half a million years ago, and not, as initially assumed, 300,000 years ago, while the common lineage shared by Neanderthals and Denisovans must have branched off from that of modern humans approximately 600,000 years ago instead of 450,000.

THE DISCOVERY OF THE Denisovans affected not only the timeline of human history and my work as a researcher but also my feelings on a personal level. One of the reasons I became interested in archaic humans was that only a few streets from my parents' house in my hometown, Leinefelde, in the Thuringian region of Eichsfeld, was the birthplace of Johann Carl Fuhlrott, who discovered the Neanderthals. Fuhlrott was one of my idols growing up. Back then, I never would have dreamed that I too would discover a new hominin, the Denisovans. Furthermore, what are the odds that the two extinct hominin forms that modern humans encountered on their way out of Africa and mixed with were discovered by two gentlemen born in the same village in eastern Germany, albeit almost 200 years apart? Even more strikingly, Johann Carl Fuhlrott and I both eventually became professors at the University of Tübingen.

CHAPTER

2

Persistent Immigrants

EVERYBODY'S DOING IT WITH *everybody else. Archaic humans make themselves understood, somehow. Modern humans conquer Europe. No chance of permanent residence. Everybody goes south for the winter. An unexpected reunion. The hunters have blue eyes.*

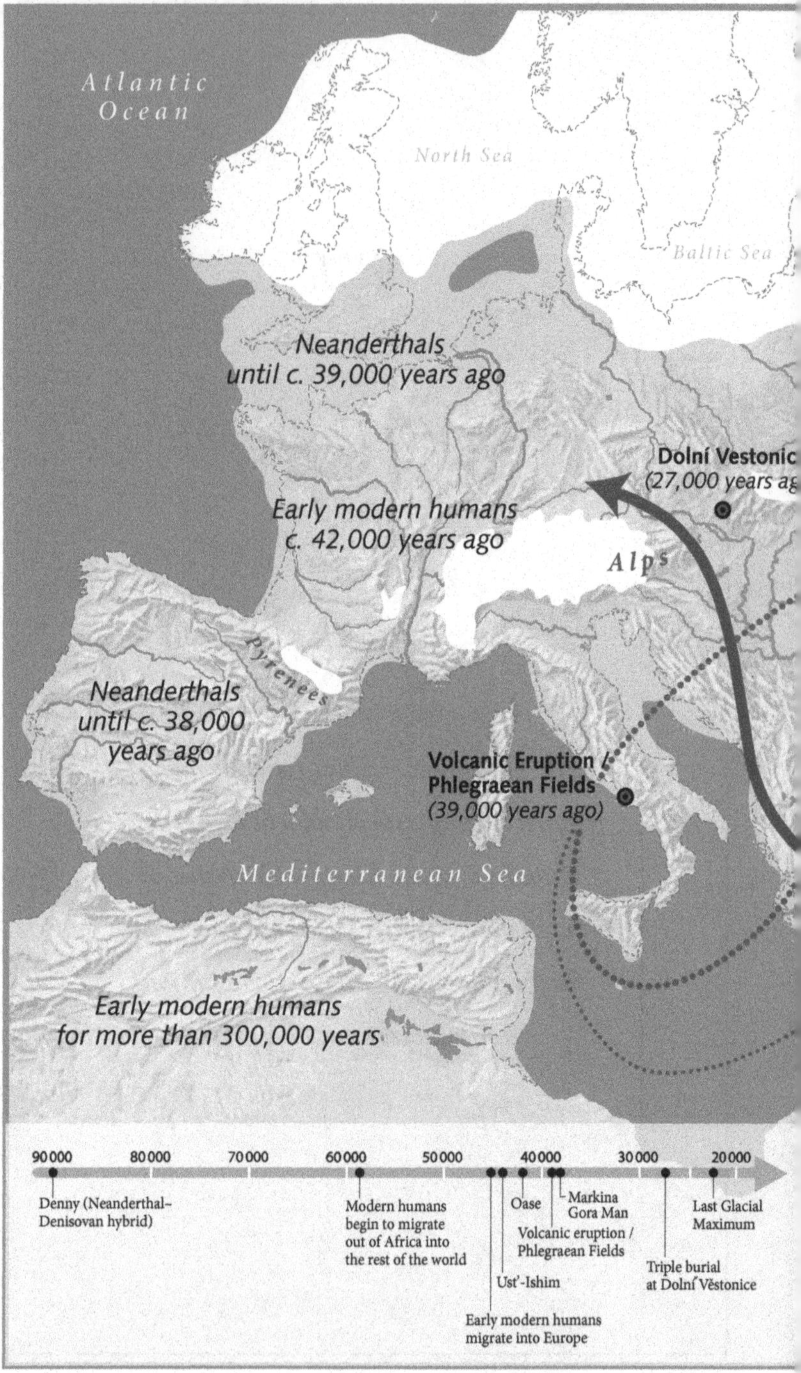

Atlantic Ocean

North Sea

Baltic Sea

Neanderthals until c. 39,000 years ago

Dolní Vestonic
(27,000 years ag

Early modern humans c. 42,000 years ago

Alps

Pyrenees

Neanderthals until c. 38,000 years ago

Volcanic Eruption / Phlegraean Fields
(39,000 years ago)

Mediterranean Sea

Early modern humans for more than 300,000 years

90 000 — Denny (Neanderthal–Denisovan hybrid)
80 000
70 000
60 000 — Modern humans begin to migrate out of Africa into the rest of the world
50 000
Early modern humans migrate into Europe
Ust'-Ishim
40 000 — Oase
Volcanic eruption / Phlegraean Fields
Markina Gora Man
30 000
Triple burial at Dolní Věstonice
20 000 — Last Glacial Maximum

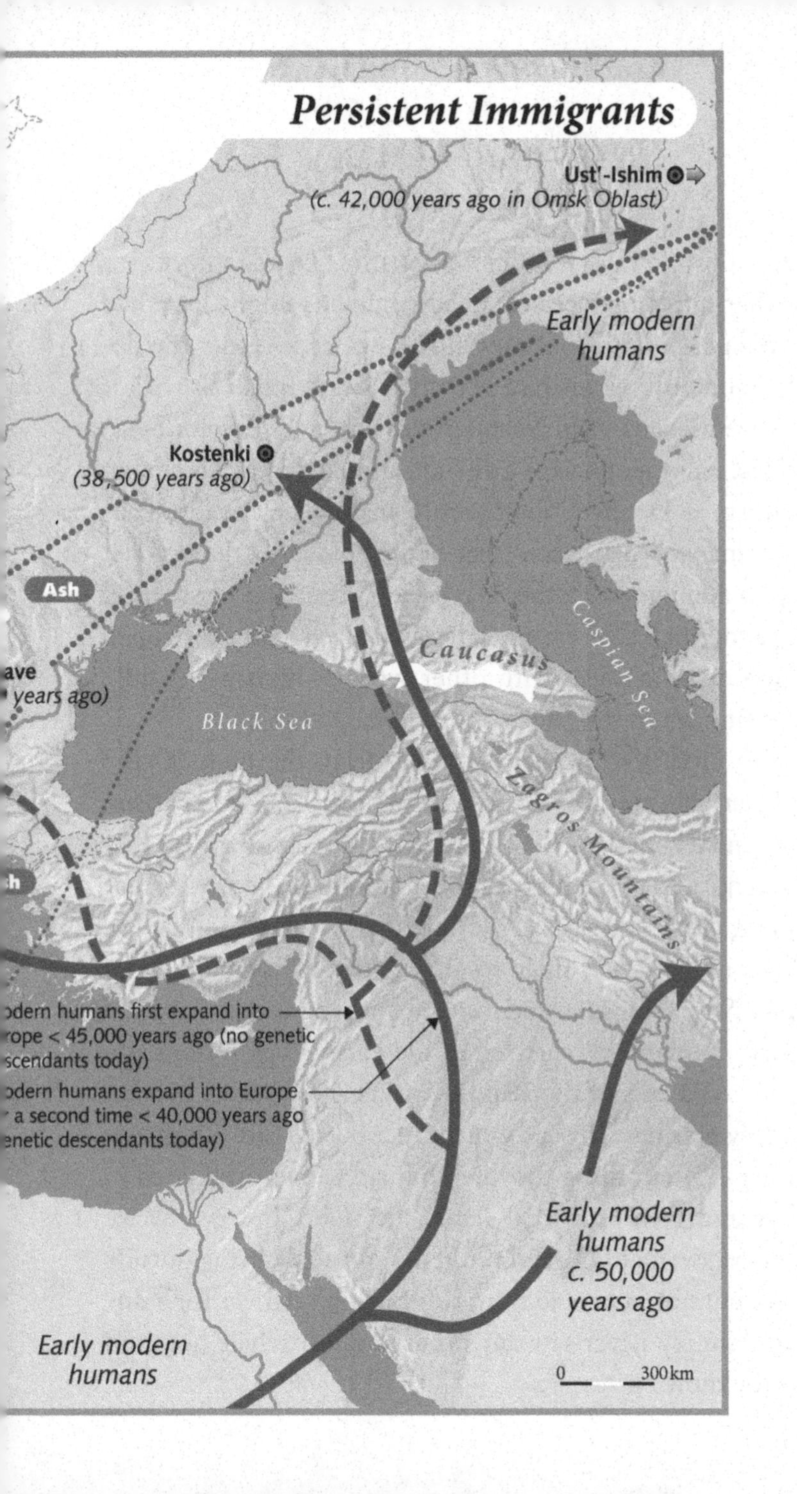
Persistent Immigrants
Ust'-Ishim
(c. 42,000 years ago in Omsk Oblast)
Early modern humans
Kostenki
(38,500 years ago)
Ash
ave
years ago)
Caucasus
Caspian Sea
Black Sea
Zagros Mountains
odern humans first expand into
rope < 45,000 years ago (no genetic
scendants today)
odern humans expand into Europe
a second time < 40,000 years ago
enetic descendants today)
Early modern humans c. 50,000 years ago
Early modern humans
0 300km

ARCHAIC HUMANS AND SEX

FOR A LONG TIME WE COULD ONLY SPECULATE ABOUT whether different types of archaic humans might have had sex with each other, but now DNA evidence settles the debate: modern humans had sex with Neanderthals as well as with Denisovans. And Neanderthals also had sex with Denisovans. Another ancient girl—affectionately known among scientists as Denny—was recently analyzed by Svante Pääbo's team, who discovered that her genome was the product of such a union: her father was a Denisovan and her mother a Neanderthal. Our early relatives were evidently very open to new acquaintances with other types of humans—hardly surprising, given the paucity of options available.

This kind of crossover was clear from the moment the Neanderthal genome was decoded. In 2010, our comparison between Neanderthal DNA and living humans revealed that between 2 and 2.5 percent of the European, Asian, and Australian genomes consists of Neanderthal DNA. Our Denisova study produced a similar result: contemporary indigenous Papua New Guineans and Australians—descendants of the modern humans who arrived in the Pacific region from Africa via Asia tens of thousands of years ago—have 5 percent Denisovan genes. This also further supported the "out of Africa" theory, according to which human beings originated in Africa and then expanded across the globe. This is why we find Neanderthal DNA in the genes of people living outside Africa but not in people from sub-Saharan Africa. Their ancestors simply never saw any other kind of archaic hominin that we know of.

It came as no surprise, therefore, when, thanks to the approximately 420,000-year-old Spanish Neanderthal, we were able to prove indirectly that his descendants had mingled with modern humans. Far more important was the insight we obtained into modern humans' earliest attempts to spread across Europe. By comparing earlier and later Neanderthal genes, we could calculate that at some point between 400,000 and 220,000 years ago, the ancestors of modern humans must have arrived in Europe—although at first they weren't able to gain a solid foothold.[1]

OUT OF AFRICA

Seven million years ago at the earliest, in Africa, the ancestral line that eventually led to today's humans split off from the line that developed into chimpanzees, who are now our closest living relatives. An array of different kinds of hominins subsequently emerged, including *Ardipithecus* and *Australopithecus*, the latter the genus to which the famous "Lucy" belonged. Living more than 3 million years ago in Africa, she looked much more like a chimpanzee than a modern human. Then, roughly 1.9 million years ago, *Homo erectus* emerged. Within a few hundred thousand years, this hominin would spread throughout the continent and across large parts of Eurasia, becoming the first archaic hominin to leave Africa. In Eurasia, *Homo erectus* evolved still further, including at one stage into the so-called Peking Man, but then died out. In Africa, meanwhile, the line that led to Neanderthals, Denisovans, and modern humans evolved from *Homo erectus* at least 600,000 years ago.

These days, nobody doubts that the common ancestors of humans and chimpanzees evolved in Africa. Until quite recently, however, many scientists disputed whether the evolution of *Homo erectus* into *Homo sapiens* took place solely on that continent (indeed, some still do). Well into the 1990s, the debate was dominated by a theory known as "multi-regionalism," which suggested that human beings from various parts of the globe were directly descended from ancestors in that specific region: Europeans from Neanderthals; Africans from the African *Homo erectus*, also termed *Homo ergaster*; and Asians from Peking Man, also known as the Asian *Homo erectus*. The "out of Africa" theory, on the other hand, posits that modern humans evolved from *Homo erectus* in Africa, then subsequently expanded outward across the planet, displacing all the other kinds of archaic hominin as they went, including Neanderthals and Denisovans.

For decades these theories jockeyed for position, with advocates on both sides beating each other over the head at conferences with their respective theses. Today, when we know more about the genetic impact of Neanderthals on Europeans and Denisovans on the inhabitants of Oceania, both theories have been proved right, albeit to very different extents. Europeans are 97 to 98 percent descended from Africans and 2 to 2.5 percent descended from Neanderthals. The indigenous populations of Australia and Papua New Guinea are about 7 percent descended from Neanderthals and Denisovans and about 93 percent from Africans. Only the inhabitants of sub-Saharan Africa did not intermix with any other type of archaic human outside the continent.

The oldest modern human fossils date from roughly 160,000 to 200,000 years ago and were found in Ethiopia. None of these, however, explain where exactly the Neanderthal and Denisovan line split from modern humans. For a long while we believed that the majority of human evolution took place in East Africa, primarily because this is where most ancient bones have been discovered. In 2017, however, evidence was found that human evolution also took place elsewhere in Africa, when the skull of an early human who lived 300,000 years ago was unearthed in Morocco. This discovery nullified the notion that East Africa was humanity's sole point of origin. The complex twists and turns of human evolution on the continent will probably remain a mystery for some time; perhaps the riddle will never be solved. What we can say for certain, however, is that all of us have recent genetic roots in Africa.

THE PROBLEM OF INBREEDING

THE NEANDERTHALS LIVED ALONG A BELT OF LAND stretching from the Iberian Peninsula to the Altai Mountains, clustered mainly south of the Alps, in today's southern France, but also in the Near East. Unfortunately, it's impossible to tell how many Neanderthals lived in Europe during any given period, but the scant number of bones indicates a small community isolated for many tens of thousands of years.[2]

This isolation was clearly not self-imposed. The Neanderthals must have been highly mobile, or they never would have pushed as far into Asia as the Altai Mountains. But they were living during the Ice Age, hundreds of thousands of years in which vast and insurmountable glaciers periodically formed. In Europe and large parts of Asia, conditions were radically different from Africa, where modern humans were evolving around the same time.[3] Many regions settled by Neanderthals were cut off from the outside world, so they interbred with relatives and harmful mutations spread. With such scarce mating options, it's understandable that they would have taken any opportunity to broaden their horizons and form new relationships—even with other types of hominins.[4] But the frequency of these encounters should not be overstated. Because Eurasia was so sparsely populated during the Ice Age, bumping into a modern human during a foray into the woods would have been like spotting a yeti. Yet these chance meetings would sometimes result in what was likely violent sexual contact.

We're still not sure whether modern humans were able to communicate with Neanderthals. Certainly, modern humans had complex language skills before they left Africa.[5] When it comes to Neanderthals, however, there's little scientific consensus regarding if or to what extent they were able to express themselves. They must have made themselves understood somehow, because they hunted in groups, which requires a coordinated strategy. Their physiology might have allowed for speech as well. A Neanderthal who lived approximately 60,000 years ago in what is now Israel was found to have a hyoid bone, important for speech that closely resembled that of modern humans. Chimpanzees, which share a common ancestor with humans and Neanderthals from 7 million years ago, have a different morphology of that bone. The power of speech may have developed, therefore, after chimpanzees diverged from humans but before Neanderthals did.

This hypothesis is supported by the so-called FOXP2 gene, which has a nearly identical version in Neanderthals. It is sometimes called the "language gene," even though scientists don't believe there's any such thing. Fish and mice also have this gene, but obviously they cannot speak. Yet we know FOXP2 plays an important role in the ability to speak. Any individual with a broken FOXP2 gene lacks the power of complex speech. Like the hyoid bone, FOXP2 changed in humans *after* the split from chimpanzees, but there is no significant difference in this gene between modern humans and Neanderthals, suggesting Neanderthals possessed at least basic language skills.[6]

NEANDERTHALS DIDN'T DIE OUT

There is no doubt that Neanderthals were human, and from an evolutionary perspective the genetic differences between them and us are minuscule. Yet these close relatives are sometimes classified as their own species. The invention of the species system was due in part to the human urge to categorize phenomena and elevate ourselves above the animal kingdom. The most popular definition of a species is probably this: a group in which two members can produce fertile offspring. Members of different species may be able to reproduce, but their offspring will not. The most famous example is probably the mule, the infertile progeny of a horse and a donkey. Because the offspring of Neanderthals and humans were clearly able to reproduce, we cannot classify them as separate species according to this definition. The same goes for the Denisovans. Yet other species concepts—including evolutionary, ecological, and phylogenetic definitions—assert that humans and Neanderthals were separate species, despite the fact that genetically the differences between them are negligible. For this reason we consider it more appropriate to refer to Neanderthals as a "type of human."

Closely related to the issue of species is the question of whether the Neanderthals ever died out at all. Of course, we no longer see them in the flesh, as though we were living in Europe tens of thousands of years ago. Yet if they produced fertile descendants with modern humans, giving us Neanderthal DNA, one could also argue that they simply merged with us. Assuming the population of early modern humans in Europe was fifty times bigger than that of the Neanderthals, our genetic makeup today reflects that ratio (fifty to one). Some of the more successful Neanderthal genes have become especially widespread, such as those affecting immunity. Some Europeans and many

South Asians, for example, inherited a gene that causes a much stronger immune reaction to a COVID-19 virus infection. Carriers of the Neanderthal gene are three times more likely to die from this newly emerged virus.

EUROPE FALLS

MODERN HUMANS LEFT AFRICA AND MOVED NORTH FOR the first time at least 200,000 years ago. For hundreds of thousands of years, however, they failed to establish much of a presence. DNA analyses have uncovered detailed evidence about at least two big pushes made approximately 45,000 years ago. At Ust'-Ishim in Siberia, 2,500 kilometers east of Moscow, the bones of a modern human whose ancestors had migrated north from Africa were unearthed at the site. A skull discovered at the Oase Cave in Romania, found to be 40,000 years old, was among the earliest modern human ever identified in Europe. The skull had an unusual shape, and a 2015 analysis revealed that it had belonged to a hybrid human with more than 10 percent Neanderthal DNA. Yet neither the Siberian nor the Romanian bones belonged to our direct ancestors. Those early humans would sometimes reproduce with Neanderthals, of course, but these cases were outliers. For a long time, archaic Eurasian hominins mostly kept themselves to themselves.

Then, roughly 40,000 years ago, the early humans who would become our direct ancestors spread across Europe and Asia. People from the Near East and along the Black Sea found their way to the Danube and then into Central Europe. Serious cyclists will know that these days you can easily travel along the Danube, biking straight from southern Germany into Romania. Forty thousand years ago, the journey from the Danube Delta to the Black Forest was no picnic, but it was one of the few corridors that offered access to Central Europe, which was mainly walled off by enormous sheets of ice. And it was worth the trip. In addition to the ice, there was plenty of green pastureland, which lured countless mammoths, woolly rhinoceroses, and giant deer, all of which featured heavily in the diets of both Neanderthals and modern humans.

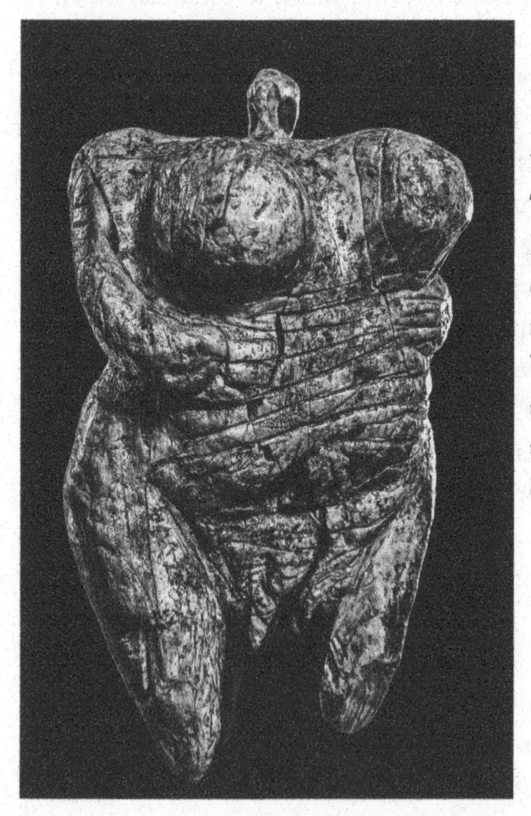

Stone Age Europeans loved Venus figurines. The Venus of Hohle Fels was carved out of mammoth ivory between 35,000 and 40,000 years ago in the Swabian Alps.

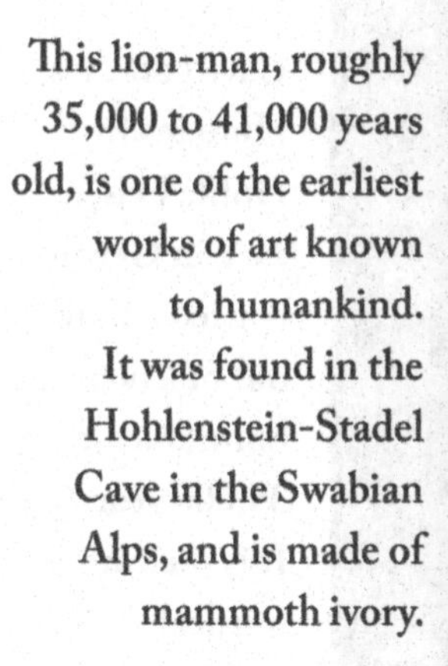

This lion-man, roughly 35,000 to 41,000 years old, is one of the earliest works of art known to humankind. It was found in the Hohlenstein-Stadel Cave in the Swabian Alps, and is made of mammoth ivory.

This first great wave of modern human migration into Europe effected an extraordinary transformation. People living in what is known as the Aurignacian period, named after early artifacts discovered in a cave in Aurignac, France, were skilled artists. They carved horses, people, and even fantastical hybrid creatures, such as the lion-man found in the Hohlenstein-Stadel Cave in the Swabian Alps. They crafted flutes out of birds' bones and developed a particular enthusiasm for "Venus" figurines, the oldest of which, found in the

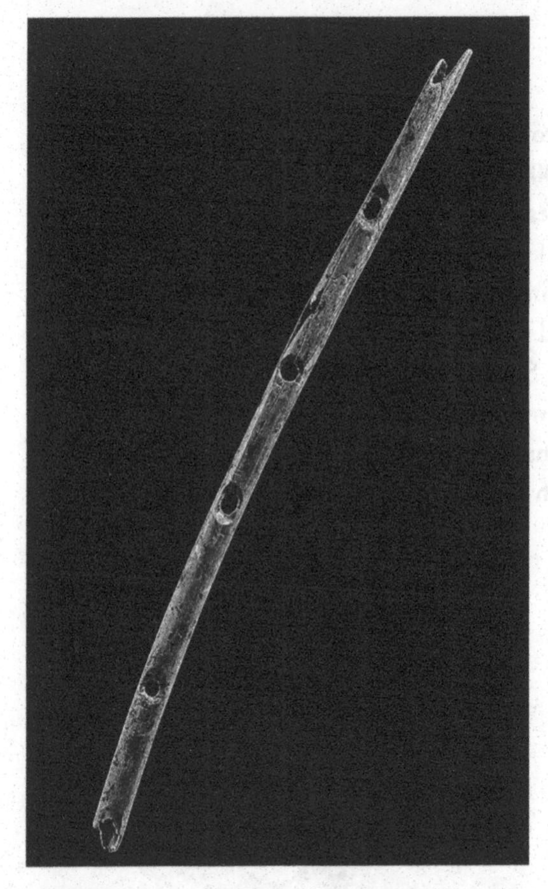

Cave concerts: Humans in Hohle Fels, a cave in Germany, crafted a flute out of a bird bone at least 35,000 years ago. It is the earliest musical instrument ever discovered.

Swabian Alps, is only six centimeters tall, but is carved with rather a large vulva and pronounced curves that characterized these statues over the next several millennia.

We don't know how the Aurignacians made this tremendous step forward in art and culture, the impact of which would be felt for another 10,000 years. Anybody familiar with Central European winters might speculate that it must have been extremely boring for our ancestors to be stuck for months in their caves, hiding from the cold. Some archaeologists think skilled artists would have had a better chance with the opposite sex, inspiring artistic competition and innovation. Whatever the reason for their cultural florescence, the Aurignacians established new artistic standards.

FLEEING AND HUNTING

Compared to our closest relative, the chimpanzee, we humans are lousy climbers. Apes have hands and feet that are perfectly adapted to climbing trees, which offer them food, a place to sleep, and protection from attack. From the moment archaic humans and chimpanzees parted ways, in humans these skills have been in consistent decline, so our ancestors developed other abilities to replace them. Instead of grip strength, for instance, we have delicate hands that can make tools and weapons. The real evolutionary breakthrough, however, came when we began walking upright.

If we think of evolution as having a conscious purpose—which it does not—then this was a bold experiment. Fundamentally, walking on two legs requires more energy than walking on all fours like an ape. Running, however, does not: humans expend roughly the same energy running over the same distance as walking. Around 1.9 million years ago, taking this evolutionary step toward efficient running made a lot of sense. The African landscape changed dramatically. Areas of trees became savannahs, predominantly grassland. There were fewer trees to climb and therefore more reasons for humans to keep their heads above the grass—to spot predators coming, for example. Unlike other types of human that did not walk upright to the same extent (and later died out), *Homo erectus* was able to hold its own on the savannah. Chimpanzees and archaic climbing humans, on the other hand, probably continued to live in areas of jungle, which have always covered large swaths of the continent—and where expert climbers have always had an advantage.

Walking upright made it possible for *Homo erectus* to employ a totally new hunting strategy—one that required further mutations, including a gradual loss of hair. *Homo erectus* could now cover almost limitless distances without overheating, becoming champion endurance athletes. It must have been easy for them to track and kill their prey across the broad expanses of the savannah. A gazelle can run fast, but not for prolonged periods, and the same is true for most mammals. They collapse after relatively short distances: horses can gallop for forty kilometers at most. Early humans would simply pursue their prey until the animal was unable to continue. In the end they would need no more than a stone to finish off the exhausted creature. The ability to run long distances also came in handy when the tables were turned and humans were fleeing something, like a natural disaster.

Even human intelligence is probably a direct consequence of walking on two legs, because the shift to consuming animal fat and protein made it possible for humans to develop an organ that consumes vast amounts of energy. In modern humans the brain demands about a quarter of the body's energy, although it usually makes up less than 2 percent of a person's bodyweight. It's these powerful brains that have enabled human beings to populate the world and fly to the moon. This evolutionary leap is quantifiable: chimpanzee brains weigh less than 400 grams, while the average human brain is at least three times heavier.

TOXIC RAIN ON A DARK HORIZON

MODERN HUMANS CHOSE A BAD TIME TO LEAVE THE heat of Africa for the chill of Europe. Europe's climate was already cooling, dropping toward what scientists call the Last Glacial Maximum, a period that began 24,000 years ago and came to a gradual halt 18,000 years ago. The last Ice Age made it difficult for humans to live in Central Europe. The temperature dropped even lower when the Phlegraean Fields supervolcano near Vesuvius erupted in a near-apocalyptic explosion approximately 39,000 years ago. Ash was carried eastward, across the Balkans and deep into present-day Russia. In places the layer of ash was several meters thick. The ash in the atmosphere was blocking the sunlight and lowering the average global temperature; geologists estimate a drop of up to four degrees Celsius. Vegetation across large parts of Europe must have disappeared for several years, and drinking water would have been contaminated by the showers of ash. Today, the region around the Phlegraean Fields—which includes Naples—is considered one of the most dangerous volcanic areas in the world, and some geologists believe there could be another major eruption in the coming centuries.

Conditions in Europe were already tough, but suddenly they had become deadly. The eruption may have been the final blow for the Neanderthals, who were already retreating before the waves of new arrivals from Africa and were sheltering primarily in Western Europe. Other natural disasters may also have contributed to their decline.

In any case, whether they died off or were absorbed into the modern human population, Europe's last Neanderthals disappeared around 39,000 years ago.

The massive volcanic eruption proved to be a boon for science, because the ash preserved one of the oldest human specimens whose genetic components can be found in contemporary Europeans. Having decoded this early human's genetic information, we now know that the Aurignacians were among our direct ancestors. The bones were uncovered in volcanic ash near Kostenki in western Russia, and were buried there just after the volcano had erupted. In 2009, for the very first time, I was able to decode the complete mtDNA of this modern Ice-Age human. The objects buried with the man, nicknamed "Markina Gora," indicate that he was probably part of the Aurignacian culture. Because he was intentionally buried in volcanic ash, he must have lived after the eruption or the layer of ash would have settled on top of him.[7]

Europe was in the midst of genetic upheaval. The Ice Age intensified and the number of Aurignacians dwindled. The shrinking population coincided with a nosedive in the variety of European fauna: some 36,000 years ago, Europe's animals underwent a strange mass extinction. Mammoths, bison, wolves, and cave bears were all affected. Hyenas vanished without trace. In their place appeared their Eastern

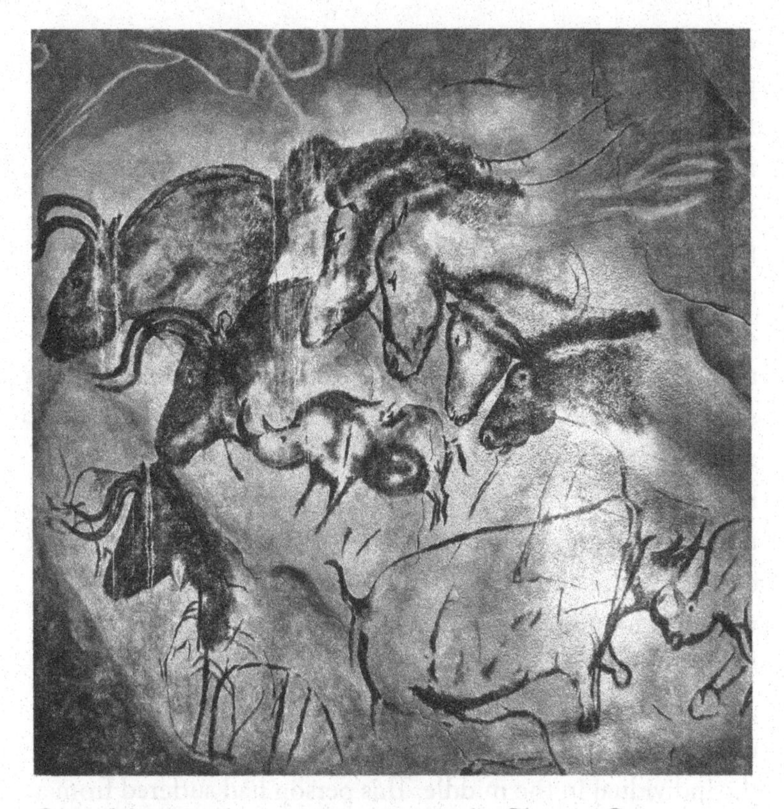

One of the countless cave paintings in the Chauvet Cave in southern France. It depicts aurochs as well as horses and woolly rhinoceroses. This impressive art gallery was created between 37,000 and 28,000 years ago.

European and North Asian relatives—and with new animals came new people. The last evidence of the Aurignacians' presence in Central Europe is 32,000 years old.

The new human inhabitants, known as the Gravettians, ushered in a new era. Like the Aurignacians, these new immigrants were big-game hunters, but they seem to have been better adapted to the increasingly cold climate than their predecessors.[8] We know they came from the east, but their precise ancestry is obscure. One of the Gravettians' most famous burial sites was unearthed in 1986 at Dolní Věstonice, in the southeast of the Czech Republic. It is a triple burial site, one of the few dating from the Upper Paleolithic, and its three resident skeletons were arranged in a puzzlingly symbolic way: buried underneath a mammoth scapula roughly 27,000 years ago, the bodies struck several archaeologists as a romantic trio. They had been laid out close together, the left skeleton's hands resting in the middle one's lap, while the middle one's hand was touching the hand of the body on the right. This is unlikely to have happened by chance, because they had obviously been prepared for burial: their faces were covered with ochre, and various carefully placed burial items were also found in the grave, including around the pubic area of the central figure.

All of this was obvious to archaeologists the moment they unearthed the site. The real uncertainty surrounded the sex of the individual in the middle. This person had suffered from a bone disease that made it impossible to determine his or her sex anatomically, unlike the other two bodies, which were both males. Because of the symbolism and positioning, most experts assumed the central figure was a woman—an interpretation we refuted using DNA sequencing in 2016. Of course, this doesn't mean the three of them weren't part of a love triangle, albeit not the kind previously supposed. The two men surrounding the man with the bone disease, incidentally, were brothers—or at least half brothers, as the mtDNA indicated. They shared genetic material with people spanning from France in the west to northern Italy and western Russia. Their triple burial displays the advanced craftsmanship and sense of symbolism characteristic of objects discovered during the Gravettian era. Gravettians are famous for their jewelry and cave paintings, but they also carried on the tradition of carving Venus figurines. Given their almost 10,000-year history, the Gravettians have a strong claim to have been Europe's most successful early settlers, but even they stood no chance against the worsening Ice Age.

A BRIDGE TO THE EAST

THE LAST GLACIAL MAXIMUM EXTINGUISHED ALL LIFE in Central Europe. For 6,000 years, the ice drove out everything. From the genes that prevailed in Europe following this extreme period of cold, we can guess what happened to the people who had previously settled on the continent.

It seems certain that the Gravettians disappeared for good; at least, there is no evidence to the contrary in the genetic makeup of contemporary Europeans. Their predecessors, the Aurignacians, however, apparently managed to flee to the Iberian Peninsula, where they sought refuge from the eternal winter. There is no genetic data from this region during the Last Glacial Maximum, but we do have some from the aftermath. This data shows that the people who lived in modern-day Spain 18,000 years ago carried the same genetic makeup that we find in Aurignacians, so it seems reasonable to suppose that the latter retreated into southwest Europe approximately 32,000 years ago to escape the increasingly aggressive cold. The glaciated Pyrenees then cut off their new homeland from the rest of Europe, making it impossible for the Aurignacians to exchange genetic material with anybody else. They would have found the route south barred to them as well. They could see across the Strait of Gibraltar to Africa, but they couldn't reach the far shore, possessing neither the technological know-how nor the physical capability to traverse the fourteen-kilometer distance (calculated using today's sea level), especially given the powerful currents.[9]

Although the relocation of some Aurignacians to the southwest meant that their genes survived, not every member of that population managed to flee the cold. It's safe to assume that the freezing temperatures in Central Europe killed the majority of the region's inhabitants. Aurignacian history, however, continued, and their genes have endured till the present day. Approximately 18,000 years ago, at the end of the mega Ice Age, they returned to Central Europe, where genetic analyses and archaeological finds show that they met and mixed with another group arriving from the Balkan region.

We can't yet say much about the genes of the people who lived in the Balkans at that time; there have been no usable bones discovered. We do know, however, that they contributed to European DNA, a fact that baffled scientists until recently. Confusingly, these immigrants from the southeast brought a genetic component that is found today in people living in Anatolia. It seemed reasonable to conclude that they originated in Anatolia before settling in the Balkans, then moving into Central Europe after the Last Glacial Maximum. Yet there was not a shred of archaeological evidence to support this hypothesis. It wasn't until we sequenced the genes of Anatolian hunter-gatherers in 2018 that we could explain what really happened. The Anatolians didn't bring their genes to Europe; rather, the inhabitants of the Balkans brought their genes to Anatolia as they spread east *before* the mega Ice Age, intermixing with the local population as they went. These genes then swept like a wave from the Balkans through Anatolia and even onward into Africa. Modern-day Turks and Kurds, as well as North Africans, share these genetic components from the Balkans with Central Europeans. These mysterious Balkan migrants are common ancestors to all these groups, spanning contemporary countries and continents.

Over the next three millennia in Europe, these genetically different populations from the Iberian Peninsula and the Balkans intermixed to form a relatively genetically homogenous group. Only recently have we been able to trace the genetic connection between Europe and Anatolia during this period. For many thousands of years, technologically highly developed hunter-gatherers with blue eyes and dark skin dominated the European continent. Genetically, this population was more closely interrelated than ever before. The dwindling Ice-Age barriers made people more mobile, beginning a process of active social exchange that eventually deteriorated into a strongly homogenized gene pool. With the ice melting, the differences and distances between humans across the world were disappearing as well.

Over the next three millennia, as the ice melted and barriers became less significant, people became more mobile, beginning a process of active social exchange. The mild climate attracted newcomers, and the next great wave of immigration was imminent: the genetic history of Europe was shifting into a new gear.

CHAPTER

3

Immigrants Are the Future

GLOBAL WARMING DRIVES PEOPLE *north. Everyone was healthier in the old days. Two kids are enough. Swabian farmers came from Anatolia. Pale skin increases chances of survival. The Balkan route proves successful. Hunters on the retreat.*

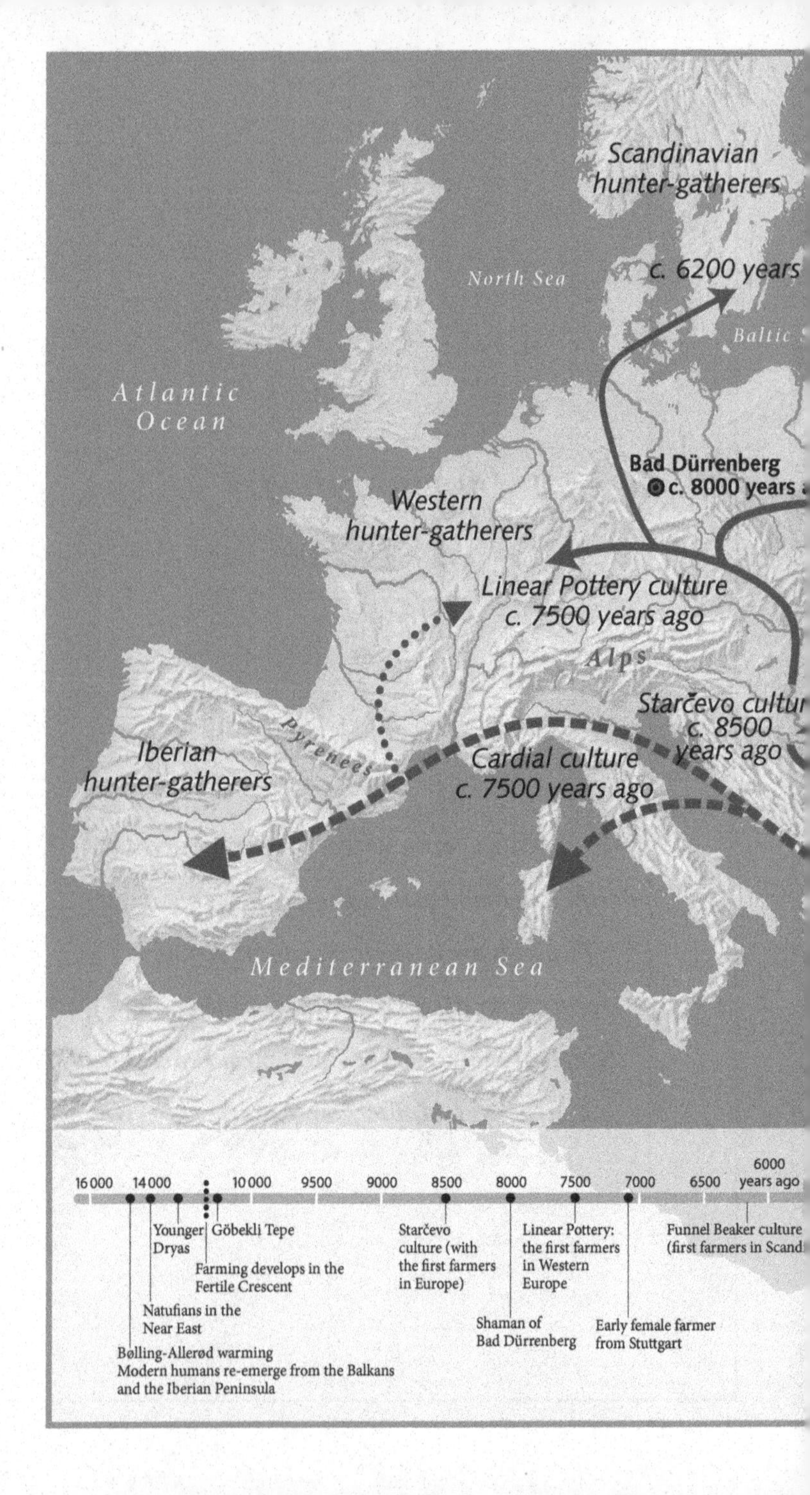
Scandinavian
hunter-gatherers
c. 6200 years
North Sea
Baltic
Atlantic
Ocean
Bad Dürrenberg
c. 8000 years
Western
hunter-gatherers
Linear Pottery culture
c. 7500 years ago
Alps
Starčevo cultu
c. 8500
years ago
Pyrenees
Iberian
hunter-gatherers
Cardial culture
c. 7500 years ago
Mediterranean Sea
16 000
14 000
10 000
9500
9000
8500
8000
7500
7000
6500
6000
years ago
Younger
Dryas
Göbekli Tepe
Farming develops in the
Fertile Crescent
Natufians in the
Near East
Bølling-Allerød warming
Modern humans re-emerge from the Balkans
and the Iberian Peninsula
Starčevo
culture (with
the first farmers
in Europe)
Shaman of
Bad Dürrenberg
Linear Pottery:
the first farmers
in Western
Europe
Early female farmer
from Stuttgart
Funnel Beaker culture
(first farmers in Scand

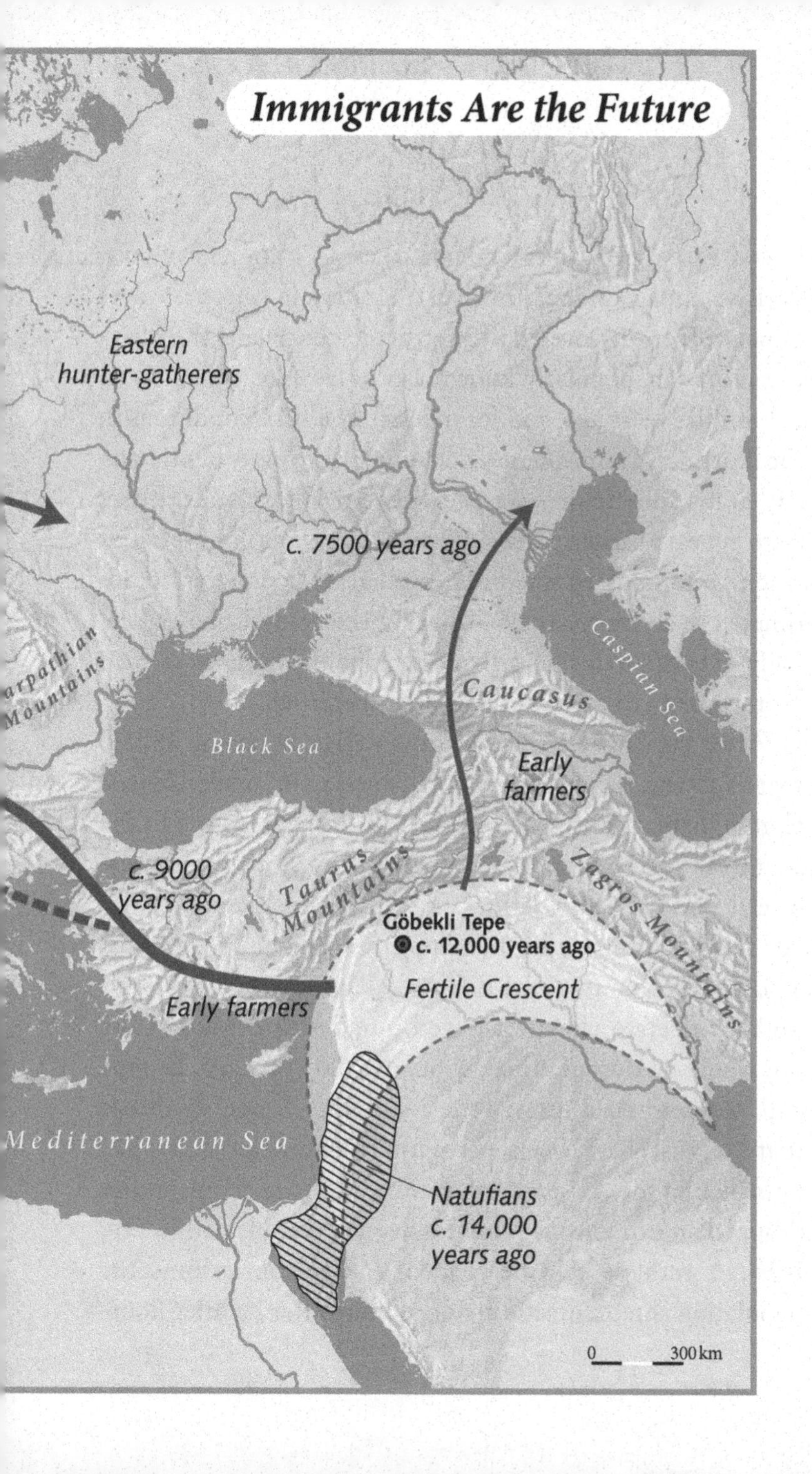
Immigrants Are the Future
Eastern
hunter-gatherers
c. 7500 years ago
arpathian
Mountains
Caucasus
Caspian Sea
Black Sea
Early
farmers
c. 9000
years ago
Taurus
Mountains
Zagros Mountains
Göbekli Tepe
c. 12,000 years ago
Fertile Crescent
Early farmers
Mediterranean Sea
Natufians
c. 14,000
years ago
0
300 km

A PLACE IN THE SUN

FROM THE VERY OUTSET, THE GLOBAL CLIMATE HAD A decisive impact on the history of migration in Europe. Waves of newcomers discovered a bitterly cold continent. The Pleistocene epoch, popularly known as the Ice Age, began about 2.4 million years ago, and for much of the time conditions in the Northern Hemisphere—including large parts of present-day Italy and Spain—were extremely inhospitable. There were repeated interglacial intervals, millennia-long periods when conditions warmed and average temperatures sometimes rose above today's, but during the coldest phases permafrost began to form north of the Alps and pack ice loomed off the northern coast of the Iberian Peninsula.

After the Last Glacial Maximum came to an end 18,000 years ago and rising temperatures once again made Central Europe habitable, people returned from their refuges in the south. As had been the case during the previous three interglacial periods, temperatures on the continent rose, slowly but steadily at first, and then, beginning about 15,000 years ago, rapidly. Known as the Bølling-Allerød warming, this period's temperate climate allowed humans to expand across the whole of Europe. Then, about 12,900 years ago, Europe and northern Asia underwent a climatic change so abrupt that it must have been perceptible within an individual human lifetime. In parts of Europe, average temperatures dropped an extraordinary twelve degrees Celsius within fifty years. A ruthless cold descended, and we can assume the population shrank drastically once more after its brief flourishing. This short Ice Age is known as the Younger Dryas. We still don't know what prompted it. Some think that the previous period of warming melted barriers of ice in the North Atlantic and poured icy water from a vast lake in North America into the ocean. This could have disrupted the Gulf Stream—the warm ocean current that has long kept temperatures mild in northwest Europe.

Not until 11,700 years ago could Europe enjoy warmer temperatures. At the beginning of the Holocene, the period of warmth in which we're still living today, temperatures finally stabilized. Though in principle the Holocene is no different from the earlier warmer phases that have occurred at regular intervals over the past 2.4 million years, the Ice Age was over, at least from a human perspective. In that view, the Holocene—which has now lasted almost 12,000 years—will be replaced by the next Ice Age following a slow drop in temperature. This, it's worth noting, does not nullify the existential threat posed by human-caused climate change.

In any case, the beginning of the Holocene was initially a stroke of luck for humanity, sparking a process of radical change that would have far-reaching effects on human evolution, comparable to the development of our ability to walk upright. The cradle of progress, however, was not in Europe but in the Near East, where it was significantly warmer than in the north. Hunter-gatherers in the region began to farm crops and raise livestock, and a once-mobile population settled down, ushering in the Neolithic period.

CLIMATE CHANGE THEN AND NOW

Global warming has always propelled migration. In the past 10,000 years, it made it possible to build a European civilization that would influence much of the world. The wave of migration that could be triggered by the current climatic changes will move in essentially the same direction as it did in our history, south to north, but with one difference. While the natural process of global warming 10,000 years ago facilitated the expansion of humankind, climate change fueled by human beings will push people to *flee* before it. The current process of warming may be insignificant from the perspective of world history, but for our global society it's an unparalleled challenge.

The reasons for this can be traced to the Holocene itself. It has allowed the population to continue growing steadily: according to current estimates, by the year 2050 we will reach the 10 billion mark. This will not only increase greenhouse gas emissions but encourage the growth of mega metropolises, most of which (for infrastructural reasons) were built in coastal areas and especially in the Pacific region of Southeast Asia. Rising sea levels could cost hundreds of millions of people their homes. Africa will likely undergo a similar process: by 2050 its population is expected to swell by half, bringing the figure up to approximately 2 billion inhabitants, but increasingly frequent droughts could make living conditions impossible for more and more of them. The pressure of migration in the Northern

Hemisphere, which has significantly more landmass, is already being felt, and it shows no signs of letting up. Of course, global warming does mean that large areas of northern Eurasia and Canada will soon be able to accommodate more people, as the thawing permafrost turns into arable land that could be used to feed more mouths. The methane released as the permafrost thaws, however, would heat the climate further still.

If you focus solely on the amount of habitable land that climate change will free up, then global warming looks like a plus—but as yet we don't know what political upheavals and conflicts may be triggered by the resulting migration. Or rather, we prefer not to think about it. The same goes for an alternative scenario: the end of the Holocene and the coming of a new Ice Age. All the climate-related data from the previous interglacial periods indicates that everything north of the Alps would rapidly become inhospitable to agriculture. Europeans, unable to feed themselves, would be forced to migrate south. With what would then be three-quarters of a billion Europeans descending on an already densely populated Africa, it seems hard to imagine that this scenario would be without conflict. Of course, this scenario is several thousand years in the future; the Holocene will probably last at least that long. Another theory suggests that human-caused climate change may even prevent the next Ice Age entirely. For this reason, many geologists and climate scientists have abandoned the terms "Pleistocene" or

"Holocene" for our period, instead calling it the "Anthropocene"—the age of humankind.

A SIMPLE LIFE IN THE WILD

AFTER EUROPE BEGAN TO GROW WARMER 11,700 YEARS ago, hunter-gatherers continued to shape the continent. Hunting and gathering wasn't just a historical phase—it's human nature. For millions of years, ever since we started walking upright, using tools to hunt, and compensating for our physical inferiority by developing increasingly powerful brains, we have been optimizing our survival strategy. Humans did what we were built for and passed on our skills and knowledge—honed by evolution—to our offspring. These days, apart from a tiny number of hunter-gatherer populations, whose lifestyles will very likely cease to exist in the foreseeable future, this expertise has been largely—and will eventually be entirely—forgotten. A two-week jaunt into the wilderness without any of the trappings of civilization would probably be fatal to most contemporary Europeans. The old hunting instinct may still be buried somewhere, but most people these days would throw in the towel if asked to catch a chicken with their bare hands.

Stone Age hunters used wooden spears and lances. Later came spear-throwers, and then bows and arrows, and their craftspeople demonstrated remarkable skill in working with materials on both large and small scales. They fashioned tools from stones and used them to fell trees, but they also produced delicate knives and deadly arrowheads. Jewelry, which had existed in Europe since the arrival of modern humans, became increasingly elaborate and detailed, incorporating shells, feathers, animal teeth, pelts, and small antlers as well as pigments.

One especially impressive picture of contemporary life—and death—is offered by a burial site in Bad Dürrenberg in central Germany, which has now been thoroughly excavated and explored. It was the final resting place of a woman around twenty-five years of age, who was buried roughly 8,000 years ago in a sitting position—and with a baby placed in her lap who evidently died at the same time she did. The bodies were surrounded by various animal products, including deer antlers. Red pigment and a kind of primitive brush were also buried with her, which scientists conjectured was an early form of lipstick. Given her extravagant appearance, the dead woman has become known as the "shaman of Bad Dürren-

The shaman of Bad Dürrenberg, Germany, may have looked like this. She was an impressive representation of the Middle Stone Age, which began in Europe 11,700 years ago, and she probably died of an infection.

berg." Like other burial sites from the Mesolithic era, which began around 11,700 years ago, the grave testifies to the complexity of hunter-gatherer culture in Central Europe. They valued aesthetics and evidently held religious beliefs, or the bodies would not have been buried with gifts. Food was also found in the graves, suggesting they imagined the dead might need provisions and indicating a belief in life after death.

In an ever-warmer Europe, food was not in short supply. A Stone Age diet consisted largely of meat, plenty of which could be found wandering through the forests and steppes, and fish, but also tubers, birds' eggs, mushrooms, grasses, roots, and leaves. Autumn would be spent stockpiling food for the winter. From observing present-day hunter-gatherer populations, we know that it only takes on average two to four hours of such work per day to survive. Early Europeans led a simple life, their possessions limited to what they carried on their bodies. As they traveled, they would leave their makeshift shelters and even their easy-to-produce tools behind; they could always make new ones if needed. Stone was everywhere. So was wood. That said, although hunter-gatherers were perpetually on the move, they did return to seasonal base camps. Operating within an area that could be covered in approximately two hours on foot, they would hunt and gather food. When there was nothing else to find, they would expand their diet, eat less, and eventually move on. As the climate turned colder, their path usually led them south, where there was more to be foraged.

The skulls of elderly hunter-gatherers are remarkable for their white, virtually flawless teeth. Sweet, cavity-causing foods such as honey were rarely eaten, and bread, which is broken down into sugar by saliva, was unknown to them. Their incisors, on the other hand, were significantly worn down. Stone Age people probably used them like a third hand—by stretching animal leather between their hand and mouth, for instance, while working on the hide with the other hand. Damaged teeth and their consequences were a common cause of death for hunter-gatherers; in fact, the shaman of Bad Dürrenberg probably died of an acute gum infection. Infectious diseases, on the other hand, were rare, since the various populations were so scattered that illness had little opportunity to spread.

The hunter-gatherers' way of life was precisely attuned to millions of years of evolution, and it kept them in excellent health. Our contemporary society's most common causes of death—cardiovascular diseases, strokes, and diabetes, to name only a few—would have been unimaginable during the Stone Age: The booming popularity of "paleo" diets, which restrict dieters to meat and plants, thus makes a certain amount of sense. Of course, today's version doesn't usually include enough insects, and nearly all meat and vegetables are in fact farmed. Only a handful of paleo evangelists eat wild herbs, roots, and wild game, so most are not really adhering to an authentic hunter-gatherer diet. Nor does calmly strolling to a paleo restaurant demand quite the same effort as chasing down your prey in the great wide open.

NATURAL CONTRACEPTION, ARCHAIC RITUALS

THE PEOPLE OF THE MESOLITHIC PERIOD HAD FEW children. Because there was no animal milk or baby food, their sons and daughters were breastfed until about the age of five or six. While they were nursing, hormonal mechanisms left women infertile. (A word of warning: these days, with food in plentiful supply, this is no longer the case for most women, so breastfeeding is not a reliable method of contraception.) When a new baby arrived, older siblings had to be physically capable enough that they no longer needed their parents' constant protection, which was often the case by the time they turned six or seven. Most women would get pregnant no more than four times, which would probably have resulted on average in two children per generation who reached adulthood. This was enough to support a stable population but not to fuel growth. In sparsely populated Europe, this meant there was little competition for food, so conflict between different groups of hunter-gatherers was rare. There was enough to go around.

There were exceptions, however, and these were significant. During the transition into the warming period especially, there were more areas of Central and Northern Europe where food was usually gathered rather than hunted. This was particularly true in coastal regions, which were teeming with seals and even, every few months, the odd stranded whale. Meat could easily be supplemented with local flora: berries, roots, and mushrooms were all in plentiful supply. These paradises were much sought after, attracting people from other regions. The established inhabitants defended them as best they could. Overall, hunter-gatherer societies were probably the most peaceful in history, but when violence did break out it was brutal. The cracked skulls and bones found in these areas testify to their warriors' ferocity. They also served to frighten intruders: the inhabitants of

Motala, in central Sweden, speared their enemies on lances and stuck them in a bog, facing away from their campsite. They even managed to put skulls inside other skulls, although we no longer understand how to interpret this symbolism. But these scattered conflicts were a very different phenomenon from the systematic and widespread competition for resources that later gripped the continent.

MAN'S OLDEST FRIEND

One of the hunter-gatherers' greatest innovations—one that is still part of our twenty-first-century lives—was the dog. For hunters, dogs were indispensable. For many of us today, they're members of the family. It's estimated that wolves were first domesticated 20,000 to 15,000 years ago, though whether this occurred on several continents in parallel or in Ice-Age Europe first is still up for debate. The oldest dog in Germany was found in a double grave in Oberkassel, a suburb of Bonn, where it was interred around 14,000 years ago beside a fifty-year-old man and a woman half that age. The grave goods buried with them included teeth from another dog, which indicates that the animal had great significance for them.

Whether his two owners looked like him—the way people these days like to say owners look like their dogs—we can only guess. Genetically, on the other hand, dogs have indeed grown more similar to humans. Like us, they can digest carbohydrates much better than their wild ancestors. Modern-day dogs have far more copies of the gene regulating the production of the enzyme amylase, which is used to digest foods such as rice and potatoes. The same mutations took place in humans as our diets came to include more carbohydrates. Unlike chimpanzees, Neanderthals, and Denisovans, who only had two copies of the amylase gene, most people today have between ten and twenty copies—more or less the same number as our four-legged friends. This parallel mutation in dogs and humans indicates that dogs have long been not only our most faithful companions but also our most convenient way to dispose of leftovers.

PIONEERS OF GENETIC ENGINEERING

IF THE CLIMATE IN CENTRAL EUROPE AFTER THE ICE Age was mild, in the Near East it was almost ideal. The warmth and increased rainfall allowed the previously barren steppes to blossom, producing large-seeded wild grasses, the ancestors of modern-day grains. The wealth of flora benefited gatherers directly; it benefited hunters indirectly, supporting more wildlife for them to kill. Gazelles, abundant and light-footed, became the most important source of meat during this period. In Anatolia and the whole region east of the Bosporus, food was in such ample supply that the hunters' urge to migrate seems to have waned, perhaps because they no longer had to look far for their next meal.

In the Fertile Crescent, which stretches from the Jordan Valley and Lebanon across southeastern Turkey, northern

Syria, and Iraq to the Zagros Mountains in western Iran, flora, fauna, and the human population flourished. Hunter-gatherers in present-day Israel and Jordan were the first to settle, establishing more than 14,000 years ago what is now known as Natufian culture. Having set up permanent homes, these hunter-gatherers picked wild grains and ground them with millstones. Evidence of this shift away from a nomadic lifestyle has also been found in southeastern Anatolia, where those early sedentary groups built Göbekli Tepe 12,000 years ago, a vast artificial mound made out of enormous blocks of stone decorated with animal reliefs and probably the oldest

An excavation at Göbekli Tepe, a complex in southern Anatolia. The first hunter-gatherers to settle lived in this region, before they later transitioned to farming.

human-made building that involved carved stones. Archaeologists believe the complex held some kind of religious significance.

As in the north, after a period of warming the Near East underwent a sudden cold snap 13,000 years ago, and rainfall decreased. This climatic shift was a harsh test for the human population: food was now in drastically short supply. Necessity may have been the mother of invention, because people now embarked on a process of rudimentary genetic engineering. Sharp-witted observers evidently realized that the genetic diversity within species of grain could be put to good use. Roughly 10,500 years ago, at the end of the cold spell, some settlements in the Fertile Crescent were growing emmer, the ancestor of modern-day wheat, as well as wild barley, from which today's barley developed. Both of these crops had to be deliberately cultivated.

For the purposes of their own natural reproduction, the seeds of wild grains don't stay in their spikes. During harvesting, this means many seeds are lost or have to be laboriously collected. Certain plants, however, underwent a specific mutation that kept the seeds attached to the spikes. Humans appear to have sown seeds of these plants in order to grow more plants with the same mutation, gradually creating a new variety. Working alongside colleagues from Germany and Israel to reconstruct the genomes of dried barley seeds from a cave near the Dead Sea, we were able to show that the barley grown in the modern-day Near East is genetically very similar to the barley cultivated in the region 6,000 years ago.

The inhabitants of the Fertile Crescent appear to have started raising livestock approximately 10,000 years ago. We find the earliest evidence of domesticated goats, sheep, and later cows in settlements dating from this era. The animals weren't primarily a source of meat but rather provided milk. Indeed, it's probable that the hunter-gatherers gradually consumed less meat as they began to settle, a trend that was dramatically accelerated by the advent of farming. Given how time-consuming farming is, there would have been few hours in the day left over for hunting. Any additional demand for meat could have been met at least in part by trading with the hunter-gatherers who still lived in the region. Several hunter-gatherer skeletons found in early farming settlements indicate the two populations coexisted peacefully and conducted trade.

THE BODY IN THE BASEMENT

ONE CANNOT JUSTLY CALL WHAT HAPPENED IN THE Near East during the Neolithic a "revolution." Farming practices developed slowly, over thousands of years. At first agriculture merely supplemented the hunter-gatherers' lifestyle, but gradually the experiment picked up steam. As of yet there was no sign of the large settlements, crops, and animal husbandry that typified the Neolithic, which can rightly be called the age of agriculture, but neither did these early prototypes resemble the activities of traditional hunter-gatherers. DNA analyses conducted by my research group have also shown that farming developed organically in the region; new techniques were not brought by immigrants, for instance, as would later be the case in Europe.

The hunter-gatherers of Anatolia were not genetically different from its farmers. They belonged to the same population. Remarkably, however, there were strong genetic differences *among* the farmers of the Fertile Crescent. Those in the east had different DNA from those in the west—and this was no marginal distinction. The two populations were as genetically distant as present-day Europeans and East Asians. The reason for this genetic gulf within a cultural space that was otherwise developing in almost the same way is still unclear. Perhaps Anatolia's mountain ranges became impassable during the Ice Age and divided the ancestors of each population.

The genetic continuity between hunter-gatherers and farmers in Anatolia did not exist in Europe. It was there that the Neolithic Revolution earned its name, transforming a culture within a few hundred years. From an archaeological perspective, this expansion has been verified beyond any shadow of a doubt for more than a century, yet the question of *how* farming practice emerged remained long unanswered. For a long time, two theories existed. The first posited that farming was a cultural technology appropriated by people in Central Europe, learned from their Anatolian neighbors, then slowly passed on from east to west. The second suggested that the Anatolians expanded west, bringing the new technology with them. The latter theory has now been proved correct, and even more unambiguously so than expected. The evidence? Extensive genetic tests carried out on hundreds of Europeans who lived between 8,000 and 5,000 years ago—and the bones of an old Swabian farmer who lived in the vicinity of Stuttgart 7,000 years ago.

Her remains were stored in the basement of my former university at Tübingen, and in 2014, an analysis of her genome revealed that her genetic roots lay in Anatolia. Her

DNA was significantly different from the DNA we found in the bones of hunter-gatherers who lived in present-day Sweden and Luxembourg before the European Neolithic. The Swabian woman, therefore, provided the first incontrovertible piece of DNA evidence that Anatolians had themselves migrated west. Since then, hundreds of DNA samples have established that around 8,000 years ago Anatolians started to settle across the whole of Europe, from modern-day Ukraine to the British Isles. They traveled from the area of modern-day Turkey through the Balkans in the south, along the Aegean and the Adriatic Seas, and then along the Danube corridor in the north. We don't know whether the hunter-gatherers were forced out or the newcomers simply outnumbered them. Either way, after the wave of Anatolian migration the hunter-gatherers' genes were less prominent in the European population. The hunter-gatherers, however, didn't disappear. They withdrew and then reemerged two millennia down the line.

PALE SKIN, NOT MEAT

THE NEOLITHIC REVOLUTION BROUGHT INTO CLOSE quarters two populations that were fundamentally—and visibly—genetically different. The hunter-gatherers, long established in Europe, had much darker skin than the Anatolian migrants. It's not immediately obvious why people from the warmer south would have lighter skin than those who had been living in the chilly north. Because people with more skin pigment are better protected from carcinogenic UV rays, the darkest skin types are found today below the equator in Central Africa. People in northern regions facing the opposite problem, a deficit of sunlight, have less pigment so they can absorb enough UV radiation to synthesize vitamin D. This is why some countries fortify foods—usually milk—with vitamin D, or require their long-suffering children to drink cod liver oil. In Germany, the Robert Koch Institute recommends people increase their consumption of vitamin D. Those with darker skin, it adds, are more likely to be deficient.

Australia, which has a majority population descended from British émigrés who arrived less than a century ago, also happens to have the highest rate of skin cancer on the planet. A third of Australians will be diagnosed with skin cancer at some point during their lifetime. As far as evolutionary biology is concerned, people with pale skin shouldn't live near the equator—or they should at least drag out the move for a millennium or two, to give their skin some time to genetically adapt. For it *can* adapt. The indigenous peoples of the Americas have much darker skin near the equator than at the southern tip of South America—although both are descended from the same population, which emigrated to the Americas roughly 15,000 years ago. In 10,000 years' time, Australia's European descendants will probably have a skin tone similar to that of the Aborigines, who arrived there much earlier, assuming there is no further immigration from Europe—and no SPF 50 sunscreen.

None of this, however, explains why 8,000 years ago Central Europeans had darker skin than the migrants from the south. The answer lies in the diets of the two populations. Hunter-gatherers absorbed plenty of vitamin D from their diet of fish and meat. The Anatolian farmers ate an almost entirely vegetarian diet, supplemented by milk products, and absorbed virtually no vitamin D from fish or meat. The skin tone of these early farmers came under selection pressure: only those with lighter skin could manufacture enough vitamin D. Several mutations were required to produce lighter skin, but the paler Anatolians in whom these genes emerged were healthier, lived longer, and had more children. The color of their skin changed along with the shift toward farming. Gradually this evolutionary development spread across the whole of Europe. The farther north we look, the paler the skin. Among hunter-gatherers, on the other hand, this selection pressure did not exist.

The skin tone of present-day Europeans, especially those in the north, is thus the consequence of a series of genetic mutations that decreased production of melanin, the pigment in human skin. This condition is especially common today in Great Britain and Ireland; certain individuals, often those with red hair, can hardly tan at all. They simply burn, which explains the strikingly high rate of cancer in Australians of British origin. Curiously, the mutation that results in less melanin production is also responsible for reduced sensitivity to cold and pain. For a long time it was assumed that this originated with the Neanderthals, who were believed to be more resistant to the cold, but there is no genetic evidence for this hypothesis: as yet, the relevant mutation in the melanocortin receptors has not been found in the Neanderthal genome.

Europe's hunter-gatherers were blue-eyed as well as dark-skinned. Although light skin gradually became the norm across Europe, blue eyes remained common even after the wave of migration from Anatolia. We still don't know why. By default, the iris is dark, so lighter eyes are always the result of mutations that lead to reduced pigmentation. Lighter eyes provide no obvious benefit, while darker ones seem to be less sensitive to light. Yet this does not explain why light eyes in Europe are far more frequent today than they would be if they were a by-product of chance. The most plausible suggestion is that people with blue eyes had better reproductive prospects. Blue eyes may simply have been considered beautiful. Genetic sequencing reveals the number of people with blue eyes declined following the influx of Anatolian farmers—then later climbed back up.

Blue eyes, incidentally, doesn't necessarily mean blue like Paul Newman's eyes. They're just less pigmented, encompassing everything on the spectrum from grayish blue to green, and green eyes simply contain a mixture of blue and brown pigment. The same mutation can thus produce very different eye colors. In terms of skin tone too, there is an infinite palette of shades between light and dark. Although the mutations responsible for lighter skin do not seem to have appeared in the genes of Central European hunter-gatherers, we shouldn't attach too much weight to that. Unfortunately, this is exactly what has happened in recent years, for instance when the DNA of "an ancient Briton" was decoded and references were made to his skin being as dark as that of modern-day West Africans. Such claims tend to be seized upon by the media and used to make wild generalizations. In fact, we do not know how dark-skinned the ancient hunter-gatherers were. The inheritance of skin color is highly complex and cannot be explained by single mutations alone. Whether early Europeans looked like modern-day people from Central Africa, or perhaps like people from the Arab world, is still unclear. All we can say for sure is they didn't carry any mutation we know of that results in light skin, so it's highly likely they had darker skin than contemporary Europeans.

If we look back further in human history, we see that dark skin was also an adaptation. Our cousin, the chimpanzee, has light skin under its dark coat. When humans shed hair, our skin evidently adapted to protect our exposed bodies from the sun. For this reason alone, using skin color to justify some sort of social hierarchy is absurd—unless those with light skin want to lay claim to a special genetic bond with chimpanzees.

THE HARDY BALKAN ROUTE

ANATOLIAN IMMIGRANTS FIRST ESTABLISHED NEOLITHIC culture in the Balkans, for the simple reason that after they left their homeland they traveled through that region first. These early farmers who settled there established what's now known as Starčevo culture, which stretched along the Danube into southern Hungary, Serbia, and western Romania. They built an entirely new kind of settlement, constructing basic—and not especially weatherproof—shelters out of clay, wood, and straw, all of which were in plentiful supply. The houses regularly collapsed, only to be rebuilt on top of the ruins, and over millennia these structures developed into small mounds. Remnants of these tells—named after the Arabic word for "hill"—still exist today, primarily in southwest Europe and the Near East. This archaeological kinship underscores the importance of the Balkans as a bridge between the Near East and Europe, providing a space for near-constant exchange. While the inhabitants of the Balkans passed their DNA to the Anatolians during the Ice Age, these genes were circulated back to Central Europe during the Neolithic period 10,000 years later. To this day, the inhabitants of Europe and Anatolia maintain a genetic connection.

The Anatolians not only introduced the Balkan people to crop farming and livestock management but also brought ceramics. Anyone who's ever moved into a new apartment without any bowls or plates and tried to eat a dignified meal without them knows how important ceramics must have been for early Europeans. Neolithic peoples were able to manufacture large quantities of bowls, bottles, and storage vessels out of fired clay. A thousand years later, this new craft was being practiced across Europe, and archaeologists have since named dozens of cultures after the distinct techniques they used to create their wares. The Linear Pottery culture, whose ceramics were decorated with bands, expanded across the whole of Central Europe within a few centuries, covering modern-day France, Germany, Poland, Austria, Hungary, and later Ukraine. Meanwhile, the area along the Adriatic coast, most of present-day Italy, southern France, and Iberia were dominated by the Cardial Ware culture, whose ceramics were usually imprinted with cockle shells.

A vast wealth of ceramic artifacts from this era continue to be unearthed, testifying to the far-reaching cultural shift that took place during the Neolithic. The Cardial Ware and Linear Pottery cultures both emerged from the wave of Anatolian migration but diverged at the Balkans. Genetically speaking, however, the difference between the two populations was infinitesimal, roughly the same as between the modern-day Irish and English. The progress 8,000 years ago of the economically superior farmers can be clearly mapped through gradual changes in DNA—but the farmers' influence was not all-encompassing. While few traces of the hunter-gatherers' DNA existed in Central Europe 7,500 years ago, today it is just as visible in certain European populations as Anatolian genes. The hunter-gatherers did not disappear with the Anatolians' arrival; they merely retreated. Until agriculture finally conquered the whole of Europe, hunter-gatherers would coexist alongside farmers for another 2,000 years. But what successfully traveled with the Anatolians was not just their genes; it was their culture, their food, and their way of life.

CHAPTER

4

Parallel Societies

THE ANATOLIANS WORK HARD ALL *day long. The hunter-gatherers search for niches. Newcomers bring violence. Sardinians are the original farmers. Learning from immigrants means learning to be victorious. Things get pretty unsanitary.*

Western hunter-gatherers
North Sea
Atlantic Ocean
Flintbek
Blätterhöhle Cave
Farmers 6200 years ago
Alps
Pyrenees
Lake Bracciano
Farmers c. 7500 years ago
Mediterranean Sea
8000
7500
7000
6500
6000
5500
Oldest boats in Europe Lake Bracciano, Italy
Settlement of Sardinia
Gold objects in Varna
Farmers migrate into Great Britain
Blätterhöhle cave site
Oldest plough
Funnel Beaker culture

Parallel Societies
arpathian Mountains
Black Sea
Caucasus
Caspian Sea
Zagros Mountains
Taurus Mountains
Mediterranean Sea
0 300 km

HUNTERS ON THE RUN

THE DNA OF ANATOLIAN FARMERS DOMINATED EUROpeans' genome for hundreds of years. Whether or not the Anatolians arrived in numbers larger than the established population, their numerical advantage would only have increased over time, as their agricultural lifestyle, with its surpluses of food, enabled them to have more children. The hunter-gatherers, meanwhile, retreated to areas inhospitable to farming: low mountain ranges with few fields, or the colder parts of Northern Europe. Local conditions during the early Neolithic were not usually ideal for farming, so there were plenty of options.

In order to live alongside each other for two millennia, the farmers and the hunter-gatherers must have come to some sort of arrangement. They lived in parallel societies; although they knew about each other, they were cautious about making contact. But they did overlap. Between 6,000 and 5,000 years ago, as a DNA analysis of remains showed, both farmers and hunter-gatherers buried their dead in the Blätterhöhle cave site in modern-day Westphalia, Germany. The two populations might have been neighbors, both agreeing to use a common burial ground. Although they clearly lived under the same environmental conditions, isotope analysis of their bones reveals that they ate the traditional diet of their respective groups. The hunter-gatherers ate predominantly fish and meat, doubtless with a good helping of worms and insects. The farmers, on the other hand, ate a mainly plant-based diet. Although they had domesticated cattle, sheep, and goats, they lived on their milk and rarely slaughtered them. Members of these different groups might not seem like the ideal pairing for a dinner date, but we know that sparks did occasionally fly between them. Though remains of their mixed offspring have been found in the same caves, it seems that male hunters lagged behind when it came to courtship: the combined offspring found in the cave carry only mtDNA from the hunter-gatherers. Since mtDNA is passed down from the mother, female gatherers must have had sex with male farmers but not female farmers with male hunters. This tallies with behavior observed in contemporary hunter-gatherer populations living cheek by jowl with farmers, in Africa for instance, where this combination—female gatherers and male farmers—is more common than the alternative.

STRESS AND POOR NUTRITION

FANS OF MEAT-HEAVY BARBEQUES WILL SURELY SYMpathize with the hunter-gatherers, who had little appreciation for their new neighbors' mainly vegetarian lifestyle. Although agriculture clearly offered the better opportunity for growth, it took 2,000 years for it to dominate the continent.

Farmers may have had more children than hunter-gatherers, but they paid an obvious price: they never had any leisure time. To keep their larders full, farmers worked around the clock for a paltry amount of grain, some vegetables, a mug of milk, and maybe a piece of cheese. The hunter-gatherers' work was no picnic, but they could do it much more quickly. And while the newcomers lived in constant fear of a failed harvest, the hunters knew how to wrest food

Agriculture was brought to Europe 8,000 years ago with migrating Anatolian farmers. During the late Neolithic, roughly 4,800 years ago, it was practiced with increasing intensity.

from nature even under adverse conditions. They also had the advantage of being well adapted to their meat-heavy diet; even today, many people struggle with grains and milk, as supermarket shelves devoted to gluten- and lactose-free products make plain. In the bones of many early farmers we have found signs of inadequate mineralization, which leads to rickets, so it's reasonable to assume that they seemed slight and weak in comparison to the powerful hunters.

Of course, it wasn't all bad on the farm. Farmers' work may have been tough and their food only somewhat digestible, but they did invent the extended family, increasing their offspring's, and so their population's, long-term chances of survival. With no alternative to the constant toil that defined their lives, farmers must have been astonished by the hunter-gatherers' easy contentment. Once farmers had started producing more food and having more children—who in turn needed more food—they had already planted both feet in their hamster wheel. More food meant more children, and more children meant more demand for food, all of which had to be cultivated and harvested. Humanity has never really reemerged from this state of overwork, and today libraries are stuffed with self-help books for stressed-out workers. And yet if we use material goods as a yardstick, farmers had a higher standard of living than hunter-gatherers. Farmers owned fields, lived in houses, kept livestock. Once they were on the path to growth they couldn't deviate without risking the lives of their children. After a few generations, it would have been impossible to return to the hunt—the skills required needed to be taught from a very young age. In a community of farmers it would have been tantamount to self-exile to join the hunter-gatherers, whom the farmers likely viewed as inferior.

In all likelihood, it was rare for the two populations to live side by side as they did near the Blätterhöhle Cave. Generally the hunter-gatherers were pushed out as the farmers settled in areas with the right conditions. Mountains, forests, and steep terrain were all out of the question. Above all, the farmers needed good soil, which ideally would remain fertile even after several years. So they gravitated toward places such as what is now the Magdeburg Börde in Germany, where the black soil is still among the most fertile in Europe. Europe was up for grabs, and the first farmers made sure to nab the prime real estate. But their heyday didn't last long. As more people competed for plum spots, the residents grew territorial.

VIOLENCE ESCALATES AT CLOSE QUARTERS

WHILE THE FIRST NEOLITHIC SETTLEMENTS WERE unfortified, subsequent generations built defenses to protect their property from outsiders. From early on there were battles over resources: mass graves populated by farmers, dating from shortly after their arrival, have been found all over Europe, and they bear the unmistakable signs of conflict. In Talheim in southern Germany, thirty people were found buried in a 7,000-year-old pit. Their attackers had beaten them with stone axes and blunt objects. In the town of Asparn an der Zaya in Austria, meanwhile, 200 individuals were executed or killed while trying to escape their enemies. No one was spared during these massacres, which are widely assumed to have been conflicts over scarce agricultural land. Small children, teenagers, women, and the elderly have all been found in the graves, as well as men old enough to fight. During the early Neolithic, humans evidently used tools designed for farming and hunting as makeshift weapons. Bows and arrows were among them, and in both Talheim and Asparn the victims' skulls were shattered with axes and adzes (the latter a tool intended for woodworking). Yet only a few centuries later, grave goods interred with farmers began to include weapons, skillfully decorated and made solely to kill. With populations rising, settlements forming, and pressures on space increasing, skirmishes became a fixture of early Neolithic civilization, although there were still no armies or organized campaigns.

These conflicts pitted farmer against farmer, but their fortifications were probably also built to deter hunter-gatherers who might otherwise have viewed the fields and pastures as an open invitation to help themselves. It's unlikely that the hunter-gatherers took up arms against the farmers—why would nomads have risked their lives for a piece of land? Based on numbers alone, they surely would have realized they didn't stand a chance. The two populations were neither conflict-free nor in a permanent state of war. This was no relationship of equals: the hunter-gatherers would have been tolerated, at best, as long as they didn't get in the newcomers' way.

SWEDISH TRACTORS

THE IMBALANCE OF POWER BETWEEN THE TWO GROUPS was starkest on the fertile terrain of Central Europe. Elsewhere, things were not so clear-cut. In southern Scandinavia and the coasts of the Baltic and the North Sea, the land was densely wooded and thus of little use to farmers. The local hunter-gatherers, on the other hand, were like pigs in clover: thanks to the warm Gulf Stream, which attracted seals and whales galore, there was abundant fishing. They saw little reason to follow the example of the farmers, who nonetheless staunchly defended their positions. In Scandinavia too, the two societies lived in parallel, albeit on different terms. Just as in the rest of Europe, they lived in close proximity at first and only later mixed. But in Scandinavia the hunter-gatherers stood their ground more effectively than elsewhere, and their DNA is better represented there today than anywhere else on the continent. Around 6,200 years ago, long after the Neolithic had begun in Central Europe, their interactions with the farmers produced what's known as the Funnel Beaker culture, named after their characteristic ceramic beakers, which tapered—you guessed it—like funnels.

Scandinavia's local hunter-gatherers weren't displaced by the new arrivals. They were open to the farmers' newly imported technologies. Over the following centuries, their willingness to innovate made the Funnel Beaker culture one of the most successful in the Neolithic. The early Scandinavians were aware of the newly invented wheel, which, combined with the use of oxen, opened up entirely new possibilities for transport and farming. The oldest identified cart tracks, dating back 5,400 years, were found in Flintbek, northern Germany, buried beneath a megalithic tomb. One of the greatest inventions given to Europe by the Scandinavians was an early form of tractor: two oxen harnessed to a plow, which carved deep furrows into the ground. Although none of these contraptions have been found, we have discovered impressions of the plows embedded in clay soil, buried beneath just twenty centimeters of earth.

Neolithic farmers could now plow large fields as well as other terrain formerly resistant to agriculture. While trees could be felled, it was impossible for humans to pull out their roots until they harnessed the power of oxen. Similarly, oxen could drag aside boulders left behind by Ice-Age glaciers, especially common in Northern Europe. Some archaeologists believe this practice inspired the construction of the monumental stone edifices that appeared across Europe during this period—the megalithic tombs, for instance, which are also known as barrows. The stones removed from the freshly tilled fields, they argue, had to go somewhere.

The Anatolian farmers had been pushing north; now members of the Funnel Beaker culture pushed south, bringing with them improved technologies as well as familiar hunter-gatherer DNA. Five thousand four hundred years ago, the Scandinavians had ventured as far east as modern-day Belarus and as far west as modern-day Saxony-Anhalt, Germany. The farmers already living there were constantly on the retreat. After several attacks, the land occupied by the Neolithic Salzmünde culture shrank to the area around present-day Halle in central Germany, finally disappearing a little over 5,000 years ago.

Generally speaking, this period of expansion from the north accompanied a decline in the sophistication of the cultures of Central Europe. It's not easy to tell cause from effect: did the people of the Funnel Beaker culture simply move into a region already in freefall, or did they rush in and subjugate it? One striking thing to note is that little human remains dating from between 5,500 and 5,000 years ago have been found in Central Europe (except for in a few regions); only artifacts and the remains of settlements have survived. This might mean that the inhabitants burned their dead, a tradition that was certainly not imported from the north. Assuming this was the case, it may perhaps be evidence of a catastrophic event, one that would later pave the way for another great wave of European migration—but more on that later.

"GENETIC FOSSILS" IN SARDINIA

THE FUNNEL BEAKER CULTURE IS STILL REFLECTED IN European DNA, primarily in Northern and Central Europe. Among Scandinavians, the hunter-gatherers' genetic material figures as prominently as that of the Anatolian farmers; in Lithuania, where the people of the eastern Funnel Beaker culture settled, it's actually *more* prominent. In the south of Europe, where the Anatolian migrants had first arrived and the Scandinavian countermovement never reached, Anatolian genes prevail. Modern-day people from the south of France and Spain have vanishingly little hunter-gatherer DNA, and people from Tuscany even less. Present-day Sardinia, however, is where the first farmers left their clearest genetic mark. There they barely mixed at all, making the Sardinians what we call "genetic fossils." They are unique. Even in Anatolia and the Near East, there are no populations that have remained virtually unchanged since the Neolithic. Chances are there were no or very few hunter-gatherers in Sardinia before that period, and no subsequent large-scale immigration.

The Neolithic settlement of Sardinia suggests that 8,000 years ago, people were capable of building boats, or at least solid rafts. Not only did they have to transport entire families to the island, but also all their belongings—including at least two cattle. The oldest boat ever discovered, built 7,700 years ago, was recovered from Lake Bracciano near Rome. Nor was Sardinia the only island to be settled during this period; the neighboring island of Corsica was too, and eventually, about 6,200 years ago, the farmers also reached modern-day Great Britain by boat. Until 5,000 years ago people in the Baltic and northern Scandinavia lived—indeed, partly still live—a hunter-gatherer lifestyle in the vast, uncultivable forests. But these groups were the exception, and by the time the farmers had crossed the Channel, their communities and way of life had expanded across the whole of Europe.

THE AGE OF INFECTION BEGINS

AS WE HAVE SEEN, DURING THE NEOLITHIC POPULATION numbers rose and people started living in increasingly close proximity with one another and with the domesticated animals that had become a mainstay of every farmer's household. During this period, Europe was home not just to wolves but also to hunter-gatherers, who would have made short work of defenseless sheep. Animals also came in handy when fending off attacks from other farmers, and provided much-needed warmth during the winter months.

Hygiene was an alien concept. The animals were not the problem—although worm infections became increasingly common when people began butchering them for their meat. The way these settlements stored food, especially grain and milk products, was the key danger. The food stores attracted rodents and the parasites that lived on them: fleas and lice. As a result, bacteria and viruses had a field day in these settlements, as diseases were passed from animals to humans more and more often. While hunter-gatherers regularly moved from place to place, the farmers lived amid animal and human excrement, raising their risk of infection. As the settlements became more cramped—and privacy a rarity—transmission from person to person became more frequent. Even as hu-

An animal being slaughtered in a farming village. Meat was actually quite rare, however; animals were first and foremost used for milk.

mans gained ascendancy over plants and animals, they bred a new enemy: infectious disease. From that point on, it would exact a terrible price.

CHAPTER

5

Single Young Men

WHAT HAPPENED TO THE *indigenous Americans? The West collapses; newcomers arrive from the East. They're strong, and they brought horses. Drink more milk!*

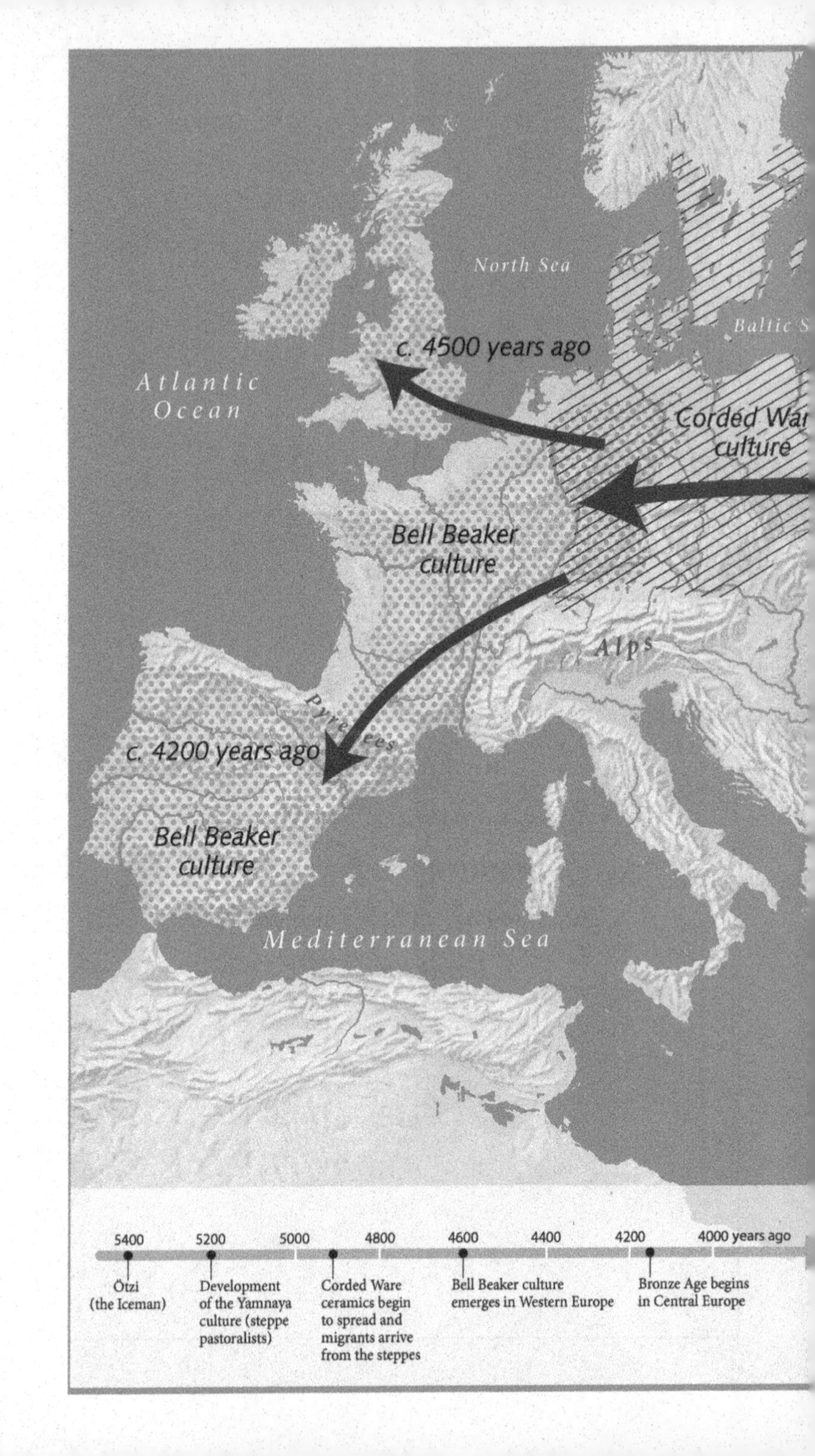
North Sea
Baltic S
c. 4500 years ago
Atlantic Ocean
Corded Wa
culture
Bell Beaker culture
Alps
Pyrenees
c. 4200 years ago
Bell Beaker culture
Mediterranean Sea
5400
5200
5000
4800
4600
4400
4200
4000 years ago
Ötzi (the Iceman)
Development of the Yamnaya culture (steppe pastoralists)
Corded Ware ceramics begin to spread and migrants arrive from the steppes
Bell Beaker culture emerges in Western Europe
Bronze Age begins in Central Europe

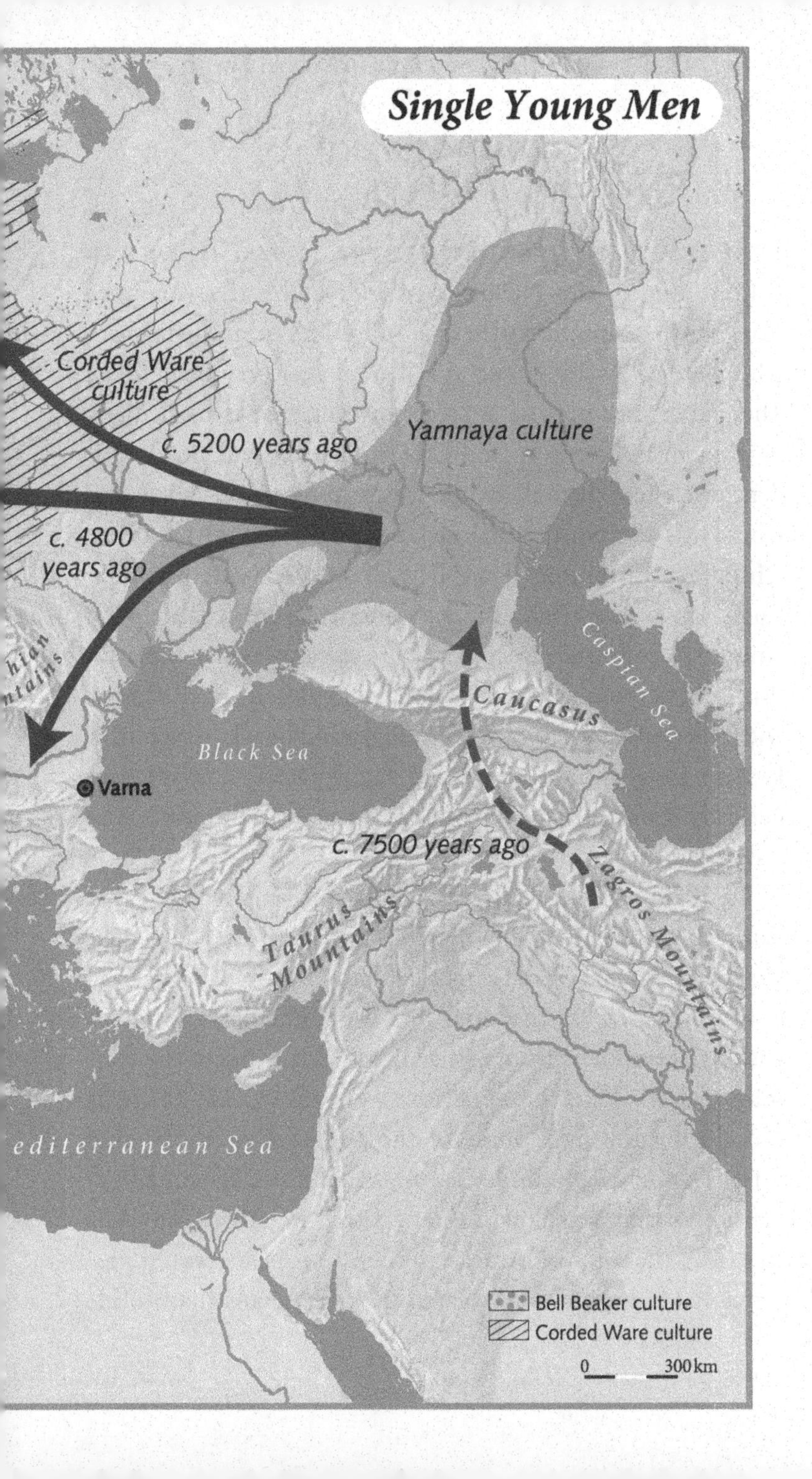

Single Young Men
Corded Ware culture
c. 5200 years ago
Yamnaya culture
c. 4800 years ago
Caspian Sea
Caucasus
Black Sea
Varna
c. 7500 years ago
Zagros Mountains
Taurus Mountains
editerranean Sea
Bell Beaker culture
Corded Ware culture
0 300 km

COWBOYS AND INDIANS

TWO GENETIC CATEGORIES WERE PREDOMINANT IN Europe during the Neolithic period: DNA that stemmed from the local hunter-gatherers, and DNA from the farmers, who were of Anatolian origin. Europeans carry both today. There is a third genetic source, however, that is particularly prominent in Northern and Eastern Europe and clearly evident elsewhere. It took awhile for us to figure out when and where this component emerged, because both early and contemporary Europeans share it with an unexpected population: Native Americans. Native Americans are definitely not among Europeans' direct ancestors, so the explanation for this genetic connection is a little convoluted. It all started with the tremendous wave of immigration into late Neolithic Europe, roughly 5,000 years ago, that ushered a new age. Genetically speaking, it's this influx that made Europeans who they are today.

In 2012, a DNA analysis of living humans revealed that Europeans were more closely related to the indigenous peoples of North and South America than to people in East and Southeast Asia. At the time this was difficult to reconcile with what we knew from archaeology. According to the conventional wisdom, the Americas were settled 15,000 years ago, during the final phase of the Ice Age, via the Bering Strait—which was still dry land—and Alaska. If human expansion had moved along a direct path from Africa into Asia and from there to the Americas, then Europeans would presumably be more closely related to East Asians than to indigenous Americans, since the latter would have split off from the Asian population most recently. Yet the genetic evidence entirely contradicts this assumption.

To resolve the issue, scientists came up with a new theory. In this view, the Americas had been settled not just by East Asian hunter-gatherers but also by people who lived in the area stretching from Northern Europe into Siberia. These people, it was surmised, had intermixed with East Asians and then migrated to North America through Alaska. This would explain the genetic similarity between Europeans and indigenous Americans. The theory never really caught on, however, because climatic and geographical obstacles during the Ice Age make it unlikely that East Siberian and European hunter-gatherers would have procreated often enough to produce a uniform population, which in this hypothesis would have been the genetic link between present-day Europeans and indigenous Americans.

When we sequenced the genome of the Swabian farmer in 2014 and compared it with the DNA of humans already living in Europe, we learned which components could be traced to the European hunter-gatherers and which to the later farmers—and none of them are found in the descendants of indigenous Americans. The hypothetical genetic bridge collapsed: no European hunter-gatherers had emigrated to the Americas.

The final piece of the puzzle fell into place with the discovery of "Mal'ta boy," a child who lived 24,000 years ago in the Baikal region of northern Mongolia. His genome provided the perfect link between Europeans and indigenous Americans, containing genes shared by both populations today. The genetic material found in the boy from Mal'ta must have mixed with the genes of the neighboring East Asians and then crossed the land bridge from East Siberia and Alaska into North America 15,000 years ago—and, somehow and at some point, also reached Europe. This would explain the genetic affinity between the two continents' populations. But what exactly happened? Why didn't the farmers who arrived in Europe 8,000 years ago or the hunter-gatherers already living there share the Mal'ta boy's genes? Why do we nonetheless find those genes in virtually all modern-day Europeans, representing up to 50 percent of their DNA?

In 2015, working alongside international colleagues, we decoded the genomes of sixty-nine people who had lived 8,000 to 3,000 years ago, primarily in the Mittelelbe-Saale region of Germany. By doing so we established genetic profiles for the various epochs during this long period, and we were able to discover when each of these three genetic components appeared in Europe. We determined that the DNA of the boy from Mal'ta was not present in Europe until 5,000 years ago. This was confirmed by the remains of a human nicknamed "Ötzi" (also called "Iceman"), who lived 5,300 years ago—he carried none of the Mal'ta genes. Four thousand eight hundred years ago, however, they appeared in the bones of early Europeans, not piecemeal but suddenly and in massive quantities. The farmers' and hunter-gatherers' genetic material almost disappeared during this period.

A vast number of people with the Mal'ta genes must have surged into Central Europe, and within barely a hundred years—about five generations—they had completely transformed the local genetic profile.[1] Genetic analyses have revealed that their DNA originated in the Pontic steppe, an area in southern Russia north of the Black and Caspian Seas.

In other words, both Europeans and indigenous Americans seem to have drawn a lot of their DNA from genetic material from Eastern Europe and Siberia. This area was home to what archaeogeneticists call "ancient North Eurasians," the group to whom the Mal'ta boy belonged. The North Eurasians' territory spanned 7,000 kilometers, from Eastern Europe into the Baikal region, encompassing the enormous Kazakh steppe, which extends as far as the flatlands by the Caspian and Black Seas. To the east, the ancient North Eurasians began to spread, probably around 20,000 years ago, mixing with the East Asians. The resulting population made its way to the Americas 15,000 years ago, and today the indigenous peoples there carry an almost equal balance of East Asian and ancient North Eurasian genes. This North Eurasian component didn't arrive in Europe until approximately 4,800 years ago, but when it did it came barreling in like a freight train. Five hundred years ago, then, when Europeans "discovered" the Americas, they had in fact come full circle: from a genetic perspective, the settlers were reunited with very, very old relatives.

FOUR-COMPONENT EUROPE

THIS RADICAL SHIFT IN THE EUROPEAN POPULATION 4,800 years ago reflects an even bigger wave of migration than that of the Anatolian farmers. Yet just like the previous wave, it was followed by a period of normalization in which the local populations' DNA partially clawed its way back. Particularly where the migrants from the steppes arrived most recently, in the southwest of the continent, the "steppe component" there is least present in the modern population, although it's still easy to measure. With this wave of migration from the east, Europe's genetic mix reached its current state.

The steppe DNA actually consists of two separate elements. The people of the Pontic steppe were descended not only from the ancient North Eurasians but also from immigrants from around present-day Iran—from the eastern half of the Fertile Crescent, where the Neolithic began and where people in the western part were genetically different from those in the east. What took place in Europe 4,800 years ago was thus a reunion of sorts between two genetic components that had previously coexisted cheek by jowl in the Fertile Crescent.

What this means is that present-day Europeans are not only descended from the hunter-gatherers of Europe and Asia; roughly 60 percent of their genetic material comes from the western and eastern inhabitants of the Fertile Cres-

Typical of the Yamnaya culture were these enormous barrows, which can still be seen today on the Pontic steppe. They probably also served as landmarks on the flat plains.

cent. Thanks to migration, our ancestors span a multiplicity of continents and radically different lifestyles.

The origin of this large-scale wave of migration from the east was the Yamnaya culture, which established itself on the Pontic steppe approximately 5,600 years ago. The Yamnaya culture not only produced pottery but also used bronze to make knives and daggers. The people of the Yamnaya culture were hugely successful. They crossed the steppe with enormous herds of sheep and cattle, stopping at each location until it was grazed down. Given the conditions in the region, their nomadic lifestyle was the most obvious form of nomadic farming. The steppe isn't particularly fertile, but it is incomprehensibly wide: often the journey to the horizon can be measured only in days marched. The immense barrows that were constructed everywhere on the steppe were another hallmark of the Yamnaya era and the primary source of archaeological and genetic information from this period. Barrows were used to venerate the dead, but they probably also acted as signposts in the otherwise boundless landscape. A barrow (also known as a kurgan) usually consisted of a single chamber buried beneath a mound of earth. Small kurgans were two meters high, while others towered up to twenty meters above the ground. Both human remains and generous grave goods have been found in the burial chambers: sometimes the dead were buried with whole wagons or the entire contents of their households. In one chamber we investigated, the wagon driver was actually still seated behind his team. His skeleton revealed more than two dozen healed breaks, much like that of a Neanderthal or a modern-day rodeo cowboy. Life as a herdsman was evidently no walk in the park.

FROM THE BRONZE AGE BACK TO THE STONE AGE

New genetic discoveries occasionally get archaeogeneticists tangled up in semantic knots. The analyses leave no room for doubt: 4,800 years ago, the people of the Yamnaya cultural region arrived in Europe. If we put this finding on the established archaeological timeline, then the eastern migrants found themselves arriving not merely in the west but in the past. The people of the Yamnaya culture had already started using bronze, so Eastern European archaeologists consider them part of the Bronze Age. In the western part of the continent, however (or at least in the Central European literature), the Bronze Age is usually said to have begun 4,200 years ago. In a sense, then, the migrants left the Bronze Age and entered the Stone Age. The fact that a smattering of objects wrought from copper and bronze were used during this period—in Central Europe, for instance—makes matters even less clear. Since the Yamnaya people from the Pontic steppe brought bronze-working techniques with them, I believe there are good reasons to argue that the Bronze Age began in Europe 4,800 years ago, but for the time being many scientists continue to refer to this period as the "Copper Age," or simply the Late or Final Neolithic.

A 150-YEAR BLACK HOLE

THE EASTERN MIGRANTS DID NOT SUDDENLY POUNCE on Europe and displace everybody who lived there. It seems more likely that they first moved into partly uninhabited areas. You'll remember that almost no skeletons have been found in Central Europe from between 5,500 and 5,000 years ago. The DNA tests carried out on the few bodies from that time that have been found there reveal the Neolithic genes from Anatolia. For the period between 5,000 and 4,800 years ago, however, it is as though the whole lot had been sucked into a black hole. We have hardly any usable DNA from Europe and hardly any objects. It seems plausible, then, that the migrants from the steppes arrived in a largely depopulated landscape.

Even today, we can only speculate about the reasons for this vast influx. For such a radical genetic transformation to be possible, it's reasonable to suppose the local population plummeted before this great wave arrived. I believe there are clear indications of an epidemic that spread through Central Europe and left few survivors. The oldest decoded plague genome dates from this period. It was found in the remains of people from the Yamnaya culture on the steppe, and spread into Europe along the same path as the steppe DNA. Of course, violent clashes between the newcomers and the farmers are also a possibility. Yet even in that scenario, the population of Central Europe must already have been decimated. Otherwise we would have found evidence of murdered people with Neolithic DNA from the period 5,000 years ago, in mass graves or on battlefields. We haven't.

Nor do we have much archaeological evidence from this

era. This gap in the record could be due in part to the new migrants' lifestyle. Assuming they maintained their nomadic habits for several generations, which seems plausible given the steppe-like landscape of Eastern Europe, then they would not have built anything for archaeologists to dig up. Indeed, almost the only structures that do survive from this 150-year gap are barrows strikingly similar to those of the Yamnaya culture. The farther we go into Central Europe, the less common these barrows become, and farther west they don't exist at all. The farther these steppe nomads ventured into the hills of Central Europe, land that was increasingly unsuitable for their herds, the less reason they would have had to stay. They might also have decided not to bother with such elaborate and time-intensive structures as barrows if they looked relatively mundane, as they would have against the hilly landscape itself.

Within a century the steppe migrants had reached the Mittelelbe-Saale region in Central Europe. Two centuries later they had reached modern-day Great Britain, and nowhere on their journey was the genetic shift more glaring than north of the Channel. While in present-day Germany 70 percent of the genetic structure changed, in Great Britain it was at least 90 percent. The immigrants from the steppe drove out the architects of Stonehenge, but they continued to use the site and even develop it further. Only 500 years after arriving in Central Europe they reached the Iberian Peninsula, the most distant point on the continent, but they arrived with considerably less force than elsewhere. Spain, walled off by the Pyrenees, continued to hold a special place in the genetic history of Europe, as it had done during the Ice Age.

Today's Spaniards, like Sardinians, Greeks, and Albanians, have the fewest steppe genes of all Europeans.

In general, this component outweighs the others in Northern Europe, while the farmers' DNA predominates across Spain, the south of France, and Italy into the southern Balkans. If the inhabitants of the steppe preferred flat country, then the most obvious path west for them ran through modern-day Poland and Germany into northern France and Great Britain. Then, roughly 4,200 years ago, the pendulum swung back yet again when steppe genes began migrating not west but east, now enriched with farmer DNA. This is why even now, people in the depths of central Russia and in the Altai Mountains have the same Anatolian genes as people in Western Europe.

NATIONALISM

RIDING ON HORSEBACK CHANGED EVERYTHING. A RADICAL innovation of the steppe people, it allowed their genes to spread farther and faster than those of any other group so far. Horses not only enabled the people of the steppes to move more quickly but made them astonishingly effective warriors. These warriors, a head taller than Central European early farmers, brought with them battle-axes and a newfangled kind of bow and arrow, made shorter than the familiar longbow, so it would be manageable enough to be fired while riding, yet still powerful. Swift horses and portable weapons were a deadly combination. Numerous archaeological sites testify to violent clashes between the established farmers and these newcomers. Axes, found regularly in burial sites in

Central Europe, most likely played a pivotal role during this initial phase of migration. As the steppe people moved farther west and south, the bow and arrow seems to have become their most common weapon.

In the nineteenth century, archaeologists in German-speaking countries as well as Scandinavia and Great Britain described this group as the "Battle Axe culture." This term was later appropriated by the Nazis and incorporated into their propaganda, reinterpreted as an early example of the Germans' superiority as warriors. For understandable reasons, other terms have been preferred since the Second World War. These days we refer instead to the Corded Ware culture, named after the distinctive cord-like patterns on their pottery.

Meanwhile, the western part of the continent was dominated by the people of the Bell Beaker culture, whose bell-shaped vessels have been found primarily in Great Britain, France, the Iberian Peninsula, and central and southern Germany. Production of these vessels was taken to Great Britain by immigrants, but elsewhere it spread purely as a cultural trend, from person to person. This runs contrary to conventional archaeological wisdom, which suggests that the production of this kind of pottery expanded northward out of present-day Portugal into Great Britain, in parallel to and independent from Corded Ware. The latest genetic discoveries, however, refute this theory. In a 2018 large-scale study involving our institute, among others, we decoded the genomes of about 400 skeletons of both cultures dating from the period before and after the influx of migration from the steppes. Our results suggest that the Bell Beaker culture came to the fore in Great Britain only once the previous inhabitants had been almost completely displaced by people with steppe DNA. At the same time, grave goods show that the Bell Beaker culture was expanding south across the entire Iberian Peninsula, where few steppe people migrated.

The average person today probably doesn't much care about when and why people in particular regions began drinking from certain types of cups. For archaeologists, however, it is a long-standing and politically charged question. Early twentieth-century archaeologists and scientists with connections to the Nazis argued that a people with a shared culture always constituted a single *Volk*—meaning they had common DNA. The implication was that superior cultural technologies went hand in hand with genetic superiority; descendants of the "Battle Axe culture," for example, could claim they had a genetic right to power and control. These cultural, linguistic, and ethnic theories carried serious political baggage in German-language archaeology after the Second World War and were roundly condemned, replaced by the notion that cultures spread not through migration, conquest, and subjugation but through cultural exchange between populations. The idea that there were massive waves of migration into Europe and that these engendered large-scale cultural shifts thus proved controversial. Nonetheless, the genetic data regarding the Neolithic Revolution—and particularly regarding migration from the steppes—is unambiguous. It has been quite a headache for many archaeologists. Our analyses of the spread of Bell Beaker pottery into the Iberian Peninsula and Great Britain reveals that the debate is not black and white: cultural change often involves migration, but migration isn't a necessary component of cultural transmission.

PRZEWALSKI'S HORSE ISN'T REALLY WILD

The inhabitants of the steppes brought plenty of horses to Europe; at least, we've certainly found a lot more horse skeletons dating from this period. On the broad steppes, horses were an ideal mode of transport, enabling the Yamnaya people to cover great distances and guard large herds of cattle. Used in conjunction with the wheel and wagon, they powered the fastest vehicles available at the time. In fact, this may have been the key technological innovation that allowed the Yamnaya to move west.

The earliest surviving DNA of any creature belongs to a horse that died 750,000 years ago and was preserved in the Alaskan permafrost. Wild horses have also been native to Eurasia since time immemorial. They were probably first domesticated on the Kazakh steppes by the people of the Botai culture, which emerged 5,700 years ago. By the Yamnaya era, domesticated horses were a fixture of daily life. For a long time it was assumed that horses from the steppes came to Europe alongside their human owners and displaced the local species. If this theory was correct, today's European domesticated horses would be descendants of the Botai animals, while the old European wild horses would have been preserved as what today we call Przewalski's horses: by the early twentieth century this type of horse had virtually gone extinct, but after extensive efforts there are now a few thousand of them in the wild.

Reconstruction of a domesticated horse from Eastern Europe, the animal from which today's Przewalski's horses are descended. The steppe migrants later switched to using the European horse.

A genetic comparison of the different kinds of horse, however, shows that this theory is inaccurate. Modern domesticated horses are not descended from the Botai animals, but Przewalski's horses are. The latter carry DNA inherited not from archaic Eurasian wild horses but from domesticated Botai horses that presumably went feral—much like the American mustang, which is descended from domesticated Spanish horses. The immigrants from the steppes seem to have preferred European wild horses; as experienced riders, they domesticated these horses within a few hundred years. Whether these horses originated in Central or Eastern Europe is unclear, but what we do know is that the horses we ride today are their descendants. By the time humans started trying to preserve Przewalski's horses, then, believing they were the last truly wild horses, it was too late: European wild horses no longer existed.

MALE DOMINANCE

THE GENETIC CHANGES THAT TOOK PLACE IN THE first century after the influx of the Yamnaya people into Europe testify not only to their superior numbers but also to the ratio of men to women in the group. The mtDNA of Bronze Age Europeans has revealed an imbalance in the sexes. If lots of women had migrated from the steppes and propelled the subsequent genetic shift, then the following generations' mtDNA (inherited solely from the female line) would have been dominated by the steppe component. But this was not the case. Instead, a pronounced shift took place in the Y chromosome, the part of the genome passed down solely from fathers to sons. Eighty to 90 percent of the Bronze Age Y chromosomes were new to Europe but had been present on the steppes. Both these factors suggest that men from the steppes came to Central Europe and had numerous children with local women. Up to 80 percent of the Yamnaya migrants were male.

Historical precedents suggest that the local male population would have been less than pleased to find themselves in competition with large numbers of strapping horsemen, and there was lots of violence. One of the most spectacular examples of violent death took place about 4,500 years ago in

Eulau, present-day Saxony-Anhalt, where inhabitants of a recently established Corded Ware village, who carried steppe genes, kept luring away the local women. Eight children, three women, and two men were executed with arrows straight through the heart. The arrowheads found in the victims clearly belonged to the previously established Neolithic population. A profiler from the Federal Criminal Police Office even inspected the Stone Age crime scene, describing it as a homicide committed by a highly skilled sharpshooter.

What prompted the attackers to kill the women and children we can only guess, but some archaeologists favor a particularly hair-raising explanation. A DNA analysis of the murdered women revealed no steppe ancestry, so it's presumed they came to the settlement from the local population. Perhaps, the theory goes, this was an act of revenge—either on the women for leaving their group or on the men for "stealing" the women. In any case, the story should be taken with a pinch of salt. Only the women's mtDNA could be examined, but it would take a fully sequenced genome to tell us precisely how the victims were related, and whether the women really had no steppe genes.

The Y chromosomes that came to Europe with the steppe migrants are still the most dominant on the continent today, meaning that a significant proportion of the population can be traced back to a number of forebears from the steppes. Yet there is a genetic border between Western and Eastern Europe. While the majority of men everywhere have a Y chromosome from the steppes, a different subtype predominates in each half of the continent: approximately 70 percent of male Western Europeans have a Y chromosome from haplogroup R1b, and approximately half of male Eastern Europeans have one from haplogroup R1a. Although we shouldn't overemphasize the significance of haplogroups, which represent a single line of descent following either mtDNA or the Y chromosome, there is a remarkable parallel here with archaeological findings. R1a predominates in areas where the Corded Ware culture was rooted, while R1b is found mainly in Bell Beaker areas. What this suggests is that, despite all the human movements that have occurred in Europe since these two cultures died out, their genetic traces, rooted in a geographical divide, still remain today. It's also interesting to note, albeit purely incidentally, that in Germany the balance between R1a and R1b men changes almost exactly along the border between the former East and West Germany.

GOT MILK?

ALTHOUGH THE WAVE OF MIGRATION FROM THE STEPPES precipitated the biggest genetic transformation Europe has ever seen, its cultural impact was less radical than the one that took place 3,000 years earlier, when the farmers arrived from Anatolia. The first cultural shake-up brought farmers face-to-face with hunter-gatherers; the second confronted farmer with farmer. If we disregard the 150-year gap in the archaeological record, settlements unearthed from the period subsequent to the incursion of the Yamnaya, such as the Corded Ware settlement from Eulau, are remarkably similar to those from earlier epochs. Like their predecessors, the new settlers lived in villages and tended the surrounding fields. In at least one key aspect, however—besides their skill with bronze—the eastern nomads were radically different from the western farmers in that they were passionate cattle herders. While the established farmers usually kept no more than two cows, the newcomers owned entire herds. Europe, with its fertile soil and verdant pastureland, allowed these former nomads to graze their livestock in one place and put down roots. This changed both agriculture in Europe and the European diet.

Cows 8,000 years ago bore little relation to today's high-yield animals, which produce an average of fifty liters of milk per day. Two liters would have been the maximum for a Neolithic cow, although humans started very early on to augment this amount through genetic optimization (read: selective breeding), and a cow in the Middle Ages probably produced around fifteen to twenty liters per day. Moreover, only a small part of that two-liter yield would have ended up in the bellies of the animal's owners—the rest would have been drunk by the calves. The remaining milk, shared among the farmer's family, would scarcely have been enough for one cup per person. This was a good thing too, because in those days Europeans weren't built to digest large amounts of cow's milk.

Even now, many people are lactose intolerant. Despite what's usually assumed, lactose intolerance is not an allergy or an illness; it's the default genetic state of all adult mammals. When humans are kept to their basic factory settings, only young children can digest milk. They produce an enzyme in their small intestine called lactase, which can break down the lactose (the type of sugar found in milk) into sugars that can be absorbed. Adults, who don't produce lactase, cannot use milk sugar as food because they can't turn it into other sugars. Instead, the lactose is broken down by bacteria in the colon, which produces diarrhea and flatulence. This process isn't dangerous, but it is extremely unpleasant and can also be painful. From an evolutionary perspective, this genetic programming makes sense—otherwise babies would be competing for their mothers' milk with other family members, including their fathers, during lean times.

Today, even the most lactose-intolerant adults can drink as much milk as they please, because lactase is available to buy over the counter. In Northern and Central Europe, however, most adults don't need these pills because they have inherited an especially widespread mutation affecting the gene that switches off lactase production as a person ages. So these Northern and Central Europeans continue to produce the enzyme even in adulthood. The spread of this mutation went hand in hand with the increasing availability of milk in Europe. Until then, it had not been necessary: even people who are lactose intolerant can drink a glass of milk a day without much trouble, although admittedly they're only digesting its fat and protein, not its precious sugar. As more milk became available with the influx of cattle herders from the steppes, the ability to tolerate lactose became a distinct evolutionary advantage and spread in the population. Lactose tolerance was propelled rather than imported by the herders, who seem to have developed the mutation once they settled and began drinking more milk. So far, we haven't found any adult Yamnaya with a tolerance for lactose; the oldest carrier of this mutation we found is an individual from the Corded Ware culture that lived 4,200 years ago in Switzerland, a region that is still famous for its delicious dairy products, including cheeses and chocolate.

The mutation traveled across Central Europe with pastoral farming, spreading faster than any previously identified mutation, including skin color. These days it's most ubiquitous in Northern Europe, where only about 20 percent of people are intolerant and don't carry this gene. The farther south we look, the more this number rises: intolerance is most prevalent in the Balkans and the Iberian Peninsula. Worldwide, adult lactose intolerance is most prevalent in large parts of sub-Saharan Africa, in Southeast Asia, and in South America. Yet even in Africa and South Asia there are still some populations where the lactase gene mutation is common, although it emerged independently from the European variant. The process of adaption to dairy farming, therefore, seems to have occurred in many regions worldwide in parallel.

The low prevalence of lactose tolerance in the Balkans is especially surprising since it was here that Europe's first farmers arrived with their cows 8,000 years ago. Their current dietary preferences would also suggest they are lactose tolerant: ayran, a drink made from yogurt, water, and salt, is extremely popular, as is yogurt itself, and sheep's-milk cheese is a major export. All these milk products have been part of their diet for thousands of years. This is also true for Italy, where most people are lactose intolerant. Yet the explanation is simple: yogurt and the cheeses in question are fermented, so most of the lactose has already been broken down by bacteria during the manufacturing process. In the south, where high temperatures encourage the growth of dairy-preserving bacteria, people likely consumed most of their milk in a bacterially predigested form. The situation in the north would have been quite different: milk would have stayed fresh for longer, so northerners would have had to break down the lactose themselves.

THE ADVENT OF LARGE-SCALE LIVESTOCK FARMING

LACTOSE TOLERANCE WAS FAR MORE THAN AN INTEResting side effect of developing agricultural practices. People with this mutation had, on average, more children than those without it. To be lactose tolerant meant having access to an additional food source. This would have led to better health and improved one's chances of having more children. In the north, where the soil was not as fertile as in the south but was highly suitable as pastureland, milk would probably have helped compensate for the lack of crops. It's no coincidence that the Celts and Teutons were known to the Romans as prodigious milk drinkers.

In the centuries after the steppe people migrated into Europe, around 4,800 years ago, pastoral farming steadily became more important. Farmers got better at farming and were able to feed more mouths, so the population grew. The Bell Beaker and Corded Ware cultures flourished; although they maintained distinctive burial rituals, their weaponry and pottery grew increasingly alike. Limited resources led to competition, but it also forced them to trade with each other. Thanks to horses, the wheel, and the wagon, goods could be transported over significantly longer distances than ever before. Approximately 4,200 years ago, in the early Bronze Age, Europe was on the threshold of a new age.

It helped that people from different regions could probably communicate with a newfound ease—as we will discover next, the steppe migrants introduced a new language to the continent. Europe, it seems, was finally speaking with one voice.

CHAPTER

6

Europeans Find a Language

DEAD MEN TELL NO TALES. *The British don't speak Slavic. Words can mutate too. The answer is in Iran. Language becomes politics.*

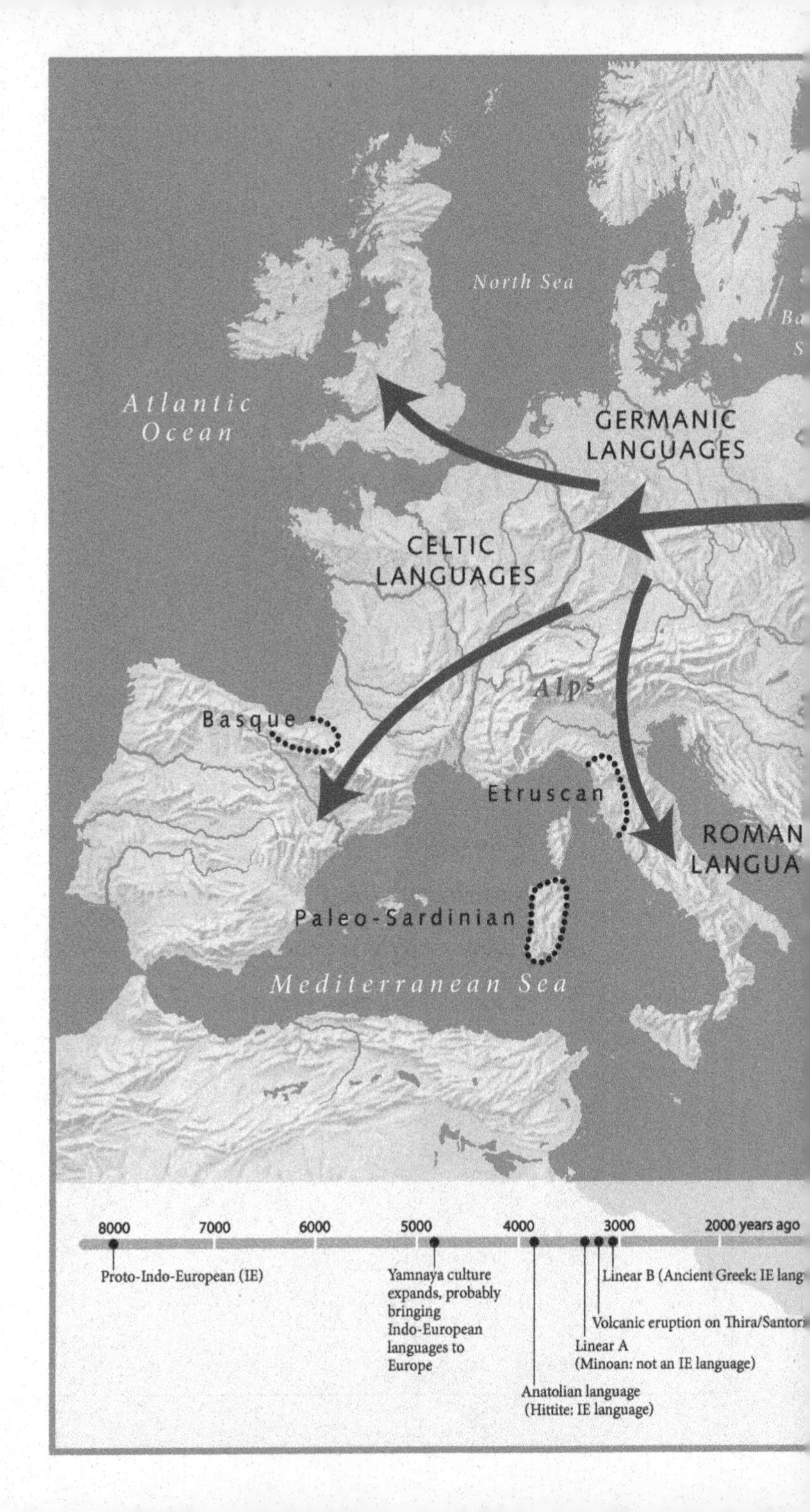

North Sea
Atlantic Ocean
GERMANIC LANGUAGES
CELTIC LANGUAGES
Alps
Basque
Etruscan
ROMAN
LANGUA
Paleo-Sardinian
Mediterranean Sea
8000
7000
6000
5000
4000
3000
2000 years ago
Proto-Indo-European (IE)
Yamnaya culture expands, probably bringing Indo-European languages to Europe
Anatolian language (Hittite: IE language)
Linear A (Minoan: not an IE language)
Volcanic eruption on Thira/Santori
Linear B (Ancient Greek: IE lang

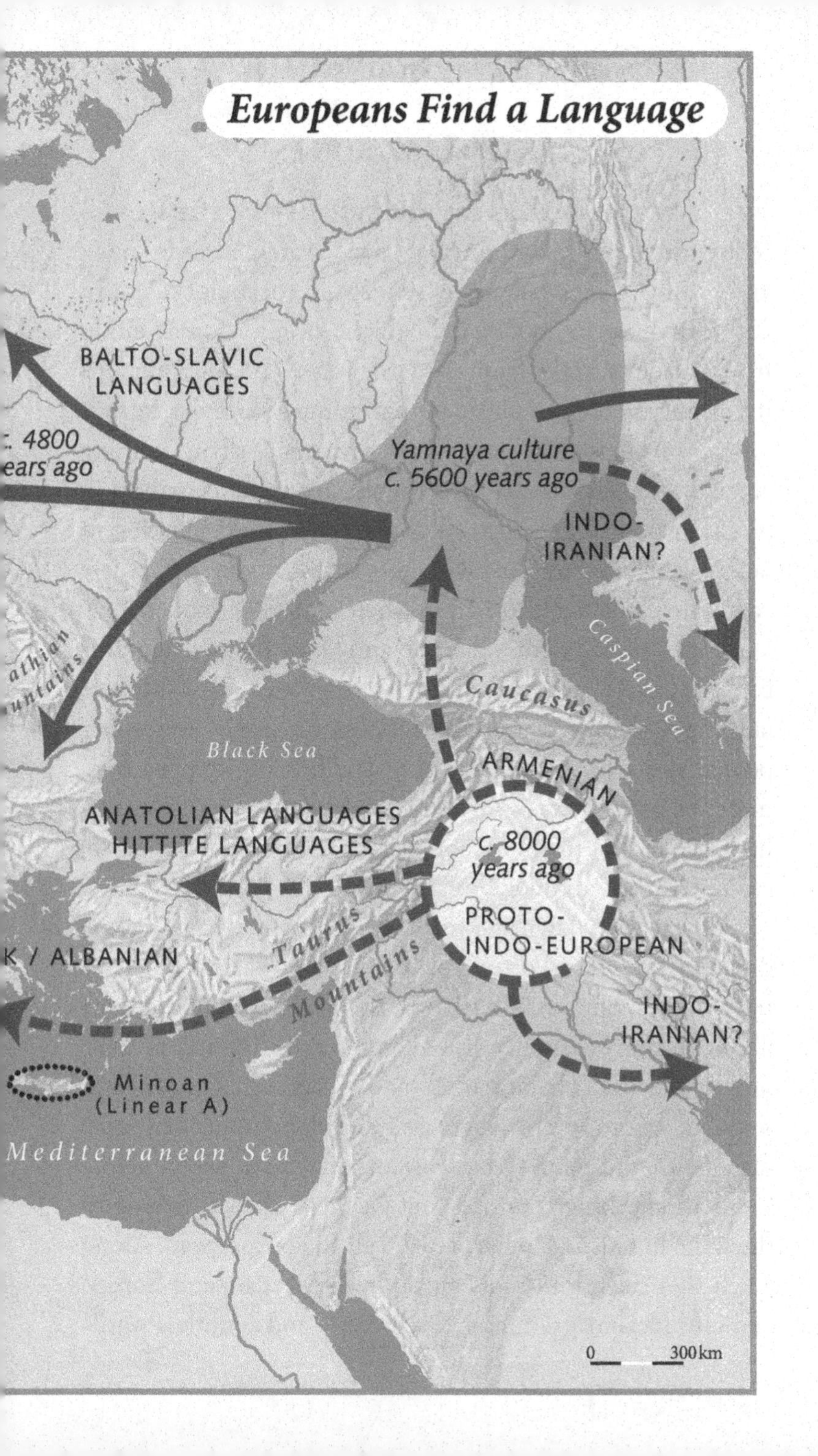
Europeans Find a Language
BALTO-SLAVIC LANGUAGES
. 4800
ears ago
Yamnaya culture
c. 5600 years ago
INDO-IRANIAN?
athian
untains
Caspian Sea
Caucasus
Black Sea
ARMENIAN
ANATOLIAN LANGUAGES
HITTITE LANGUAGES
c. 8000
years ago
PROTO-INDO-EUROPEAN
K / ALBANIAN
Taurus
Mountains
INDO-IRANIAN?
Minoan
(Linear A)
Mediterranean Sea
0 300km

SPEECHLESS BONES

THERE ARE 6,500 SEPARATE LANGUAGES IN THE WORLD today, give or take, and linguists have examined every nook and cranny of each language's syntax and vocabulary. Almost everything we know about linguistic origins comes either from ancient texts or from modern usage. Although humanity's ability to communicate in this uniquely complex form is rooted in our genes, bones can obviously tell us nothing about how their owners used to talk. Yet genetic analysis in recent years has managed to advance our understanding of languages. Drawing on DNA as well as language trees, we can now explain quite better when and how modern-day languages spread across Europe and Asia. Steppe migrants brought likely a new family of languages to Europe—languages that were the predecessors of nearly everything people speak on the continent today. But the steppes were merely a way station. Our modern-day languages appear to have originated in the region around Armenia, Azerbaijan, eastern Turkey, and northwest Iran.

Almost every language you can hear today—from Icelandic to Greek, from Portuguese to Russian to Hindi—derives from a common root. We all learn this at school, but it doesn't jibe with our experience. There are areas in Bavaria or Saxony where the inhabitants of one village can't understand somebody from seven villages away, let alone someone speaking one of the many other variants that have arisen across German-speaking countries. Yet all these dialects belong to the same linguistic family: they are all Indo-European. Along a belt that runs from India and Iran across mainland Europe and into Iceland, grammatical structures and countless words can be traced back to a single point of origin. Going back further in time, we reach the base root of all Indo-European languages, a common language known as Proto-Indo-European. Basque, Hungarian, Finnish, Estonian, and a few smaller languages in northeastern Europe are exceptions to this rule.

The proto-language is a theoretical construct, of course. We will never know exactly what it sounded like. Researchers have had to fall back on written sources, but writing developed only after the Indo-European languages were already distinct. Ancient texts and modern languages offer clues, but our understanding of the origin and transmission of Indo-European languages is ultimately based on conjecture. Archaeogenetics hasn't changed that, but certain linguistic hypotheses are more consistent with the genetic data than others.

For decades, there have been two main competing theories about how Indo-European languages came to Europe. One theory suggests that they arrived with the Neolithic Revolution 8,000 years ago. The other dates their arrival to 5,000 years ago, with the influx from the steppes. Both theories were put forward, incidentally, before we had genetic proof of these two epochal waves of migration. The steppe hypothesis presupposes that this wave actually happened, which is why it was long discredited, especially by archaeologists, most of whom disputed any such migration had taken place. Instead they favored the Neolithic view, arguing that Indo-European languages reached western Eurasia with the cultural shift toward agriculture. This theory does not necessarily presuppose an influx of migrants, because it operates on the premise that language, like other cultural technologies, can be transmitted from person to person.

Recent analyses have established a new set of facts, but they have not settled the debate. Though we now know definitively that colossal waves of migration took place 8,000 and 5,000 years ago, and that in both cases the local population was largely displaced, the question of which wave brought Indo-European languages remains an open question. I find the steppe model more supported by the genetic data, as I will explain shortly.

A VOLCANIC ERUPTION ON SANTORINI

TO UNDERSTAND THE DEVELOPMENT OF INDO-EUROPEAN, it helps to take a look at the ancient Greeks—the very ancient Greeks. Linguists in the twentieth century not only painstakingly uncovered the relationship between Indo-European languages but also decoded the world's earliest known written records. The oldest Indo-European language preserved in written form was spoken by the Hittites, a people who lived in Anatolia until about 3,200 years ago. For a century we have also been aware that the oldest Indo-European written language found in Europe was an ancestor of Ancient Greek and thus Modern Greek: Mycenaean. It was written in a script known as Linear B and spoken by the people of the Mycenaean culture, who established one of the first advanced civilizations in Europe about 3,600 years ago.[1] Resident on the Greek mainland, they were ancestors to the Greeks—along with Minoans, members of an advanced civilization that developed even earlier on the island Crete. The Minoans used a different script, referred to by researchers as Linear A. Linear A and Linear B have characteristics in common, and the individual signs are also alike, but only Linear B has been deciphered; Linear A continues to baffle linguists. We know that the Linear B script represents a language that is a predecessor of Greek, and is thus an Indo-European language. Linear A uses a similar script, but the language it represents is a mystery.

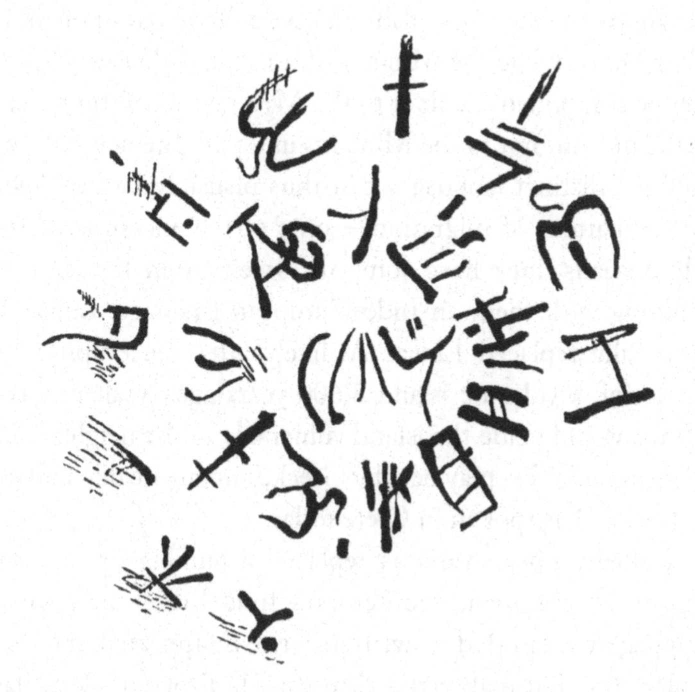

The Minoans used the script referred to as Linear A. To this day it has never been decoded. Unlike the language spoken on the Greek mainland around the same time, the language recorded in Linear A was likely not an Indo-European one.

What do these fundamental differences between the two scripts mean, given that the two cultures were so closely intertwined? To explore this question thoroughly, we have recently examined the DNA of people from both civilizations who lived on the Greek islands and around the Aegean. From the outset it was clear that the Minoans and the Mycenaeans were both descended from Neolithic migrants from Anatolia, so the two populations were closely related. Nonetheless, there were some significant genetic differences. The Mycenaeans on the mainland also carried the steppe component in their DNA, while the Minoans did not. In other words, the steppe component made it to the Mycenaeans on the Greek mainland, but not to the Minoans in Crete. The neighboring cultures' distinct languages can thus plausibly be explained by the pattern of migration—some of the ancestors of the Mycenaeans must have come to Greece from the steppes, bringing with them an Indo-European language. Linear B eventually replaced Linear A, likely after the eruption of Santorini, a volcanic island 3,600 years ago, weakened the Minoans and made the island vulnerable to the neighboring Mycenaeans. This may be why Greek, a linguistic descendant of Linear B, is spoken in Crete today.

Indo-European variants replaced a number of regional languages. Etruscan, another non-Indo-European ancient language transmitted in written form, disappeared and was replaced by Latin after the Etruscans' territory, modern-day Tuscany and surrounding regions, was conquered by the Roman Republic, which was expanding outward from modern-day northern Italy. Two non-Indo-European languages from this era, however, have survived to the present day. Paleo-Sardinian is one, even though just a few words remain. One can find numerous villages, rivers, and mountains on Sardinia with names that are clearly not of Indo-European origin. The other is Basque, which is still spoken

A Bronze Age fresco from the volcanic island of Santorini, depicting a procession of Minoan ships. They lived primarily on Crete. The Minoans' language vanished with their culture.

today in parts of northern Spain and southern France. Other languages that held on after the arrival of the steppe people still exist in Scandinavia, the Baltic, northern Russia, and Hungary. These Finno-Ugric languages probably arrived from northern Asia after Indo-European was already established on the continent. Historical documents and archaeological data suggest that they most likely reached Hungary in the late first millennium CE and Scandinavia even earlier.

BEFORE INDO-EUROPEAN

TO ANSWER THE QUESTION OF WHAT LANGUAGES PEOPLE in Europe spoke before Indo-European came to predominate, it's worth looking at Paleo-Sardinian and the Sardinians themselves, the only population in Europe largely descended from Anatolian farmers. They have virtually no hunter-gatherer DNA, a clear sign that nobody (or almost nobody) lived on the island prior to the farmers' arrival. It therefore seems reasonable to assume that a precursor to Paleo-Sardinian, the latter probably still spoken on Sardinia until about 2,000 years ago, reached Europe from Anatolia 8,000 years ago. This doesn't mean that this is when all the languages spoken in Europe during the Neolithic arrived; languages spoken by the hunter-gatherers may also have survived. Yet it hardly seems likely that the Anatolians adapted to communicate with the hunter-gatherers by learning their language—the language of a culture that historical and contemporary experience suggests they viewed as inferior. Still, the hunter-gatherers, living in their parallel societies, may well have clung to their own languages.

Basque is thus occasionally seen as a holdover from the age of European hunter-gatherers, but the genetic data does not bear this out. The Basques do have more hunter-gatherer DNA than Central Europeans, but it is vastly overshadowed by steppe and farmer ancestry. Genetic analyses of early Basque farmers likewise reveal a very high proportion of Anatolian genes, higher even than among present-day inhabitants of the region. It's likely that Basque, Paleo-Sardinian, Minoan, and Etruscan developed on the continent in the course of the Neolithic Revolution. Sadly, the true diversity of the languages that once existed in Europe will never be known.

Some researchers think Indo-European was imported by Anatolian farmers, but this seems unlikely as well. We know a second wave of migration—the newcomers from the steppes—took place after the farmers' arrival, so we must ask what language this new population brought with it. Some proponents of the Anatolian-origin hypothesis argue that the steppe people could have brought Slavic, which is a branch of Indo-European. In this scenario, the Indo-European languages would have come from Anatolia 8,000 years ago, spreading westward into Europe as well as north onto the Pontic steppe. While branches of Indo-European were developing in Europe during the Neolithic, the hypothesis goes, Slavic was developing in parallel on the steppes, only arriving in Europe 5,000 years ago. Yet this is not supported by the evidence: migrants from the steppes displaced 90 percent of the local population in modern-day Great Britain, but today there is no trace of Slavic influence on the languages spoken there.

To be clear: detours, interactions, and staggered developments in the formation of a language are not inconceivable. Languages rarely move simply from A to B, then on to become C and D. Like the genes of the people who transport them, they are an amalgamation of highly diverse influences. A new theory on the origin of Indo-European languages that my colleagues and I developed is similarly based on this fundamental premise, and we do believe that the steppes were a way station in the spread of Indo-European—just not in the same way as in the model just described.

LANGUAGE IS MATHEMATICS

MANY YEARS' WORK, AND PLENTY OF DEBATE, LED MY colleagues and me to develop a new hybrid theory on the origin of Indo-European. For our model, we used genetic data about the waves of European migration during the

Stone and Bronze Ages and drew on a method that allowed us a glimpse of our linguistic past. We incorporated techniques usually used in genetics, on the basis that what's true for DNA is true for languages as well: they mutate with relatively consistent frequency. A geneticist can calculate from the DNA of two individuals when their most recent common ancestor was alive. In linguistics we can take two closely related words—the German *Leiter*, let's say, and the English "ladder"—and work backward, figuring out how many steps there must be between the two variants and their single word of origin. These rates of mutation were calculated for thousands of words from numerous Indo-European languages, to produce a family tree that shows when the various languages branched off from one another. Its shape often mirrors the family tree of human populations: German, Danish, and English, for example, have more recent common ancestors than German and Italian.

Russell Gray, my colleague at the institute, was able to extend the linguistic family tree much further into the past than the first written sources of Indo-European. Together with his colleagues he analyzed the differences between the oldest known Indo-European languages—Mycenaean, Hittite, Ancient Greek, and Ancient Latin—and worked out how often they must have mutated since they'd diverged. The most recent common ancestor of all Indo-European languages, according to their calculations, was spoken roughly 8,000 years ago.

This figure has been public knowledge since 2003 and strongly suggests that Indo-European migrated west with the Anatolian farmers. Yet genetic data unearthed in recent years has refuted this thesis. It's clear that Indo-European languages were spoken not only in Europe but also in India, Afghanistan, and Pakistan. While it's true that agriculture spread both west and east from the Fertile Crescent 8,000 years ago, if Indo-European originated during this period then it follows that people in the east as well as the west would have spoken the same or very similar languages, which they then exported in both directions. Until recently, there was no evidence to the contrary; after all, the Fertile Crescent represented a homogenous cultural milieu between present-day Israel and Iran. Yet, as we now know, genetic data suggests that the eastern and western populations of the Fertile Crescent were two fundamentally different groups—groups as different as modern-day Europeans and Chinese—and must have diverged much more than 11,000 years ago; the same must be true of their languages. The origins of Indo-European must therefore date back at least 11,000 years, not 8,000, making the Anatolian theory moot. Proponents of the steppe theory had a similar problem, because their model was equally irreconcilable with the evidence that the most recent common ancestor of all Indo-European languages existed 8,000 years ago. Though they assumed that what's known as the Maikop culture, located in the region between the Black and Caspian Seas, transmitted Proto-Indo-European eastward and westward, that culture dates back no more than 6,000 years.

ROOTS IN IRAN

NONETHELESS, IT'S HIGHLY LIKELY THAT INDO-EUROPEAN languages were brought to Europe from the steppes 5,000 years ago. Wherever Indo-European languages are spoken

FAMILY TREE OF INDO-EUROPEAN LANGUAGES

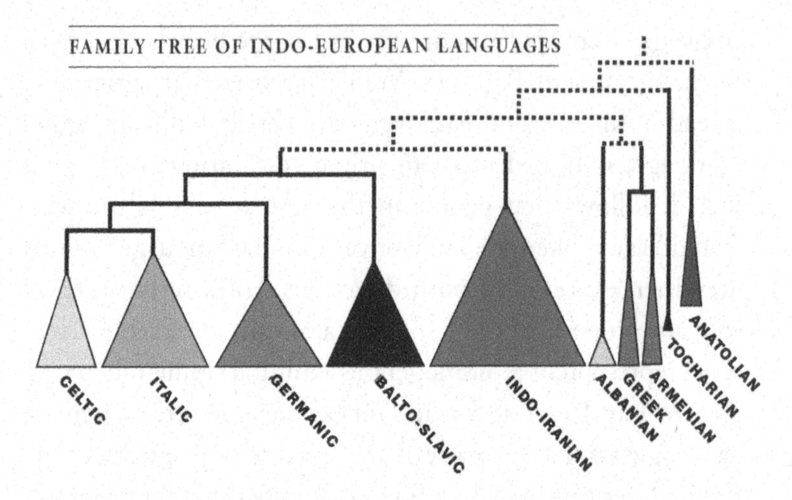

According to the hybrid theory developed at Jena, Indo-European languages originated in present-day Iran. Anatolian and Tocharian (then spoken in western China) no longer exist today.

today, there is a significant proportion of steppe DNA: more precisely, the genetic components that arrived on the Pontic steppe from modern-day Iran during the Neolithic. This is true for modern-day Iran, Afghanistan, and Pakistan as well as for Europe. On the Indian subcontinent, home to a sixth of the world's population, the steppe genes figure heavily. In the north, they constitute a third of most people's DNA. Those in the south have a significantly lower percentage, corresponding perfectly with the distribution of Indo-European languages. Southern India is dominated by Dravidian languages, which are not part of the Indo-European family, while in the north a branch of Indo-European is widespread. This region also holds the key to settling the debate over the most recent common ancestor of all Indo-European languages.

The spread of agriculture from the east of the Fertile Crescent is sometimes referred to as the Iranian Neolithic, because this expansion took place in parallel with—but independently from—the movement of Anatolian farmers. People from what is now Iran moved eastward into northern India and northward across the Caucasus. Approximately 8,000 years ago, in other words, these migrants became the ancestors of people in regions including present-day Pakistan, Afghanistan, and northern India—and of the Yamnaya people. This is presumably how Indo-European spread to all these areas. Then, 5,000 years ago, the Yamnaya brought this language to Europe. It is furthermore possible that the Yamnaya and their descendants brought the Indo-Iranian languages to the East. Genetic analysis revealed that Yamanya genes spread into Central Asia and the Altai mountains around the same time that they spread to Europe. There is an extinct language called Tocharian that was spoken in western China until 1,000 years ago and it is well possible that most of Central Asia spoke a form of Indo-Iranian during the Bronze Age. It is therefore also plausible that the Indo-Iranian languages were brought to India and Pakistan from the steppes of Central Asia during the Bronze Age. Even though we are not sure about the exact route that those languages spread, we are quite certain that the Indo-European languages ultimately originated in the Fertile Crescent, as proponents of the Anatolian theory suppose, but not, as they suggest, in western and central Anatolia; rather, it emerged from northern Iran. Similarly, advocates of the steppe thesis are probably right to suggest that Indo-European came to Europe and maybe Central and Southern Asia from the steppes. But that doesn't mean it originated there. This is also why we called our new hypothesis the hybrid hypothesis, as it includes both an East Anatolian origin for Proto-Indo-European and a spread through the steppes.

Anatolia plays a remarkable role in the history of European languages. Our hypothesis suggests it gave rise to Proto-Indo-European in the east and was the source of what became the Neolithic languages in Europe 8,000 years ago in the west. In Anatolia itself, the languages of the Anatolian farmers were probably replaced as the people of the Iranian Neolithic expanded into the region 6,000 years ago—as shown by our genetic data. Europe could have remained home to the languages originating with the Anatolian farmers while Anatolia itself adopted Indo-European. Today, however, Turkey is one of the few European countries where Indo-European languages, such as Kurdish and Zazaki, are actually in the minority, whereas the area where the Turkic languages are spoken as a majority stretches from Turkey across Azerbaijan and Uzbekistan into the Altai region. The beginning of the end of Indo-European linguistic history in Anatolia can be dated to the eleventh century, when Turkic-speaking warriors began to conquer the region. Today, only about 20 percent of the population of modern-day Turkey speaks Indo-European languages.

LANGUAGE AS AN INSTRUMENT OF POWER

AS MIGRANTS ARRIVED FROM THE STEPPES, THE GERmanic languages—including English and German—began to develop in Northern and Central Europe. The Italic languages—including Vulgar Latin, the ancestors of all modern-day Romance languages—emerged, as did Albanian and Armenian. These hold a special place in Indo-European linguistic history because they are the only examples of their specific type of language; in other words, they are a direct subgroup of Indo-European, without any additional branches. The Balto-Slavic group developed, as did Celtic, which has been preserved in a few corners of the British Isles and in Brittany. During the age of the Bell Beaker culture, Celtic was probably spoken widely in Western Europe until the Roman Empire advanced into the northwest. Of the Hellenic languages to emerge then, only Greek now remains. And the Middle East is home to the large Indo-Iranian branch of Indo-European languages.

Today, with 3 billion speakers worldwide, Indo-European is the family of languages most spoken. European colonial powers took these languages to Australia, parts of South Asia, and Africa, where European languages are often spoken as a second language if not a first, and to the Americas. Anybody who has ever tried to understand the English spoken in India (where Hindi is also an Indo-European language) will have noticed how rapidly languages develop. The French spoken in what was once French-colonized Africa differs from that spoken in France, and the Spanish spoken in former colonies is different from the language used in Spain.

If language were static, you could take a train trip through much of Southern Europe armed only with Latin—or, better still, with Proto-Indo-European. The reality, however, is that even parents sometimes find it frustratingly difficult to follow their teenage children's conversations. That said, languages these days don't develop anything like as quickly as they once did, because they have long been obliged to adhere to strict standards. Spanish, for instance, has been a relatively stable language for 500 years, because it took a fixed written form quite early on. In Germany, this development began with Luther's translation of the Bible, and hard-and-fast rules for spelling were eventually laid down by the Duden dictionary in the nineteenth century. The standardized languages we know today are thus a far cry from their common Indo-European roots. The dominance of English, however, may now be making languages more similar after a long period of divergence.

Five thousand years ago, then, the linguistic landscape of Europe was significantly altered by migration for the final time. While the Romans later disseminated their language from the Atlantic to the Black Sea, they never migrated there in large numbers. The vast wave of migration from the steppes had the same impact on the language of Europeans as on their genes: it laid the foundations of the house in which we live today. And so the journey of our languages is also the journey of our genes, which have shaped what we speak and how we communicate who we are. The house itself, however, was built not by migration but by the huge empires that arose after the third millennium BCE and shaped the subsequent history of Europe. With the arrival of these empires, the Bronze Age had begun.

CHAPTER

7

Refugee Ships on the Mediterranean

EUROPE MAKES THE LEAP FROM *the Stone Age. Fathers pass on everything; daughters leave the nest. Turmoil in the Near East. Nowhere is beyond the law.*

Tin deposits in the Bronze Age
Copper deposits in the Bronze Age
North Sea
Baltic
Atlantic Ocean
Tollense Valley
Nebra sky disk
Unetic culture
Augsburg
Alpen
Pyrenees
Mediterranean Sea
5000
4800
4600
4400
4200
4000
3800
3600
3400
3200 years ago
Unetice culture
Akkadian Empire
Migration from the steppes
Bronze Age begins in Central Europe, ushering in an era of intensive trade in raw materials
Nebra sky disk
Battle in Tollense Valley

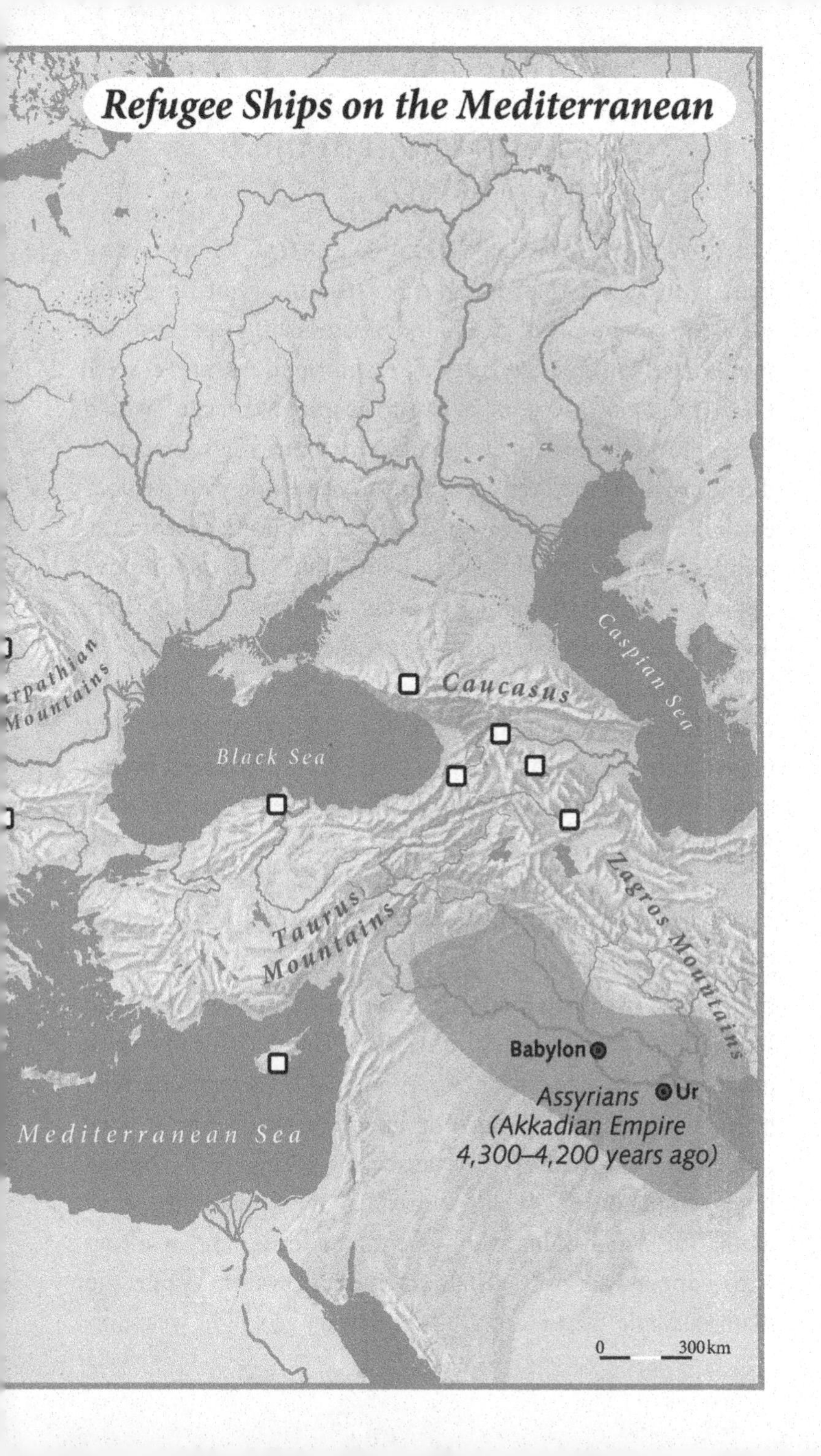
Refugee Ships on the Mediterranean
Caucasus
Caspian Sea
Black Sea
Taurus Mountains
Zagros Mountains
Babylon
Ur
Assyrians
(Akkadian Empire
4,300–4,200 years ago)
Mediterranean Sea
0
300km

PROGRESS THROUGH BRONZE

EUROPE HAS PROBABLY NEVER EXPERIENCED GREATER genetic upheaval than it did upon the influx of migration from the steppes. It is all the more astonishing that it didn't immediately trigger a cultural revolution. As we've seen, there is a gap of 150 years in the archaeological record, which has prompted all sorts of speculation about what happened during that period. Yet according to the evidence that does exist, life went on just as it had before. The nomads from the steppes became settled farmers, living much like their predecessors, their settlements scarcely distinguishable. Then, 4,200 years ago in Central Europe, the Bronze Age was set in motion, catapulting the planet into a new era. Unlike the Neolithic Revolution, however, the cultural shift was not preceded by migration. This new age was introduced by the same people who had developed the Corded Ware and Bell Beaker cultures over the previous 600 years. Genetically, nothing had changed; culturally, everything did.

The transitional phase between the Neolithic and Bronze Ages is referred to as the Copper Age. It was during this era that people first began mining natural resources, hacking the soft, reddish metal out of the earth. In Europe, this first took place in the Balkans. Progress, then, had once again derived from the same area as farming and ceramics before it. Ceramics in particular were crucial to working with copper: high temperatures were required to manipulate the new metal, for which kilns were essential. Mining and working with copper was only a half measure, however. While the material could be used to produce jewelry and light weapons, it remained too malleable for tools and weapons after it had been forged. One could harden copper by adding tin: the resultant alloy was bronze. This technology first became widespread 5,000 years ago in the Near East. The new metal paved the way into the future, offering entirely new possibilities for weapons, tools, and agricultural implements. Bronze was not simply a new material; it enabled people to enter a previously unknown sphere of production.

The discovery of copper and the development of bronze were important—albeit not the only—prerequisites for the emergence of the first advanced civilizations. The foundations of these had already been laid in the Near East and around the Mediterranean in the fourth millennium BCE, even as hunter-gatherers were still stalking through the woods in parts of Central and Northern Europe. Cities such as Ur and Babylon sprang up on the banks of the Euphrates and the Tigris, while the empire of the pharaohs blossomed in Egypt. In Anatolia the Hittite Empire held sway and in Europe the Minoans and Mycenaeans developed the first civilizations.

The north was lagging behind economically, but it wasn't isolated. During the third millennium BCE, the societies of Europe began to trade more and more intensively, and bronze played a key role. Although the techniques of bronze production were developing in the south, that region had only meager reserves of tin. That raw material was concentrated mostly in areas far north of the earliest civilizations, primarily in Cornwall, Brittany, the northwest of the Iberian Peninsula, and the Ore Mountains in Germany. A lively system of exchange developed: tin went south, while expertise was channeled to the north and west of Europe. Bronze and the products wrought from it had an increasingly profound impact on societies, families, and individuals, propelling a transition into a world of property, hierarchy, and patriarchy. These wholesale changes in the way we lived can be traced in our genes.

INVENTING THE PATRIARCHY

FROM APPROXIMATELY 2200 BCE THE BELL BEAKER AND Corded Ware cultures fused into the Unetice culture, concentrated mostly in central Germany, which left the famous bronze Nebra sky disk to posterity. The shores of the Lech, a river near Augsburg in southern Germany, was another place where those two cultures lived in close proximity, though each had its own settlements, customs, burial rites, and probably languages. They developed into another early Bronze Age culture during the same period as the Unetice culture, in this region around the Lech River. It's likely that their way of life resembled that of other Central European societies at the time. People lived on farms that mostly consisted of a house, an outbuilding, and a stall for animals and buried their dead in cemeteries nearby. The DNA preserved in these graves has survived to the present day, roughly 4,000 years later, offering glimpses into their living conditions and social organization.

We examined the DNA of almost 100 people buried in the Lech settlements who died between 2500 and 1500 BCE, during the transition into the Bronze Age. We sequenced their genomes and performed a strontium isotope analysis on their teeth. This analysis takes advantage of a simple principle: different forms of strontium can be absorbed into the human skeleton through diet—in other words, through eat-ing plants and animals. These isotopes have different masses and are found in different relative concentrations according to geographical area. Because human beings during this period obtained their food solely from local sources, the relative concentration can tell us where they grew up. Certain parts of the skeleton—for example, the enamel of the molars—develop during childhood and absorb strontium, so we can also find out whether a person spent their whole life in a specific place or lived a more mobile existence. The process doesn't work on modern-day humans, because the majority of our food is sourced from places far beyond our immediate environment.

We carried out a strontium isotope analysis on eighty-three people buried near the Lech: twenty-six men, twenty-eight women, and the rest children. One might have expected to see a similar ratio of locals to newcomers in adults of both sexes. Yet this was not the case. Seventeen of the women (almost two-thirds) and only one man came from elsewhere sometime in late adolescence. This clear disparity in the ratio of male to female arrivals could not be dismissed as coincidence. It looked like evidence of a deliberate process of exchange between regions. If the settlements we examined are in fact typical of the early Bronze Age, then this hints at an entirely new relationship between the sexes. While the men remained in their settlements, the women they married often came from elsewhere; this suggests that likely a hierarchy had emerged, with men at the top. Many wives were outsiders, and must likewise have often sent their own daughters away when they reached marriageable age.

Nonetheless, the burial sites do not indicate discrimination against women. As both parents, mothers and fathers received the same number of grave goods. The dead who were not related to other people buried in the cemeteries, however, were given very few, if any, grave goods. This suggests that they had low social status and were probably workers and outsiders. Households thus would have had a similar structure to what later evolved in Greece and Rome, consisting of nuclear families and bond servants or paid workers. Using DNA analysis, we were able to identify men from five consecutive generations in some family graves, but we did not find a single adult female descendant, confirming that the daughters of the families were likely sent away before they became adults. Evidently sons, instead, inherited the farmsteads from their fathers. Whether these sons were the firstborn, however, is impossible to determine genetically. There were several brothers found in the graves, but the younger ones could have set up their own farms in or near the settlement. In all, this genetic data reveals patriarchal and hierarchical structures that became widespread during the Bronze Age and continue to shape some familial and social conventions even today.

CONSUMERISM AND MASS PRODUCTION

THE BRONZE AGE USHERED IN A NEW CULTURAL ERA, not just near the Lech but across the whole of Europe. Prior to the discovery of copper, people had worked primarily with clay. The production of ceramics was not trivial, but it wasn't an advanced technology. The development of bronze, however, signified a tremendous technical and social leap for humankind. Mining the earth for raw materials and then alloying copper with tin in extremely hot kilns demanded increasing skill specialization. It also required miners, kiln builders, metalworkers, and traveling traders who could fetch the tin from the farthest corners of Europe.

In the Neolithic, it was common to be a jack-of-all-trades. Knowledge of farming and animal husbandry was ubiquitous; at the most there would have been a few select experts in the manufacturing of ceramics, yet even their skills were hardly exclusive. Nor would the people of the Stone Age have contended with a scarcity of resources for crafting tools and weaponry—the wood and stones they used were everywhere. The early farmers were living in the most nascent form of a consumer society: virtually everything they produced was for their own use, and their possessions were of negligible value. There were exceptions, of course, such as the odd piece of gold or silver jewelry. But there is no archaeological evidence, at least in Central Europe, that these pieces were concentrated in the hands of a few individuals or families.

Nature provided stone and wood, but bronze took effort to manufacture, and the raw materials had to be obtained first—unless you happened to be sitting on them. Regions with copper deposits grew rich, and those with the even rarer tin were practically booming. Tin from Cornwall was traded all across Europe, as were copper and tin from the Ore Mountains in Germany. Interregional trade had existed prior to the Bronze Age, but now it picked up speed. Trade spurred development, and materials and expertise for that development were in limited supply, intensifying the competition between societies and individuals. Those with valuable commodities defended them; those without did everything they could to obtain them.

The greatest innovation of the Bronze Age was the ability to mass-produce goods. Molds for bronze could now be made from stone to manufacture identical products. Nothing of the kind had ever existed before, as a glance at earlier ceramic artifacts makes abundantly clear. To understand the impact of batch production in the Bronze Age, it helps to picture the inverse happening today: imagine if every hammer in your nearest hardware store suddenly had a unique shape. These new Bronze Age wares not only looked identical but were more stable than anything that had gone before. And what did people make with this new technology? The answer is unsurprising: primarily they produced more effective weapons.

THE END OF THE LONE WARRIOR

INSTRUMENTS OF DEATH HAD, OF COURSE, ALWAYS been a part of human life. Spears, lances, arrows, and bows, as well as small daggers made of wood and stone, were used for hunting. Copper made it possible to produce higher-quality knives and halberds, but these were limited in length by the softness of the material. Not until the advent of bronze were people able to produce long, stable stabbing weapons, especially daggers but also new kinds of spears and lances. It was easier to kill, but it was also easier to defend oneself with bronze helmets, shields, armor, or greaves. Accelerating a trend toward inequality was the fact that this equipment was expensive. Well-armed warriors clearly had the advantage, even if their opponents could dispatch more men into battle. The Bronze Age almost unavoidably prompted an arms race.

There was more to conquer and more to defend, and

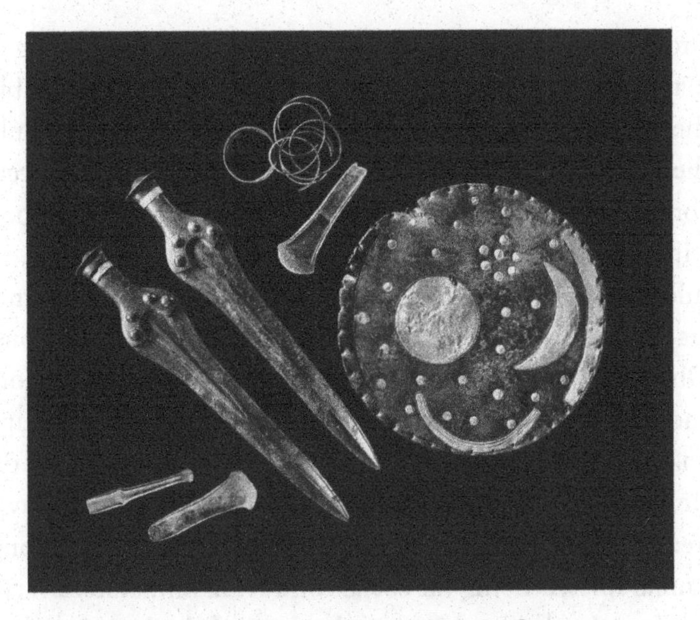

A world-famous find from Saxony-Anhalt, Germany: in addition to weapons and jewelry, looters discovered the Nebra sky disk in 1999. It is about 3,600 years old, and the earliest known concrete depiction of the sky.

clashes between different settlements were increasingly common. Paradoxically, though, the drastic surge in weapons production may have made life safer, at least off the battlefield. During the Neolithic, most Central European villages constructed large fortifications, shielding themselves from attackers vying for control of their farmland. Many early Bronze Age settlements lacked this form of protection, suggesting they felt less threatened. The farmsteads on the Lech, for instance, were arrayed along the banks of the river, not even separated by fences. The most likely explanation for this sense of security is the establishment of military structures, for which there is evidence dating from the beginning of the

Bronze Age. Territorial rulers, often referred to as "kings," may have guaranteed the various regions' safety. It's possible these leaders levied taxes on the populace, financing not only their lavish lifestyles but their armies as well. And so the celebrated lone warrior was replaced by foot soldiers armed with arrows and lances, under the command of a king. A ruler could call upon mercenaries or, in wartime, gather farmers from the settlements and provide them with weapons. Obedience to the ruler was a condition of this protection, and such a king would have been prepared to turn his weapons on opposition from within. The first state monopoly on violence was looming, as was the end of the potentially law-free zone. The patriarchal system on the farms was run along similar lines, echoing the social contract in miniature. Everyone remained subservient to the man of the house, and in return he went into battle during wartime and risked his life for the safety of his kin.

These rulers were almost certainly in constant competition with other kingdoms but probably not in a constant state of war. After all, they profited from trade and would have wanted to keep the productivity of their own populations high. They must have held parleys to negotiate issues of trade and draw political spheres of influence. War would probably have been a last resort, provoked only if the chances of victory seemed good and valuable land or natural resources were at stake. The concentration of power and resources led to ever bigger, more prosperous, and more populous realms.

The Bronze Age Unetice culture is a typical example. During the roughly 700 years this culture thrived, between 2200 and 1500 BCE, the Uneticeans seem to have revered their leaders as godlike beings; at least, their graves, full of countless weapons and large amounts of gold, seem to indicate as much. These stand in sharp contrast to the graves of simple farmers, which contain no weapons. Nor were soldiers laid to rest lying down, like the kings; rather, they were buried in a crouching position. Ordinary Uneticeans seem to have lost the right to possess weapons of their own. Axes, hatchets, and halberds were stockpiled by the king, only to be distributed during wartime. Hoards from this era have been discovered in many areas of Europe and include hundreds of daggers, lances, and axes. It's likely these stockpiles were hidden by rulers to prevent their subjects from rebelling. They may also have worried that farmers would forge their swords into plowshares, another reason to keep a supply of weapons to hand. As these weapons grew more sophisticated, military conflicts could now be fought with ever more deadly efficiency. The same innovations that created networks of industry and progress in the Bronze Age also bred hierarchies, distrust, and sociopolitical divides.

THE FERTILE CRESCENT

THE BRONZE AGE BEGAN JUST AS A CLIMATIC SHIFT, called the 4.2-kiloyear event, took place. The climate became more humid in the Mediterranean region during this period, and colder and drier in Northern Europe. In the Near East, a 300-year period of drought led to political upheaval and the collapse of advanced societies, especially in modern-day Iran and Iraq. The Akkadian Empire crumbled into dust within decades, as its population fought to survive, and archaeologists estimate that around 300,000 people lost their homes in the course of three centuries. To the south, during the Third Dynasty of Ur, the Sumerians built a 100-kilometer wall to keep out the refugees fleeing the climate crisis. But they could not prevent the collapse of the Sumerian Empire in 2000 BCE. Toward the end of the dry period, the people the Sumerians had tried to repel built a flourishing civilization farther north, one that would later come to dominate the entire region: Babylon.

A mural relief in the mortuary temple of Ramses III at the temple complex of Medînet Hâbu. It depicts the Egyptians in battle against the attacking "sea peoples." The Bronze Age began an era marked by struggles over power and resources.

Over the second millennium BCE, war became a common means of exercising power, bringing with it all the attendant ills so familiar to us today. Vanquished opponents were killed or enslaved, while increasingly deadly weapons systems were developed. There were abductions, genocides, rapes. The rulers of the major empires, mostly still concentrated around the eastern Mediterranean, sent armies tens of thousands strong into battle, dispatching chariots that could slaughter even distant opponents. In short, the world grew more complicated and conflicts grew more deadly, not only around the Mediterranean but elsewhere. In the Tollense Valley in northern Germany, archaeological evidence reveals that in 1300 BCE between 2,000 and 6,000 men fought a violent battle. In the aftermath, hundreds of rotting bodies would have turned the valley into a place of nightmares.

As the population continued to grow exponentially, there were always reasons to fight over raw materials and land. Around 1000 BCE, at the end of the Bronze Age and the beginning of the Iron Age, the world was home to about 50 million people, twice as many as had existed a thousand years before. The civilized world was no longer big enough to make space for everyone. People fleeing wars, droughts, or plagues could no longer be sure of finding a new home at their journey's end. Over the centuries and across the continent there must have been countless refugee movements, but one of the most historically significant of these occurred at the end of the Bronze Age. It found its way into the Old Testament, and continues to affect political disagreements today. Around 1200 BCE, a huge number of refugees suddenly appeared on boats in the eastern Mediterranean region—and for a long time historians have been wondering where these people came from. Thanks to DNA analysis, we finally know more.

A REFUGEE CRISIS IN THE MEDITERRANEAN

THE PERIOD PRECEDING THESE REFUGEES' ARRIVAL had been a phase of consolidation in the Near East. In the middle of the second millennium BCE the region had largely stabilized from the upheavals of the 4.2-kiloyear event. The Assyrian Empire reigned on the Euphrates and Tigris Rivers, the New Kingdom of Egypt reached as far north as Lebanon, the Hittites were holding their ground in Anatolia, and the Mycenaeans were doing the same on the Aegean. Yet somewhere between 1300 and 1200 BCE, peace came to an end. The ruler of Alashiya wrote from modern-day Cyprus to the allied king of Ugarit, a city-state in present-day Syria, advising him to beware of hostile ships that were making the Mediterranean unsafe. Panic gripped the entire Near East, and it was not unfounded: around 1200 BCE the Hittite Empire collapsed, and over the following decades its neighbors fell like dominos. Egyptian sources report skirmishes with what they called "sea peoples," and Ramses III wrote about a triumphant battle against a group of enemies who had defeated all the other rulers in the region.

Yet even the Egyptian Empire couldn't keep its northern territories. The region of Canaan, which corresponds almost exactly to modern-day Israel, was abandoned. Archaeologists had concluded from texts and finds dating from this period that the ominous "sea peoples" settled in the area, but it was impossible to say for sure. We have virtually no written records or documents for about a century and a half of what was clearly an important epoch for the Near East; the only things remaining are ruined cities and states. It wasn't even clear whether the sea peoples really existed. Yet there was plenty of evidence that they were connected to the Philistines, a group that plays a central role in the Old Testament—Goliath, David's opponent, was a Philistine. Goliath's description in the Old Testament paints him as a strong, well-equipped warrior. His helmet was made of bronze, as was his "coat of mail," which weighed "five thousand shekels." He also had bronze greaves on his legs, and "between his shoulders" was "a target of brass." Moreover, "the staff of his spear was like a weaver's beam; and his spear's head weighed six hundred shekels of iron." Clearly, Goliath was an extremely impressive Bronze Age warrior.

The riddle of the sea people is much more than a historical exercise. Whether the documented cultural changes in the region were caused by an influx of migrants displacing the local population is one question. But there's an existential aspect as well: the Philistines are considered by many to be the ancestors of modern-day Palestinians, while according to biblical tradition Canaan is also where the Israelites settled after they left Egypt. The issue of the sea people is thus bound up with a highly current political conflict, which, despite being rooted in the biblical age, is present in many forms today.

In order to shed light on this 150-year period after the empires of the Near East collapsed, we examined the skeletons of people who lived in what is now Israel and Lebanon both before and after the crisis. We managed to obtain usable DNA from half a dozen individuals from three of the biblical Philistine settlements and saw a clear shift in the region's DNA after the presumed arrival date of the sea peoples. A new genetic component from the south of Europe had been introduced. We can infer from this that the Philistines' homeland may have been located in the Aegean, since the Mycenaeans living there had a similar genetic structure. At the start of this 150-year dark age, the Mycenaean civilization was among the first to crumble, just before raids by the sea peoples were reported in the empires farther east and south. In other words, the sea peoples do seem to have existed, and evidently they came from the area around the southern Mediterranean. The idea that they were Mycenaeans is only conjecture, however, because as yet we haven't examined enough Mediterranean civilizations from the late Bronze Age to narrow down the origin of the Philistines more precisely. Theoretically, the seafarers' new genetic component could have come from Cyprus or Sicily. As we don't currently have enough sequenced genomes from these regions, we can't rule them out. On the other hand, archaeological findings have suggested a connection between the Philistines and the Aegean. Our analysis revealed another surprise. We found almost no traces of the newly introduced southern Mediterranean DNA in individuals from those Philistine cities a few hundred years after their initial arrival, suggesting that those migrants did not keep to themselves over the following centuries; they rather admixed with the local population. We could not find any significant differences between the local Philistine and Caananite population by 800 BCE, debunking ideas of genetic separation between people from those different cultural groups during the Iron Age. Like everywhere else during this time, they were highly connected through trade and marriage.

The few historical accounts from this era don't support the idea that the groups arriving in the Levant from more westerly Mediterranean regions consisted solely of warriors. This may have been one of the biggest refugee crises of the ancient world. Victory inscriptions and battle reliefs from the Egyptian Empire hint that women and children migrated with the soldiers along the perilous Mediterranean route, trying to find their way inland through the Nile Delta.

According to reports, entire families as well as soldiers were killed or captured by the locals. Living conditions in their homeland must have been so dangerous that men and women were willing to risk their own lives, and the lives of their children, for the chance to escape.

THE FUNDAMENTALS REMAIN

AS OF FEBRUARY 2019, ARCHAEOGENETICS HAS REVISED and retold the story of European ancestry and how it is intertwined with that of the Neanderthals, explained the roots of the Neolithic Revolution, and proved that the Bronze Age was preceded by a wave of migration from the steppes on a scale hardly anyone had thought possible. We now know that the major genetic changes that took place on the continent 8,000 and 5,000 years ago were the last, and that even the vast empires that later flourished and fell in Europe had no comparable genetic impact on a continent-wide scale.

Archaeogenetics has, however, also helped identify more recent patterns of migration, albeit using a fundamentally different technique. Codeveloped by scientists at our institute, this method has recently helped us to trace domestic migration in Europe over the last two millennia. It focuses not on the fundamental commonalities between genomes, which prove a relationship among populations, but rather on very tiny genetic variations that distinguish one group from another. Using this method, we were able to prove with genetic data one of the most famous waves of migration: that of the Angles and Saxons into present-day England. It emerged that modern-day inhabitants of England owe about 30 percent of their DNA to migrants who originated in the Netherlands, Denmark, and northern Germany and came to the island in the fifth century. It's a safe bet that archaeogenetic studies such as these will increasingly shape the way European history is written. Using ever more subtle methods of DNA analysis, we should be able to describe patterns of movement even after the Bronze Age. There are many new and more detailed discoveries in the offing, especially for this migration period and the early Middle Ages.

Needless to say, there's more to the story of Europe's genetic journey. There's extensive evidence to suggest that the numerous waves of migration within and into Europe, especially that from the steppes, is closely connected to the history of disease. The journey of human genes was followed very rapidly by a stream of viruses and bacteria, shaping the history of the continent perhaps even more profoundly than any king could ever hope to do. For most of our history these enemies were invisible, and it's only recently that—thanks to genetic analysis—we are beginning slowly to understand the little critters.

CHAPTER

8

They Bring the Plague

FLEAS VOMIT BLOOD. THE PENTAGON *provides a jump-start. The plague comes from the east. The horse comes under suspicion. Body parts fly through the air. Europe closes its borders. Foreign rats to the rescue.*

1350
North Sea
Cambridge
London
East Smithfield
Atlantic
Ocean
1348
c. 4(
years
Nabburg
Aschheim
and Altenerding
Alps
4700 years a
Toulouse
1347
Pyrenees
Lunel
Barcelona
Valencia
Mediterranean Sea
1346
3000
2500
2000
1500
1000
500
v. Chr. 0
n. Chr.
500
1000
1500
Stone Age
plague pathogen
Plague pathogen
during the Yamnaya
culture (not the
bubonic plague)
Oldest Bronze Age
bubonic plague
pathogen (Samara, Russia)
Most recent
Stone Age plague pathogen
Hittite plague
Plague of
Athens
Antonine
Plague
Justinianic plague
beginning of the
1st pandemic
Black Death,
beginning of the
2nd pandemic

They Bring the Plague
3600 years ago
in the Altai Mountains
Earliest bubonic plague
3800 years ago
Laishevo
4800
years ago
after 1350
Bolgar
Yamnaya culture
rpathian
Mountains
Caspian Sea
1346 Kaffa
4900 years ago
Caucasus
Black Sea
Constantinople
542
Hittites
Zagros Mountains
Genome:
Stone Age plague
Black Death
(1346–1351)
Justinianic plague
(541–549)
Pathways of expansion
Mediterranean Sea
Pelusium 541
Egyptian Empire
0
300 km

HUMANS ARE THE NEW BATS

NO OTHER DISEASE IN EUROPE'S COLLECTIVE HISTORICAL memory gives rise to anything approaching the horror of the plague. There are several good reasons for this, and the fact that every year between 2,000 and 3,000 people worldwide still get infected with plague isn't even high up on the list. The plague earned its fearsome reputation primarily in the fourteenth century, when the "Black Death" killed an estimated one in three Europeans—or perhaps even one in two—as historical accounts of patients coughing up blood and body-strewn alleyways describe. Many contemporaries assumed that it would wipe out humankind. Similar concerns were reported during the Justinianic plague, which was first recorded in sixth-century Egypt and rapidly spread throughout the Mediterranean. For many hundreds of years the disease continued to haunt Europe, with thousands of documented outbreaks. It was the scourge of humanity, only losing its terrifying reputation a little over seventy years ago, when antibiotics came into widespread use.

Only recently, thanks to genetic analysis, have we discovered how the plague arrived in Europe. It spread here much earlier than previously supposed. In fact, we have discovered that a plague outbreak in the Stone Age most likely cleared the way for the great wave of migration from the Pontic steppe.

For a long time, the plague was a ghost. Scientists knew about the pandemic that raged across many European countries between 1347 and 1353, but they weren't sure if it was caused by the bacterium *Yersinia pestis* or some other patho-

The plague was a constant presence among Europeans during the Middle Ages, and death was everywhere. *Dance of the Skeletons* by Michael Wolgemut, dating from 1493, reflects the widespread sense of impending doom.

gen, such as smallpox. However, in 2011, working at Tübingen, we decoded the genome of a historic plague pathogen for the very first time, examining material found in a medieval mass grave in London. The city was particularly badly hit by the Black Death. According to written sources, victims of the epidemic were buried in East Smithfield Cemetery that we analyzed. The plague pathogen could be sequenced because the bacteria multiply in huge numbers in the host and can be found in a very high concentration in the blood.

Using the technique tested and refined on Neanderthal and other human bones, we used parts of the skeleton that were well supplied with blood—specifically, the teeth—to fish out and decode the *Yersinia pestis* genome.

To understand the plague bacterium, we should momentarily ignore its deadly effect on the body. *Yersinia pestis*, like any other living being, is fundamentally interested in one thing: to propagate and spread as widely as possible. The bacterium lives inside foreign organisms, multiplying before moving on to new hosts. The death of the host is not the pathogen's goal; in fact, it can even be a hindrance.

A good example of this is the Ebola virus, one of the most deadly pathogens known to humankind. It kills extremely quickly, giving the virus only a short span of time to leap from an infected person to someone else. Since Ebola outbreaks rapidly burn out, there isn't time for the virus to reach faraway populations, so historically they haven't covered much ground. The flu, on the other hand, is a more adept traveler. The virus rarely kills, so it travels great distances, as the annual flu epidemics testify. New strains originating from Southeast Asia migrate across the planet nearly every year. So, counterintuitively, compared to the flu Ebola is at an evolutionary disadvantage, precisely because it is more deadly. There's still no cast-iron guarantee that Ebola outbreaks will burn out quickly, as we saw during the devastating epidemic of late 2013. For the first time, the virus crossed several national borders, possibly because it broke out in densely populated areas—or perhaps because of the strain's unique properties. Even then, human casualties are, from the virus's point of view, simply collateral damage. The same was true of the plague.

Yersinia pestis diverged from its nearest relative, the soil-dwelling bacterium *Yersinia pseudotuberculosis*, approximately 30,000 years ago. Human beings, scattered sparsely across the world tens of thousands of years ago, were a potential—albeit not especially promising—host for the plague and all other pathogens. A human infected with a virus or bacteria may have decimated whatever small hunter-gatherer group they were traveling with, but that would probably have been the extent of the damage. Pathogens first adapted to humans when we grew more numerous and began to settle down and live in close proximity to one another.

At the dawn of human history, pathogens needed other hosts in order to multiply, and that usually meant nonhuman animals. Bats, for instance, lived, as they do now, in close quarters in colonies of tens of thousands, dripping with all kinds of fluids as they cling to their perches, and they are still the most common source of new pathogens, especially viruses, as was also speculated for the coronavirus that caused the 2020 pandemic. The process of a pathogen leaping from animal to human—if human food is infected with infected animal feces or if infected flesh is eaten—is called zoonotic transmission. Most pathogens found in modern-day humans are probably descended from a zoonotic origin. Today, human beings, like bats, can be relied upon to spread viruses and bacteria widely throughout our now-gigantic, densely packed population.

VIRUSES AND BACTERIA

Viruses and bacteria both make humans and animals ill, which is about all these hugely diverse pathogens have in common. While bacteria are living creatures, amassing wherever they find the most nutrients and the best conditions to multiply, viruses are simply packaged molecules without their own metabolism. Think of viruses as the zombies of the pathogen world: they're not alive, but they can wreak terrible havoc on contact with an organism by making the body work for them. Viruses can affect not just humans but bacteria too. The reverse is not the case.

Viruses are usually a piece of DNA inside a shell. They bind to human cells at the first opportunity—when a virus is inhaled, for instance, and latches onto a cell in the mucous membranes of the lungs. Once attached, the virus introduces its DNA into the cell and changes its genetic information. The cells then no longer reproduce their own genetic information but that of the virus. The virus spreads throughout the body and, if recognized by the immune system, will be destroyed—along with the infected cells. What antibiotics are to the struggle against bacteria, immunizations are to the defense against viruses. By giving the immune system a weakened version of the virus or its building blocks, the system can be trained to identify and fight it. Without immunization, however, the body takes longer to respond, sometimes long enough for the virus to attack the whole body and bring it to the point of collapse.

POOR OLD FLEAS

TO UNLEASH ITS HORRORS ON HUMANKIND, THE PLAGUE bacterium first had to employ another organism, one that dies an agonizing death as it transmits the disease: the flea.

During the era of the great plague pandemics, humans in Europe lived in extremely unhygienic conditions. Sewers were rare, settlements were cramped, and the conception of hygiene as a means of preventing illness was unknown. In villages and cities, grain was commonly stored in attics, while the streets swam with feces and the whole place teemed with rats. Rodents, we can assume, were the first hosts to the plague pathogen, which could have passed to humans via their bites, droppings, or flesh. The fatal moment came when the pathogen mutated, allowing it to pass more effectively from rats to human beings via the rat flea.

Fleas were crucial to the widespread transmission of the bubonic plague. To pass from one mammal to another, the bacteria had to reach the flea and then enter the bloodstream of the other organism. But fleas don't naturally expel blood—they only consume it. The bacterium cleared this final hurdle by evolving "virulence genes," which enabled it to survive in the flea's stomach. More ominously for the flea, several of the virulence genes also prompt the bacteria to produce a biofilm in the animal's foregut, which blocks the flea's stomach and infects every fluid that touches it. The infected flea's suffering begins when it tries to suck blood from another organism after its foregut has been blocked. The flea ingests the host's uninfected blood and then vomits the now-infected blood back out, infecting its prey.

While a healthy flea only feeds a few times a day, infected

fleas make hundreds of attempts. Slowly starving to death, as they cannot ingest blood, they become increasingly aggressive, until they cause mass infection in humans and animals. The death of the human being is thus a means to an end for the bacteria: the more bacteria in the host's blood, the higher the transmission rate to the next potential victim. This method of transmission turned the disease into the infamous bubonic plague. After a person is bitten, the plague bacteria multiply in the lymph nodes, making them visibly swollen. Within ten days, the bacteria spread throughout the body, causing organ failure and ultimately fatal blood poisoning. The extremities usually darken, hence the name "Black Death." The pneumonic plague, another form of the disease, is a side effect, and that form can be transmitted directly from person to person. As the lungs of the bubonic plague victim degenerate, aerosolized bacteria are exhaled. If these droplets find their way into another person's lungs, that individual will be dead within one or two days.

HELP FROM THE PENTAGON

THE MUTATIONS NECESSARY FOR THIS APPALLING PROCESS of transmission and disease had already taken place in the pathogens that caused the Black Death, as well as the Justinianic plague, the first historically documented epidemic of the plague. Beginning in the sixth century, the Justinianic plague is estimated to have killed dozens of millions of European victims and is considered one potential cause of the permanent downfall of the Western Roman Empire.

In 2016, we successfully reconstructed a bubonic plague pathogen from this period. It was found at a burial site near

Munich, where a young couple who reportedly died around the same time as each other in the sixth century had been laid to rest. This discovery of the plague north of the Alps ran contrary to historical sources, which suggest the pandemic only hit the Mediterranean.

Searching for the plague genome in a London cemetery was an obvious step, since the Black Death ravaged the area and countless victims were buried there in mass graves. Tracking down the Justinianic plague near Munich took more luck. During periods in which there were no written records, it was entirely unclear which areas had been affected by the disease. Researchers weren't just searching for a needle in a haystack; they didn't know which haystacks to search. Extracting DNA from dead people is the easy part: you can find it in their bones. But if you're looking for ancient pathogens, you have to know which skeletons to examine and which dead people suffered from a particular ailment. Until recently, scouring every sequenced skeleton for any pathogen would be a highly uncertain undertaking and much too expensive.

Then, in 2012, the US Department of Defense launched the Defense Threat Reduction Agency's Algorithm Challenge, which offered a $1 million prize to anyone who could develop a computer algorithm that would quickly discover and identify bacterial and viral DNA. (The Pentagon wanted to be better prepared for biological warfare.) More than a hundred contenders entered the competition, but only three made it to the finals. The winning three-person team was announced in autumn 2013, and it included one of my colleagues at the University of Tübingen, Daniel Huson, a specialist in bioinformatics. Huson later worked with our institute to develop a related algorithm that could match a billion DNA sequences to their organism of origin within twenty-four hours. The program indicates how much of a skeleton's DNA is human and how much derives from microbes, bacteria, or viruses—and, crucially, which ones—and it is 200 times faster than older algorithms; instead of waiting nearly a year for results, you wait one day. The algorithm recognizes whether DNA contains bacterial or viral genetic material known to belong to human pathogens. This only works if this material is similar to known pathogens and their sequences already exist in scientists' data banks—unknown, extinct diseases will remain undiscovered. Previously, microbes were superfluous to the sequencing of human DNA; now they are the focal point. Several thousand skeletons have been examined at our institute, and not only the plague but a whole set of other diseases have been detected, helping us to understand how epidemics have traveled between humans and societies in the past, so that we can predict and prepare for the pandemics of our future.

THE PLAGUE FOLLOWS THE MIGRANTS

IT WASN'T UNTIL 2017 THAT, THANKS TO MY COLLEAGUE'S algorithm, we identified the earliest plague pathogen discovered to date. We examined more than 500 Stone Age teeth and bones from Germany, Russia, Hungary, Croatia, and the Baltic for the plague, which returned several positive results. The first and biggest surprise was from the Pontic steppe, where we reconstructed the genome of a plague pathogen from a roughly 4,900-year-old Yamnaya individual. This means that the plague afflicted human beings much earlier than previously supposed and was already on Europe's doorstep in the Stone Age, before it accompanied migrants from the steppes. The disease has now been identified in skeletons throughout Europe dating from between 4,900 and about 3,800 years ago, including in the Baltic, Croatia, and Augsburg in Germany—but also in the distant Altai Mountains and in the Lake Baikal region, where it appeared roughly around the same time. The path traveled by the bacteria, which was constantly evolving along the way, corresponds to the route we believe was taken by the migrants from the steppes. Thus, the plague and the steppe peoples must have made their journey west and then east around the same time. Was the spread of the plague connected to human patterns of migration?

There is reason to believe that the plague was expanding into Western Europe before the wave of human migration. After all, the people who lived in these regions were already in contact. The bacterium could have piggybacked on traveling traders and attacked an unprepared population. The impact that unfamiliar bacteria and viruses can have on humans is well documented: during the European settlement of the Americas, for example, the native population died in huge numbers from illnesses brought by the new arrivals. The same may have happened to the people of Western Europe.

This cannot be proven genetically, because few skeletons have been found in Central Europe dating from between 5,500 and 4,800 years ago—which might indicate that the plague was already ravaging the area. Perhaps people started to burn their dead, hoping to ward off the obvious danger posed by infected bodies. It's also conceivable that they simply stopped touching the lethal corpses, leaving them to decay unburied, in which case the bones would not have survived.

Of course, there could have been many reasons why the population was decimated. A climatic shift might have caused poor harvests and famine; violent clashes between farmers over scant resources could have resulted in vast numbers of unburied dead. Or another pathogen, one that no longer exists and is thus unidentifiable, may have been responsible. Or perhaps—though this is least likely—nothing happened at all, and archaeologists have simply been unlucky in not finding human remains from this period. All we know for sure is that there was a sharp decrease in the number of dead bodies.

If the plague was to blame, how did it spread? The Stone Age plague had not yet evolved the brutally efficient method of reaching new hosts via flea bites. It's possible that the disease was airborne—like the flu or COVID-19. If it did reach Europe this way, an epidemic could have worked up significant momentum on the densely populated continent. This scenario fits with the archaeological evidence, which suggests not only that there were fewer people but that entire settlements—for instance, on the coast of the Black Sea—were depopulated at a single stroke, as though the occupants had fled from a mysterious disease. A plague genome discovered in 2018, which at 4,900 years old is the earliest such genome found in Northern Europe, suggests a similar chain of events. The man's ancestors had not yet mixed genetically with the Yamnaya population. Perhaps many of his compatriots died the same way he did; the illness could have preceded the great wave of migration, leaving essentially uninhabited land in its wake.

ON THE BACKS OF HORSES

THERE IS FAR MORE GENETIC DATA AVAILABLE REGARDING the European plague after the great steppe migration, but it still leaves room for at least two, mutually exclusive interpretations. The plague may have already ravaged Europe prior to the influx of migrants, passing from person to person. Or perhaps the majority of pathogens were brought to Europe by migrants and were *not* transmitted between humans but carried on the backs of horses. I favor this theory, although it still leaves a lot unexplained. The evidence against human-to-human transmission is that pneumonic plague, as we know it today, is found only concomitantly with the bubonic plague. As this form of the disease had not yet evolved during the steppe migration, the bacteria were probably passed from animals to humans. The three species that likely accompanied them on their trek west were cows, sheep, and horses. The steppe horses, as you may remember, were later replaced by domesticated European horses, and exist today only in the form of the now-wild Przewalski's horse. This wholesale replacement of the equine population took place in the third millennium BCE, in parallel with the expansion of the steppe migrants—and the plague.

This theory could also explain why the migrants started using different horses around this time. It wasn't an obvious thing to do. After all, they had brought already domesticated horses to Europe and could easily have continued to breed them. Instead, it seems they were compelled to tame wild horses and to cut themselves off from the horses that had carried them west.

Historical experiments with animals may offer a clue as to why this was. In 1894, the famous bacteriologist Louis Pasteur sent Alexandre Yersin to Hong Kong, where the world's third and—so far—final great plague pandemic was raging. The plague was a notorious scourge, but its causes were unknown. Having illegally obtained a couple of plague victims from the morgue, Yersin discovered the bacterium that would later be named after him, *Yersinia pestis*. For two years Yersin tried to develop a vaccine, infecting several types of domesticated animal in the process. The only one that survived was the horse—specifically, the domesticated descendant of the European wild horse. This breed, the one we ride today, may be more resistant to the plague.

This could explain why people in the centuries following migration from the steppes preferred European wild horses, while the nonresistant Asian horses nearly died out. In this scenario, the reservoirs of the Stone Age plague would be the Asian horses, which continually infected humans.[1] Riders spent a lot of time on their horses, inevitably coming into close contact and swapping bacteria. And in those days, nearly every single man from the steppes was a rider. With only one exception, all of the Stone Age plague pathogens have been discovered in men with steppe DNA.

All these narratives about the Stone Age plague are based on suppositions and deductions. What we do know is that the disease was on the threshold of Europe even before the great sea change in population, and that something either before or during the process of migration caused the population to plummet. For me, the Asian horse offers an obvious explanation, albeit certainly not the only one. If Alexandre Yersin had infected a Przewalski's horse with the plague as

For a very long time, people had no idea where the mysterious plague originated and how exactly it was transmitted. When Arnold Böcklin painted *The Plague* in 1898, the bacterium had just been discovered by Alexandre Yersin.

well, we might be a little wiser. The unfortunate test animal, on the other hand, would probably be dead.

CONDITIONS IN LATE ROME

THE EARLIEST KNOWN FORM OF THE BUBONIC PLAGUE emerged 3,800 years ago at the latest, in the Samara region. The earlier non-bubonic form that had emerged in the Stone Age died out about 3,500 years ago; at least, that's the age of the most recent example we found. No one can be sure how potent the new bubonic strain was in those early days; at least our genetic analysis revealed that it carried all virulence genes that were necessary for infecting fleas and looks virtually identical to plague strains found throughout the world today. We therefore can't rule out the possibility that waves of bubonic plague assailed Europe and the Near East from this point onward. Ancient drawings, for instance, depict not only the collapse of empires during the migration of the sea peoples but also a "Hittite plague" that beset the empire shortly before it disintegrated. It's pure speculation, of course, whether the plague bacterium or some other pathogen was responsible for the Hittites' decline and that of other Near Eastern civilizations. If it was indeed the plague, then the sickness was probably already being transmitted by flea.

Fleas and the bubonic plague were an efficient team, but they were still missing one crucial factor: the black rat, which significantly expanded the bacterium's territory. All signs indicate that black rats migrated into Europe with the expansion of the Roman Empire. The Eastern Roman Empire, in fact, was the site of the first historically documented plague epidemic in human history. As with the Black Death, researchers were initially unsure whether the Justinianic plague, which started in the sixth century—and was named after the reigning emperor, Justinian, who caught the disease but survived—was really an epidemic of the plague or some other illness. The historian Procopius of Caesarea recorded detailed symptoms of the sickness, which afflicted millions of people from the mid-sixth century onward. These included swellings known as buboes in the groin, attacks of madness, and hallucinations. The victims' only slim chance of survival was burst buboes. Writing in the capital city of Constantinople, modern-day Istanbul, Procopius described tens of thousands of people dying every day. It's no wonder contemporary witnesses believed the end of the world was nigh. Our genetic analyses of victims of the Justinianic plague, in which we could recover genomes of the bacteria from Bavaria and southern England as well as France and Spain, proves that the Justinianic plague was, in fact, an outbreak of bubonic plague, and that death swept far north and west across the continent.

The Justinianic plague first proliferated in Constantinople. The proximate cause was probably a terrible earthquake in 542, which reduced parts of the city to rubble. One theory suggests that corpses—as well as food that had tumbled out of storehouses—may have triggered a sharp rise in the rat population, creating ideal conditions for the spread of the flea-infested rats. Because Constantinople was extremely well connected to other Mediterranean port cities by sea, the epidemic that eventually swept across the whole of Europe probably moved along shipping routes. This plague also coincided with the late stage of the migration period that had picked up again after the collapse of the Western Roman Empire at the end of the fifth century. As humans migrated, they transmitted and propagated disease. The bubonic plague could even have been carried across the Channel into southern England by Angles and Saxons.

Outbreaks of what was most likely the bubonic plague continued to flare up well into the eighth century. People everywhere were afraid, not just of the repeated, deadly epidemics but of the political instability that followed in their wake. Historians have attributed, in part, the waning influence of the Eastern Roman Empire to weakened, plague-bedeviled garrisons. The Franks were perpetually edging north, and the once-great metropolis of Rome had diminished until it was just a small city in the area settled by the Lombards. It would be overly simplistic to ascribe all of this solely to the plague, but there's no doubt the disease had a profound impact on human experience and social structures.

Europe underwent at least eighteen more severe epidemics well into the eighth century: approximately one outbreak per decade. Why the plague then disappeared until the fourteenth century is still unexplained, but there are some clear archaeological indications that the black rat population slumped during this period. During the dark ages of the waning first millennium, there may have been fewer people and fewer settlements, and thus worse conditions for rats. Maybe the plague bacterium, temporarily, ran out of steam.

AIRTIGHT BORDERS, SUSPICIOUS FOREIGNERS

THE PEOPLE OF THE LATE MIDDLE AGES (APPROXIMATELY 1250–1500) may have felt reasonably safe from catastrophic plagues. After all, more than 500 years had passed since the nightmares of the sixth to eighth century. The line of the *Yersinia pestis* bacterium that had caused the Justinianic plague was actually extinct, proven since by our genetic analyses.

The story of how the Black Death came to Europe has been told many times, yet its horrors are still difficult to comprehend. One of the grisliest episodes took place in Crimea, in the port town of Kaffa (now called Feodosia), a trading colony that belonged to the maritime republic of Genoa.

Since 1346, Kaffa had been besieged by Mongolian troops of the Golden Horde Empire, which was then a major power in Central Asia and Eastern Europe. In the spring of 1347, the Mongolians reportedly catapulted corpses and body parts over the walls of the city. Many of the attackers had the plague—indeed, sources report that it had been rampant among the Golden Horde for several years—so the Mongols knew the deadly potential of the mysterious epidemic felling their comrades. This early form of biowarfare was brutally effective, and plague spread through the streets of Kaffa. Panicking, its inhabitants boarded ships, fleeing what seemed like certain death.

The plague would presumably have killed a majority of the people on board the ships, but the remaining survivors would have tumbled into the ports where they arrived and infected a totally unprepared population. From these Mediterranean ports the plague was carried north, often by people trying to escape it. It wasn't long before the news spread like wildfire: foreigners, it was said, were bringing death and corruption. Contemporary witnesses reported that people became wary of all outsiders—the mere whisper that refugees were on the way would be enough to cast whole cities into uproar and inspire border controls and communication bans.

Perhaps here we are witnessing the historical beginnings of the questionable links made by politicians between immigration, violence, and disease.

Bizarre ideas about the origins of the plague were rife. All foreigners were suspect, but the Jewish community bore the brunt of this suspicion. They were accused of having poisoned wells, and hundreds of Jewish households were slaughtered in outbreaks of unchecked violence. Lepers and the poor were targeted, but sometimes the wealthy and the nobility were as well—in essence, anyone who didn't belong to the social majority was stigmatized. Although they didn't know how the plague was transmitted, observers could see that it was highly infectious and struck indiscriminately. The Italian scholar Gabriele de' Mussis described the implacability of the disease, which afflicted "inhabitants of both sexes in every city, every place, and every country." Many observers speculated about a "pestilential miasma" that drifted from country to country, claiming the lives of its victims. Over the following centuries, the plague struck certain cities with particular frequency, including Venice, where traders from across the world did business. Shortly after an outbreak, Venice would ban foreigners from entry; captains who disobeyed were fined and threatened with ship-burning. Closing the port was the authorities' preferred way of preventing the spread of disease in many places, although it was mostly ineffective.

Quarantine, which involved isolating newcomers for forty days (*quaranta* in Italian), was invented during this period. Many cities set up health authorities, but the people they put in charge knew nothing about the deadly potential of rats and fleas. They focused on segregating people who were sick,

Doctors were harbingers of death: the beak-like mask worn in this seventeenth-century copperplate engraving is evidence that people at least suspected there might be a risk of airborne infection.

which mostly meant cooping them up with other victims and leaving them to their fate. Corpses were quickly disposed of, usually dumped into graves—now, morbidly, a reliable source of plague samples for archaeogeneticists.

Trying to estimate a body count, some historians believe that contemporary witnesses might have exaggerated the number of victims because the circumstances were so appalling and so utterly new. It may be that, in fact, less than two-thirds of all Norwegians and 60 percent of the English, Spanish, and French populations died as has been claimed in some accounts. Yet even conservative estimates go far beyond anything we can imagine today. Only the Thirty Years' War, which was also accompanied by the plague, caused fatalities on a comparable scale. According to today's more modest calculations, a third of Europe's population died during the Black Death, 27 million people out of a population of approximately 80 million. We can only guess how ferociously the plague devastated certain regions and especially port towns, but in some cases it may have wiped out half the population—as it did in London, for instance. Virtually everybody (or at least well over half of Europeans) must have been infected with the bacteria, because we know today that without medical treatment—and nobody was treated in the Middle Ages—the bubonic plague is fatal in "only" about 50 percent of cases. The other 50 percent develop a lifelong immunity.

IMMUNITY

Without the immune system, there would be no human beings. There would be no mammals, and probably not even primitive multicellular organisms. The world is full of bacteria, viruses, and other pathogens that necessitate a response from the body—and respond it does. It has two primary defense systems. The first is the innate immune system, a mechanism that complex creatures have used for about 400 million years. Humans have this system in common with many other animals, including the horseshoe crab. It enables the organism to recognize and combat proteins that cause damage to the body. Before a pathogen can multiply in the blood, it is surrounded and eventually digested by macrophages, also called scavenger cells.

The innate immune system, however, can only destroy bacteria and viruses it recognizes as such. One characteristic by which macrophages recognize bacteria are the tiny propellers, also called flagella, they use to move themselves through the bloodstream. Part of the plague bacterium's success is due to a mutation that occurred when it diverged from its closest relative, *Yersinia pseudotuberculosis*. It lost its propeller, meaning that the innate immune system could no longer recognize it. It also gained the ability to evade the macrophages themselves and multiply inside them. The bacteria produce a protective protein shield to avoid being digested.

The innate immune system cannot cope with such well-equipped viruses and bacteria, so this is where the adaptive immune system steps in. The latter is a more recent evolutionary development, and has to form within individual human beings—a process that requires infection. The white blood cells come to recognize certain features on the surface of the pathogen and respond with a range of countermeasures that ultimately flood the blood with antibodies and destroy the attacking bacteria or viruses. Yet this process takes nine to fourteen days, and during this time the body must somehow stay alive. It usually copes well with the flu virus, but when it comes to the plague, the outcome very much depends on luck and the fitness of the person infected. The adaptive immune system then produces not only antibodies but memory cells, which enable the body to respond instantly the next time it is attacked. This protection can last for up to forty years after the initial infection—this is the mechanism exploited by vaccines. Once somebody has survived the plague, the pathogen will be defeated by the adaptive immune system if the person gets reinfected. If the plague wins the battle, however, the bacteria spread throughout the body and the person dies of sepsis or organ failure. It is only possible to tell if someone had the plague if they died of it. If they survived, then their antibodies would have wiped out all the bacteria, leaving no genetic residue.

THE CLONE WARS

AFTER THE INITIAL OUTBREAK OF THE BLACK DEATH, the plague dogged Europe for centuries. Totting up all the historical reports of major and minor epidemics, there were an extraordinary 7,000 outbreaks during this period. These are collectively referred to as the "Second Pandemic." The last great wave probably took place between 1720 and 1722 in

Marseille. It had long been unclear whether the disease described by eyewitnesses as the plague was in fact the same pathogen as the Black Death, but by sequencing various plague genomes, we were recently able to confirm their diagnoses. Even in eighteenth-century Marseille, people were still dying of the strain of bubonic plague that arrived in Europe in the fourteenth century.

In fact, during the period of the Black Death itself, we now know that it wasn't just the same strain—it was actually a clone. Everybody who died during this initial pandemic was attacked by identical versions of a single bacterium. This came as a tremendous surprise, because pathogens mutate very frequently (this is why flu shots are redeveloped every year). Yet genetic analyses show that the plague bacterium could not have mutated during the six-year ordeal, because it mutates at an unusually slow rate: one mutation every ten years. The clone also tells us that the plague bacterium only came to Europe once. Previously it was thought that the Black Death might have been brought to the continent repeatedly on ships or through trade. But if this were the case, we would have found various different strains dating from this period and not an identical bacterial clone that caused millions to die.

Europe, not Africa or Asia, became a plague hotspot. Over the following centuries, there were repeated flare-ups. These outbreaks probably occurred just when people had dropped their guard because a few decades had passed since the last epidemic. These long pauses were a result of the immunity acquired by those who had survived the plague. As soon as the number of people with immunity dwindled and the population was once more vulnerable to the bacterium, the next epidemic would erupt. Children, whose immune systems had never been exposed to the bacterium, would have been more likely than average to be victims. Between outbreaks, the plague probably hunkered down in Europe's huge population of rats.

The Black Death, then, was the mother of the European plague. It was the origin of all later European strains, slowly collecting mutations before it disappeared from Europe in the eighteenth century for good.

BACK TO ITS ROOTS

SPREADING OUT PAST EUROPE, THE PLAGUE THEN edged back toward its birthplace—Asia. Our genetic analyses proved that a descendant of the European clone appeared in the empire of the Golden Horde at the end of the fourteenth century (the same Golden Horde that had fired corpses into Kaffa fifty years earlier). Central Asia's rodent population is the world's largest reservoir of the bacterium even today.

In nineteenth-century China, the European-born medieval strain of the plague reemerged and caused the third major bubonic plague pandemic in human history. It massacred an estimated 12 million people in roughly fifty years. The Hong Kong plague, as it's known, affected more than just China: it was especially severe in the Pacific region and across large swaths of Asia, but the disease was also carried to the Americas and Africa on steamships. It exists in both places still. The outbreak in Madagascar in December 2017 can be traced back to the Hong Kong plague, and in the United States signs at the Grand Canyon warn tourists of the same pathogen that once evolved in Europe during the Black Death. We now know that other strains must have existed in China in the late nineteenth century—indeed, most still exist today—but only the bacterium descended from the Black Death was capable of spreading all across the globe.

In most areas of Europe, the pathogen is considered extinct, but in others it is still relatively widespread: in Central Asia there are more than two dozen rodent reservoirs of the bacterium, while in North America it is commonly carried by prairie dogs. These days the disease can be treated with antibiotics, so it has lost much of its medieval horror, but it still proves deadly in many cases, especially if the victim is infected with pneumonic plague, which usually kills its host even before it can be identified or treated.

Researchers today still argue over whether black rats were in fact a reservoir of plague during the Middle Ages. But there is a good deal of evidence to suggest that they were. The plague disappeared with the collapse of the Roman Empire, just as the rat population plummeted, and returned during the late Middle Ages, as Europe's cities and rat populations grew. It would also explain why the plague ravaged Europe for the last time in the eighteenth century. During this period, the black rat was supplanted by its nearest living relative, the brown rat, which challenged its much smaller foes over territory and occasionally even ate them. Much like the Black Death centuries earlier, this aggressive species was probably carried to Europe via shipping routes—only this time with positive consequences for humanity. Brown rats can transport the plague too, but they don't live in anything like such close proximity to humans, so this may be one contributing factor behind the elimination of the plague in Europe. Today, black rats are restricted to only a few boltholes in Europe and are even considered an endangered species in some countries around the world.

Regardless of whether the black rat was responsible for one of the greatest disasters in European history, fear of the animal is now seared into Europe's collective memory. Yet the creatures that inspire such disgust today, the brown rat, may in fact have saved us from the plague. Sadly, they only bought us some breathing space: the next deadly epidemics were already in the wings, waiting to take up the mantle of horror.

CHAPTER

9

New World, New Pandemics

MOTHER TERESA PROBABLY *had leprosy. Tuberculosis swims to the Americas. The arms race between humans and pathogens. Epidemics rush on ahead of settlers. Your neighbor's STDs.*

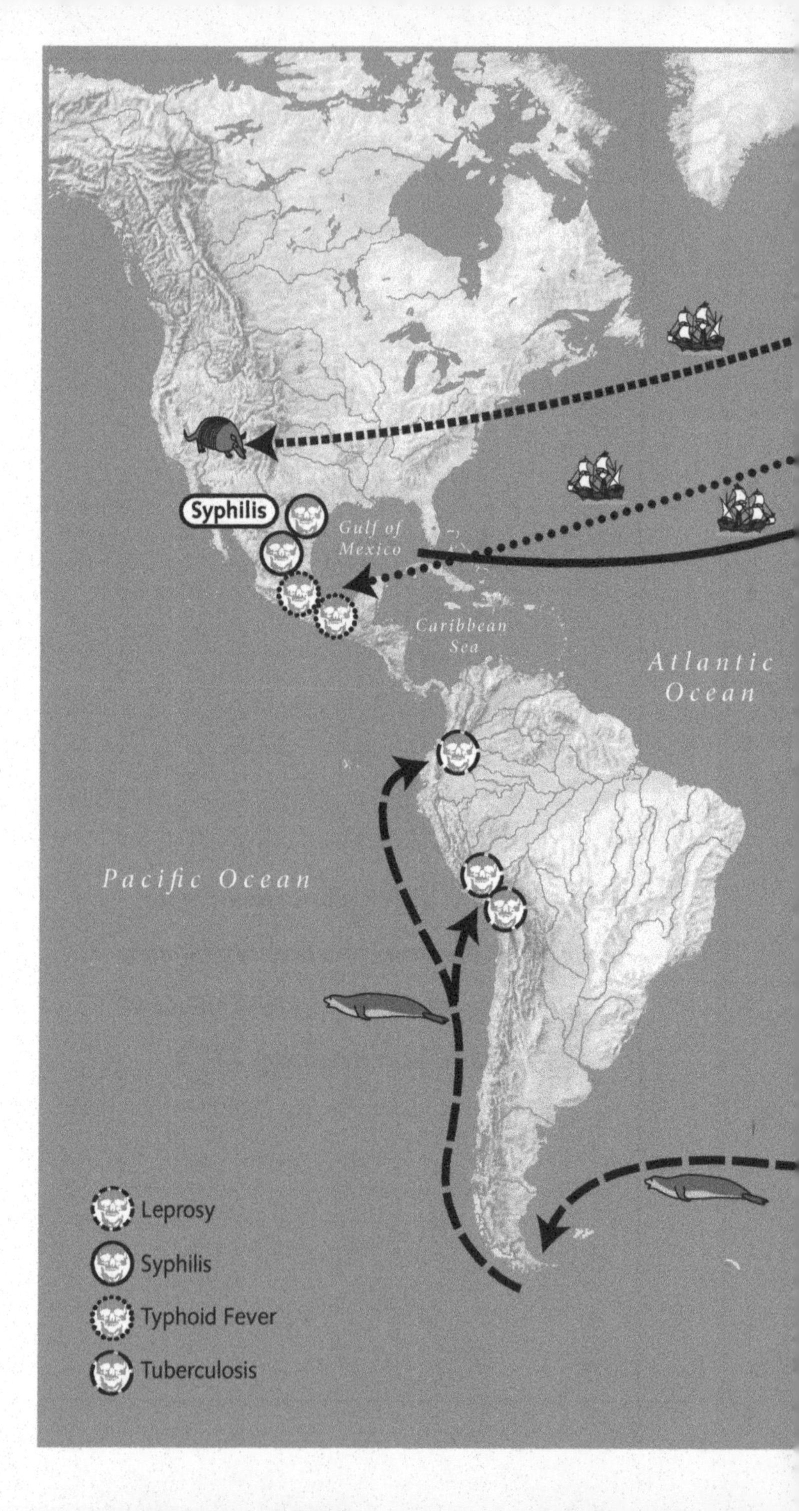
Syphilis
Gulf of Mexico
Caribbean Sea
Atlantic Ocean
Pacific Ocean
Leprosy
Syphilis
Typhoid Fever
Tuberculosis

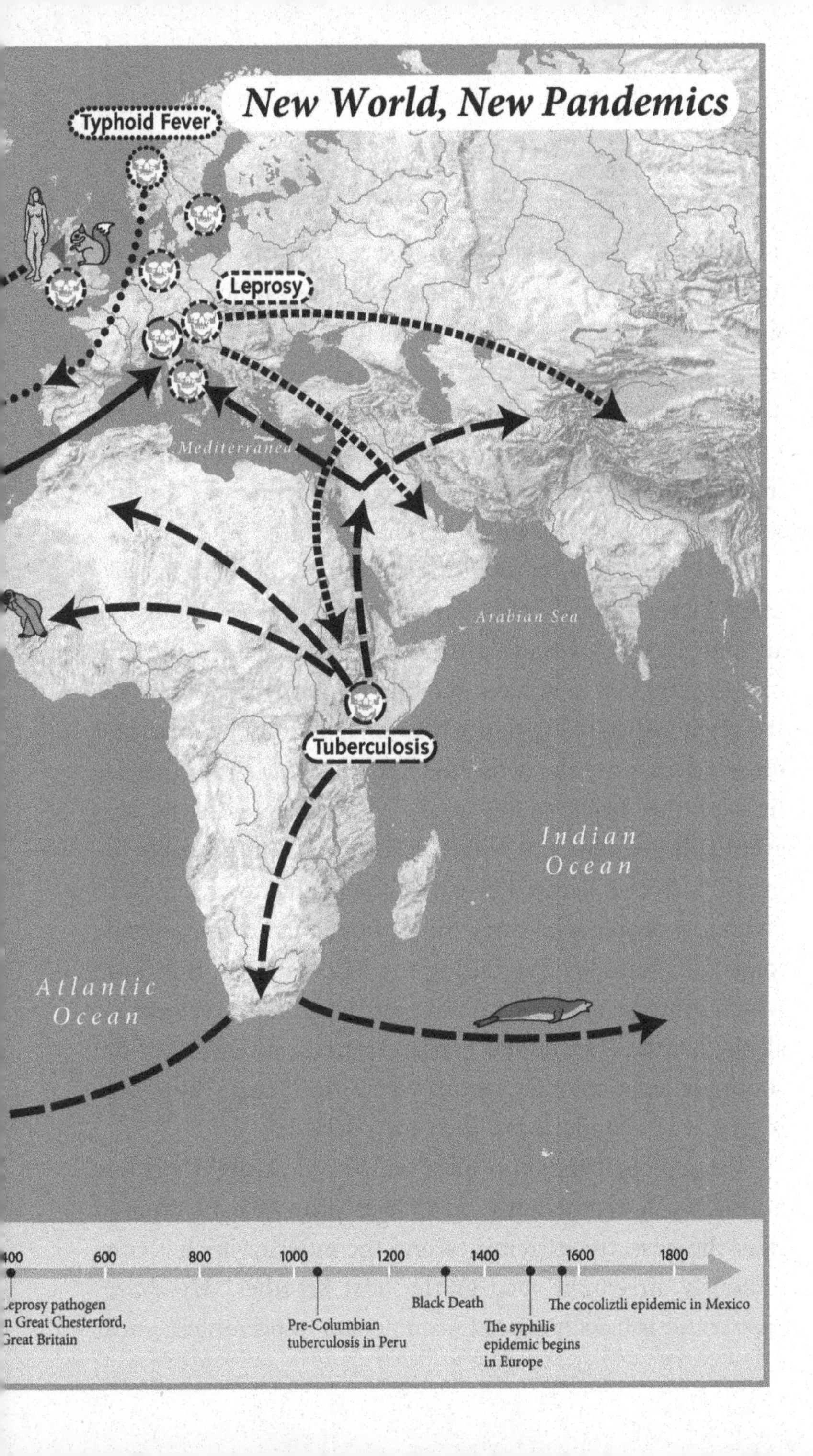
New World, New Pandemics
Typhoid Fever
Leprosy
Mediterranean
Arabian Sea
Tuberculosis
Indian Ocean
Atlantic Ocean
400
600
800
1000
1200
1400
1600
1800
Leprosy pathogen in Great Chesterford, Great Britain
Pre-Columbian tuberculosis in Peru
Black Death
The syphilis epidemic begins in Europe
The cocoliztli epidemic in Mexico

DEATH AT THE LEPER COLONY

THE PEOPLE OF THE MIDDLE AGES LIVED IN FEAR OF another appalling disease: leprosy. For those afflicted, leprosy was perhaps an even worse fate than the plague. Although most people did not die as a direct consequence, it was nearly always tantamount to a death sentence. And while the plague killed its victims within a few weeks or even days, leprosy inflicted years of torture, in which the victim was dead to society well before his or her physical demise.

Like the plague, leprosy is one of the oldest surviving diseases. It was probably already spreading havoc among the ancient Egyptians and Hittites, and today there are still roughly 200,000 new cases per year, primarily in South Asia. It's often associated with the missionary Mother Teresa, and for good reason—she dedicated her life to caring for the victims of this bacterial infection. Mother Teresa, who was eventually awarded the Nobel Peace Prize, was probably infected with the disease herself, although she never fell ill. In fact, most people who carry the pathogen never show symptoms. This was also true during the Middle Ages. But those whose immune systems did not pass the leprosy test were hit all the harder. They awaited near-certain death in one of the countless leper colonies, camps where the "lepers" were segregated and abandoned to their own devices.

The leprosy bacterium likes temperatures slightly below normal body temperature, so it lives primarily on exposed skin: the nose, the extremities, and the mouth, which is continuously air-conditioned as the host breathes. *Mycobacterium leprae* is usually passed from person to person via smear transmission, which requires close contact. A healthy immune system recognizes the pathogen but cannot kill it—the bacterium's extremely thick, waxy coating protects it. Instead of destroying the intruder, the cells are encapsulated by the body's defenses. They cannot multiply, but they are still alive. The host is infected with leprosy, but the disease is held in check by the immune system, where it can wait for decades.

If a person is weakened by another infection or a lack of food, the leprosy bacterium can break out of its stranglehold and spread. The immune system then attacks not the bacterium itself but the healthy tissue around it. At first the skin is blighted, then the soft tissue beneath, and then, in particularly nasty cases, the bones. Contrary to popular belief, the extremities of those suffering from leprosy do not drop off; instead, they are eaten away by the host's own immune system. Social exclusion usually exacerbates the disease by further weakening the body's defenses: victims lose their social relationships and eat a poorer diet; they may become homeless and receive limited medical care. Today, this is only a problem in deeply impoverished regions, where leprosy is most common. In medieval Europe, this vicious circle was the norm.

Because leprosy can affect the bones, the skeletons of many victims show visible signs of the disease, which is not the case with the plague. The earliest bones showing possible signs of leprosy were found in the remains of a 4,000-year-old skeleton from India, but the marks on these bones are ambiguous, so the diagnosis is not certain. The earliest medieval European leprosy case we have been able to examine so far comes from Great Chesterford in England, where the disease struck between 415 and 545 CE, but we were also lucky in finding a 2,000-year-old Egyptian mummy that preserved leprosy DNA. Historical leprosy pathogens are relatively easy to detect, because their waxy cladding helps preserve their genetic material better than human DNA.

It's likely that a majority of Europeans in late medieval Europe were infected, the disease hanging like the sword of Damocles over a population already beset by outbreaks of the plague every decade or two. Many medieval European skeletons show signs of leprosy, and a large number of leper colonies were set up in Europe from the sixth century onward. Especially in the densely populated and dirty cities, which had no sewage systems or running water, death and disease could descend on the population at any time and without any warning, even without the frequent military conflicts.

THE ARMS RACE BETWEEN HUMANS AND PATHOGENS

The idea that human immune-response genes help us adapt to pathogens is still only a theory. There is much to recommend it, but we're missing definitive proof. According to this hypothesis, when deadly bacteria or viruses attack the body, the variants of the immune-response gene best able to deal with the pathogen will gradually prevail. The suggestion, for instance, that the plague came to Europe from the Pontic steppe and killed vast numbers of people there 5,000 years ago—either before or after the great migration—is tenable only if the populations in the east were more resistant to the plague than those in the west, or if their lifestyle was better at hindering the spread of the bacterium. Thus far we have found no signs of genetic adaptation in Stone Age samples, but we also know that mutations offering protection against pathogens can occur outside the immune-response genes.

Better resistance against diseases can even be linked to harmful genetic changes that are advantageous under certain circumstances. On Sardinia, for example, one in nine people carries a gene causing thalassemia, a genetic disorder that hampers the development of red blood cells. Sufferers are usually less physically resilient, which ordinarily is an evolutionary disadvantage. Yet clearly on Sardinia it wasn't, because a side effect of thalassemia is resistance to malaria. Malaria, transmitted by mosquitoes, once devastated the ancient Mediterranean world. The high incidence of thalassemia on the island reveals that the evolutionary disadvantages of the genetic defect were outweighed by the advantages of resistance to malaria. In other words, while the less-fit people with thalassemia may have had fewer children, those without the defect died more often of malaria.

A similar, even more pronounced version of the phenomenon has been observed in East Africa, one of the regions most badly affected by malaria today. In some areas, half the population has inherited a genetic condition called sickle cell anemia from one parent—and, with it, resistance to malaria. People who inherit the condition from both parents, however, have little chance of survival. Statistically, in regions where half the population carries the sickle cell trait, one in four children dies of the disease. Yet despite this, the condition continues to be a selective advantage—evidently because malaria is a much bigger threat.

There is even a useful genetic defect that provides protection against HIV. In certain individuals, the CCR5 receptor is damaged. People who inherit the defect from both parents are virtually completely resistant to HIV—in Europe this is roughly one in every hundred. About one in ten Europeans has the defective gene from one parent, possibly offering increased protection against the virus. However, it's likely that the mutation makes carriers more susceptible to the West Nile virus and the influenza pathogen.

LEPROSY OUT, TUBERCULOSIS IN

LEPROSY RETREATED FROM EUROPE, PERHAPS IN PART because of improving standards of hygiene, but the population had no respite. It may not be a coincidence that around the same time leprosy diminished, tuberculosis (TB) took hold. Tuberculosis and leprosy are both caused by closely related mycobacteria. It's conceivable that TB, which is transmitted by inhaling airborne droplets, immunized its victims against leprosy, so one illness was overlaid on the other. In any case, from the seventeenth century onward, tuberculosis killed countless numbers of people, and remains to this day one of the most dangerous and widely spread infectious diseases. Roughly 8 million people fall ill each year and 1 million die from TB infection. As with leprosy, the actual rate of infection is significantly higher than what can be recorded. It's estimated that one in three people across the globe is currently harboring the bacterium. Like the leprosy pathogen, it is surrounded by a kind of waxy coating that the human immune system can surround but not penetrate. In a person with a weakened immune system, the TB bacteria spread inside the lungs and other organs. Patients with advanced TB cough up blood and become increasingly exhausted, until the bacteria have depleted the body, causing particular damage to the airways. Tuberculosis is often associated with pale skin, an emaciated figure, and, in bad cases, bloody sputum, which may have partly inspired the literary vampire mythos of the nineteenth century. Until the discovery of antibiotics, the only recourse was to strengthen a patient's immune system—by keeping them in sanatoriums, for instance.

Few infectious diseases are as thoroughly researched as tuberculosis. Yet only within the last few years have we begun to understand how TB first affected human beings. Until relatively recently, it was considered collateral damage of the Neolithic, because of bovine tuberculosis, another form of the disease. Bovine tuberculosis remains widespread even today, which is why we pasteurize milk and advise people not to drink untreated milk. The cow has always been considered the original carrier of the tuberculosis bacterium, and it was believed that humans became infected when they domesticated cattle.

In the early 2000s, this theory was overturned. Medical researchers began sequencing the tuberculosis genome in samples taken from both humans and animals, in order to build a family tree. Tuberculosis samples taken from humans in Africa showed the greatest genetic diversity, and all human

European and Asian strains are derived from this source. Bovine tuberculosis, meanwhile, branched off from a human strain of the bacterium, also in Africa. It appears that we infected cows, not the other way around. Tuberculosis, it was concluded, must have emigrated out of Africa with human beings. Yet even this is not quite right.

In Peru in the early 2000s, archaeologists dug up the mummified remains of several people, three of whom had evidently suffered from tuberculosis. Their thousand-year-old spines showed the customary deformations that occur when thoracic vertebrae, eaten away by bacteria, break during violent fits of coughing. In 2014, we were able to confirm the diagnosis with genetic analyses of samples from the mummified bones. It was clear that TB had been rife in the Americas long before the arrival of Christopher Columbus, although this had previously been considered unlikely. If tuberculosis existed in the pre-Columbian Americas and was brought there by people from Africa, only one possibility remained: the disease must have crossed the Bering Strait roughly 15,000 years ago, carried by migrants from Asia.

Yet this did not fit with the genetic origins of the tuberculosis pathogen found in the Peruvian mummies. This pathogen was descended from the same branch as bovine tuberculosis. By comparing modern tuberculosis bacteria from across the world with pre-Columbian American pathogens, we were able to establish when and where their common ancestors existed: approximately 5,000 years ago somewhere in Africa. None of this fits with the idea that tuberculosis was brought to the Americas by humans 15,000 years ago. Five thousand years later the land bridge to Alaska was underwater, so tuberculosis could not possibly have come to the

Americas that way, and certainly not in a cow, because we know that there were no cattle in the pre-Columbian Americas. Similarly, it was clear that TB could not have been brought to Europe by people migrating out of Africa, because this wave of migration took place between 40,000 and 50,000 years ago.

What this tells us is that in the past millennia, TB must have taken different routes to the Americas and Europe than previously assumed. In the case of the Americas, we are now quite sure that it swam across from Africa. Pathogens similar to the bovine tuberculosis bacterium have since been found in other animals, including sheep, goats, lions, and wild cattle, but also in seals, and the strain found in seals was the most similar to the variant in the human mummies from Peru. In one of those animals, the bacterium must have found its way from Africa to South America by crossing the Atlantic. In some coastal regions of South America, seals were a popular source of human food, so their resident bacteria would have easily infected the local human population. Over the following millennia, tuberculosis spread across the whole of the Americas, probably evolving into an American variant of the disease. It was this strain that infected—and likely killed—the three mummified individuals in Peru.

Today, the pathogen is still found in seals all over the Southern Hemisphere. Human beings in the Americas, however, no longer carry this pre-Columbian strain; so far, tests have revealed nothing but European tuberculosis since colonization began. Clearly this was brought by settlers after the arrival of Columbus, and it could have contributed to the devastating loss of life among indigenous peoples, in an age when European diseases decimated the unprotected local population. If this scenario is accurate, it makes sense that there is no evidence the American pathogen transmitted to settlers or spread widely in Europe—European tuberculosis must have been significantly more aggressive than the American type. Even now, the European strain is prevalent across the globe. When and precisely how the TB pathogen found its way from Africa to Europe is still unclear. TB was probably already among us in the Middle Ages, if not earlier, long before it unleashed its terrible power.

A HUNDRED-YEAR WAVE OF DEATH

AMERICANS WERE SEPARATED FROM EUROPEANS FOR AT least 15,000 years, although both had common ancestors in the region around Lake Baikal where the Mal'ta boy was found. The long separation may be one reason so many indigenous people died after the arrival of their distant European relatives starting in the late 15th century. It's difficult to judge the number of these victims, not least because the epidemics were often accompanied by a brutal policy of conquest that destroyed countless lives and even whole cultures. The invaders might even have viewed these diseases as helpful allies. It's estimated that up to 95 percent of the indigenous American population died within the first hundred years of colonization. Many European settlers described diseases that killed the inhabitants of the New World but left them untouched, or at least still standing.

The written record we have of the colonialists as they moved south and west from the East Coast of North America may give us a sense of how the plague entered Europe 5,000 years ago—if the plague did indeed originate on the steppes. Though many indigenous Americans died after direct contact with European explorers, some of them recount arriving in towns already denuded by disease. These scenarios are reminiscent of those archaeologists have reconstructed of the steppe migration in settlements around the Black Sea

While we can only speculate about Stone Age Europe, we have a clearer picture of more recent history in the Americas. The deadly effect of the smallpox and flu viruses is well documented. Until recently, however, we didn't know what had caused some of the deadliest epidemics in colonial history, including the cocoliztli epidemic that raged between 1545 and 1550 in what is now Mexico and Guatemala. An estimated 60 to 90 percent of the population suffered from a mysterious illness; now DNA sequencing tells us that they likely died of bacterial enteric fever, a form of typhoid known as paratyphoid.

The illness is caused by the bacterium *Salmonella enterica paratyphi C*, which lives primarily in the gut and can spread outward, colonizing the entire body. Sufferers develop a high fever, dehydration, constipation, and later extreme diarrhea. It is transmitted through physical contact or via food or drinking water contaminated with feces. Even today, more than 10 million people—generally those living in impoverished countries with poor sanitation—fall ill with the disease every year, and roughly one in a hundred patients will die as a result.

The people of Central America in the mid-sixteenth century were clearly suffering from a very severe manifestation of this disease. Here too, inhabitants fled the diseased cities. The citizens of Teposcolula-Yucundaa in southern Mexico fled into the neighboring valley and left behind an enormous

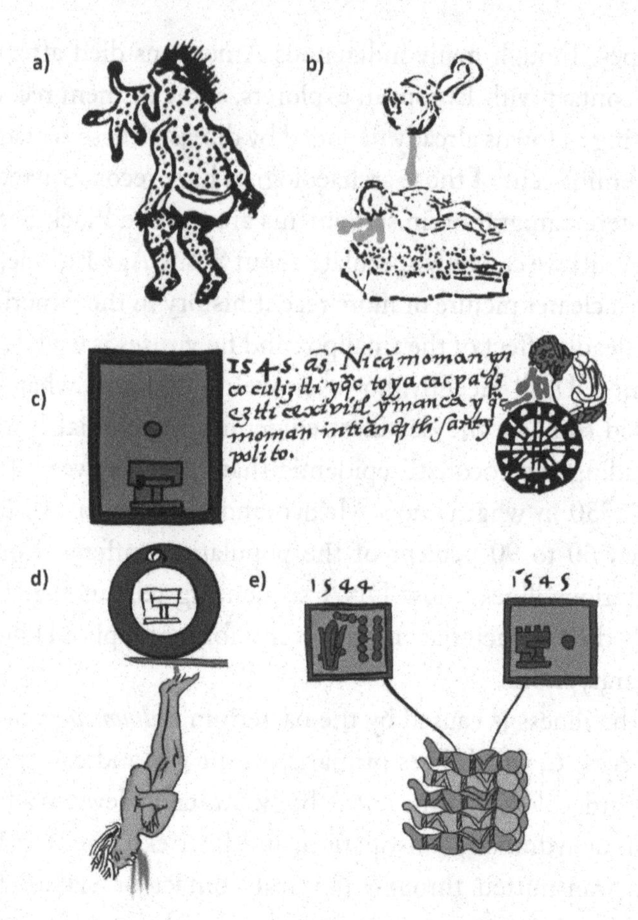

Indigenous pictograms from Mexico's early colonial period. They illustrate the cocoliztli epidemic during the mid-sixteenth century. Blood is shown flowing from the nose and mouth, and the artist also depicts years and mass graves.

cemetery that has remained largely undisturbed. In 2018, we examined the remains of twenty-nine people buried there, and in ten of them we found paratyphoid bacterial DNA. The epidemics in Central America were probably among the deadliest in history. There were also outbreaks of typhoid in Europe, including in the early twentieth century in the industrialized and densely populated west of Germany, but these never even approached the scale of the cocoliztli epidemic.

NOT REALLY SYPHILIS

THE EUROPEAN AND AMERICAN EARLY MODERN ERA IS in part a history of disease, mostly concerning European pathogens that migrated with its people to afflict those on the other side of the Atlantic. Syphilis took the opposite route, arriving in Spain in 1493 with the return of Columbus's first expedition. The sailors had brought back to the Old World the most feared sexually transmitted disease of modern times, syphilis—or, at least, that was how the story was told in Europe. Conversely, American researchers argued that Europeans carried the bacteria into the New World. In fact, the most recent genetic analyses of syphilis pathogens from the Americas and Europe suggest a degree of back-and-forth far more complex than previously realized by either side.

The year Columbus returned from the Americas, there were reports in Mediterranean harbor towns of a formerly unknown disease. War had broken out between France and Naples, and a vast French army comprising soldiers from many countries met in Italy. When these soldiers marched back north in 1495, they spread this disease, syphilis, throughout Europe, where it would continue to plague people for decades—in fact, over the next fifty years, it became more and more prevalent. People came up with nicknames for the sickness, revealing how strongly they associated the scourge with foreigners. The "French disease," it was termed in most of France's neighboring countries, including in Italy; the "Neapolitan disease," said the French. The Scottish spoke of the "English disease," while the Norwegians ascribed it to the Scottish. The Poles laid the blame squarely on the shoulders of the Neapolitans and French, but the Russians located the problem in Poland. There was, however, general agreement as to where syphilis had originated: the New World, from which it was brought back on the ships of the returning conquerors.

The spread of the disease in the sixteenth century was particularly ruthless. Syphilis bacteria, which are transmitted primarily through sexual contact, reproduce mainly in the genital area. The body's defense systems destroy the cells surrounding the bacteria, creating painful lesions in the flesh—and that's just the mild version. During the fifty-year epidemic, up to 16 million people died of a particularly virulent form known as neurosyphilis, which is virtually nonexistent today. Fleeing the body's immune response, syphilis bacteria retreat into the nerve cells before getting attacked by the immune system and the body's own response consumes part of the brain, often taking the roof of the skull for good measure. Sufferers are driven insane and die an agonizing death.

The bacterium's ability to retreat into nerve cells makes it hard for archaeogeneticists to detect it in skeletons. Even if the bones do display the lesions typically left by the disease, there is usually no pathogen DNA to be found. In fact, the bacteria are difficult to isolate even in living patients. In 2018, in order to map the pathogen's historical genome for the first time, we examined some highly unusual skeletons. They belonged to five Mexican children who died between 1681 and 1861, most of them no older than nine months. They had been buried in a former monastery in Mexico City and showed clear signs of congenital syphilis, which is passed from the mother during pregnancy and can cause severe disabilities and deformities. The bacteria had not yet retreated into the nerve cells, because the children's immature immune systems had not attacked them. In three of the five skeletons we found bacterial DNA—and, surprisingly, not just syphilis. One of the children had actually died of yaws. Yaws and syphilis bacteria are subtypes of the same bacterial strain, meaning they are closely related and can cause very similar damage to babies in the womb.

This discovery suggests that in the past, skeletal changes caused by yaws may have been misattributed to syphilis. This suspicion was supported by recent research on five monkey populations in East Africa. Scientists had studied individuals showing clear signs of syphilis, including lesions in their genital parts. But when we sequenced the pathogens present, every single one of the animals was suffering from yaws.

Sequencing the pathogens in the Central American babies and the African monkeys gave us a new perspective on syphilis. The disease could have had a very similar sister that was wrongly diagnosed during centuries past. If so, this permits another interpretation of syphilis and its history. The disease could have come from the Americas with the returning sailors, but in return, Europeans could have brought yaws to the New World. These deadly sexually transmitted souvenirs would in this case have been a reciprocal feature of our early transatlantic relationship.

African monkeys may originally have played host to the common ancestor of both yaws and syphilis. According to this theory, they would have passed the bacterium to human beings. Then, 40,000 to 50,000 years ago, the two kinds of bacteria diverged—in other words, the split occurred as modern humans were spreading out of Africa across the globe. The original inhabitants of the Americas, who crossed the Bering Strait, could have carried the disease that developed over the subsequent 15,000 years into modern syphilis. In Africa, meanwhile, yaws evolved. When exactly it arrived in Europe is unclear, but there's plenty of evidence to suggest the disease was around during the Middle Ages. Numerous skeletons dating from the period before 1493—in Great Britain, for instance—show clear signs of syphilis. Until now, these finds have usually been taken as evidence that the disease existed in Europe before the discovery of the Americas, but I am almost certain that the dead people in question suffered from yaws.

AN UNDERESTIMATED THREAT

FOR MOST PEOPLE IN THE MODERN WEST, PLAGUE, leprosy, paratyphoid, tuberculosis, and syphilis are little more than ancient ghosts. Bacterial infections such as these are no longer viewed as potentially fatal, having been largely replaced in the public consciousness by appalling viral pandemics. The Spanish flu was one example, claiming almost as many human lives between 1918 and 1919 as the First World War. Or smallpox, which was only eradicated in the 1970s after a nearly 300-year campaign to vaccinate against the disease. Or HIV, which has cost the lives of roughly 40 million people since the 1980s. And still fresh in most people's memory is the COVID-19 pandemic of 2020.

Although bacterial diseases have been held in check in Europe for about a century, there's no reason to sound the all-clear. We are still far from having made bacteria harmless. In fact, we should assume that the scourges of the Middle Ages may return, perhaps even within a few decades. There are signs this is already happening.

The tuberculosis epidemic that began in the sixteenth century is still raging today. Even though millions of people still carry the bacterium, we don't fear TB because we have antibiotics. Discovered in the mid-twentieth century, antibiotics seemed like a good defense against virtually all bacterial infections.

We now know that this sense of security was false. More and more bacteria are developing a resistance to antibiotics because we have so massively overused those drugs, both in livestock as a growth stimulant and in human medicine. We are now aware of a whole series of tuberculosis strains that are resistant to several antibiotics. Bacteria are remarkably quick to adapt. Often they will show the first signs of resistance barely a year after a drug's introduction. Medicine has only a few years' head start on the tuberculosis pathogen. To a bacterium that has persevered in the human population for roughly 5,000 years, the groundbreaking development of antibiotics was just a minor setback within a much longer race. As early as the mid-twenty-first century, many tuberculosis patients may be infected with fully resistant bacteria.

Multi-drug-resistant bacteria and the looming antibiotics crisis are part of the emerging "third epidemiological transition" facing the world today. The first transition took place when humans became farmers. Living in close proximity to animals, they caught their pathogens and spread them among the settlements. The second transition occurred only recently, with the implementation of hygiene standards in the nineteenth century and the introduction of antibiotics in the twentieth. Bacterial diseases faded into insignificance and diseases of affluence came to the fore, especially in the West. Cardiovascular diseases and diabetes, instead of tuberculosis, plague, or cholera, are now leading causes of death. In the next phase, the old diseases could soon return, even in affluent regions of the world. In many poorer, countries, deaths from leprosy, typhoid, tuberculosis, or even the plague are still part of everyday reality. Syphilis is slowly but surely making new headway in Europe. In part because HIV is now treatable, albeit not curable, more people are deciding not to use condoms—a dangerous game, because the syphilis pathogen, like the microorganisms that cause other STDs, is increasingly becoming resistant to antibiotics.

Bacteria descending on an untouched and thus especially vulnerable population is, however, a thing of the past. What happened during the wave of migration 5,000 years ago and during the colonization of the Americas at the end of the fifteenth century are no longer plausible scenarios. Today, the world's population is about 500 times bigger than it was during the Stone Age, and 15 times bigger than at the time of Columbus. People are increasingly mobile. In the past three decades alone, the number of flights per year has doubled worldwide, and Europeans are one of the most mobile groups. Traveling the globe as tourists, we ensure the continued globalization of viruses and bacteria. Mobility and infectious disease have gone hand in hand since the Neolithic, and that does not look set to change.

Archaeogenetics has a role to play here that goes well beyond scholarly interest. By comparing ancient and modern pathogens, we can begin to understand how they have evolved over the preceding years and centuries, as well as what human DNA does to counteract them. In doing so, we can help the medical community keep pace in the constant biological arms race. One of the many fascinating twists of human evolution is that, within less than a century, we managed to transform ourselves from defenseless victims of bacteria and viruses to worthy opponents. Now we need to make sure we don't squander that competitive edge.

CHAPTER

10

Conclusion

The Global Melting Pot

EVERYTHING WAS WORSE IN *the past. We're not one people. Africa is misunderstood. Fear of the mobile human. Intelligence is unfairly, but evenly, distributed. Humans create their own evolution. Borders fall.*

Net migration 2012 (in thousands)

- Increase of 100 or more
- Increase between 20 and 99
- Between a decrease of 19 a
- Decrease between 20 and 9
- Decrease of 100 or more

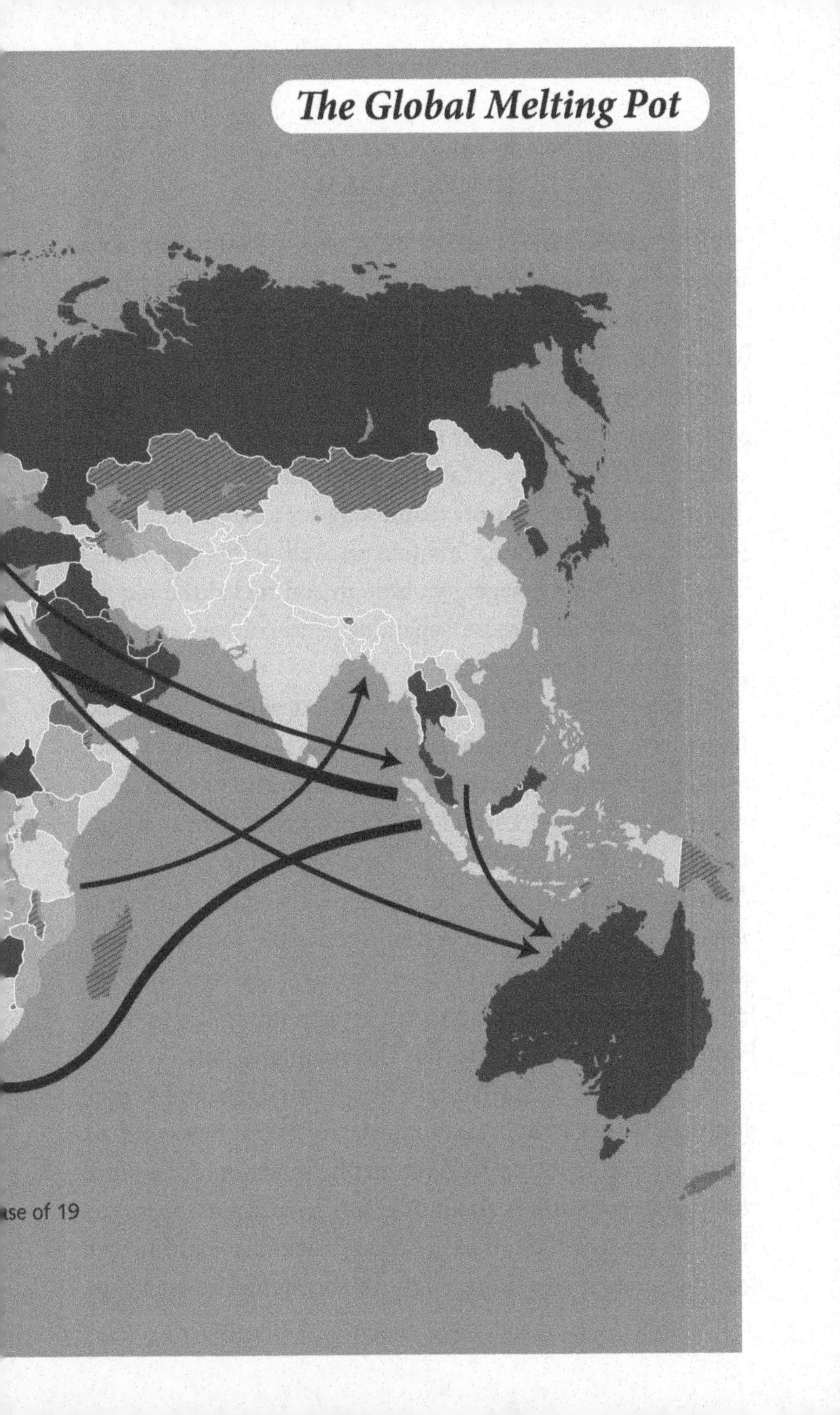
The Global Melting Pot
se of 19

NO ROMANTICIZING, NO FATALISM

IN JUNE 2018, DONALD TRUMP WENT ON TWITTER AND appealed to a widespread, deep-seated fear: that immigration is synonymous with the importation of violence and disease. Criminal gangs, tweeted the grandchild of Scottish and German immigrants, would "pour into and infest" the country with violence. It's probably no accident that Trump went for maximal ambiguity by using the word "infest," which is usually used in a medical context and suggests an infectious danger. The reaction among his fans as well as his opponents showed that the message got through and fueled the big divide that more and more separates conservatives and progressives over the last decade.

In Europe too, equating immigration with violence and disease is no longer a phenomenon of the far-right fringe but a guiding principle of several governments who have come to power by making anti-immigration promises. Their message, to use Trump's metaphor, has been spreading throughout Western society for years like an aggressive virus. Immigration, violence, and disease are an inseparable mixture in the minds of many people: diseases "attack," societies are "infested" with violence, refugees are "overrunning" Europe and North America, the "fortress" is threatening to fall.

In large parts of the Western world, immigration has predominantly negative connotations. This isn't new, and of course it's not exclusively a Western phenomenon. All around the world, reservations about migrants have always been justified by anxieties about violence and sickness—and by the fear that one's own culture might be threatened or even suppressed by a foreign one. Countering this argument is no trivial matter. Even archaeogenetic evidence about the history of migration seems to offer something for everyone: those who view migration as a vital part of an evolving culture and population and those who view it as humanity's perpetual malaise.

Genetic analyses have given us a highly accurate picture of what happened during the Neolithic Revolution, which began in Europe 8,000 years ago. Archaeologists had known for ages that people had begun to farm around that time. Though they had their detractors, many researchers theorized that this revolution was less a major upheaval than a fluid transition. Agriculture, they argued, was carried like a torch from the Near East to every corner of Europe, bringing new knowledge and sowing the earth with grain. With the genetic evidence we've gathered, however, we can say with certainty that agriculture was brought to Europe from the Near East by large families of migrants who sidelined established populations. Because old and new populations had virtually no contact for centuries, it *does* make sense to talk about cultural suppression. The Neolithic period is a prime example of the decline of the "West" and the triumph of the "East"—although at this point the West was an extremely modest society in which people lived as nomads in the woods and grasslands, while migrants from the Near East imported a significantly more advanced lifestyle.

While the Neolithic Revolution can still be considered a largely peaceful—albeit imposed—takeover of Europe by foreign populations, this picture becomes altogether more complex when we reach the second major wave of migration, which began around 5,000 years ago. In the Neolithic period, migrants from the Near East found themselves on a sparsely populated continent that offered both them and the established population enough space and food for all. Three thousand years later, however, when the new Europeans arrived from the steppes, they encountered a population weakened—probably by the plague they'd imported. The history of immigration in the Bronze Age is thus an example of migrants who brought either disease and death or violence and destruction in their wake.

Europeans today are therefore the product of large-scale patterns of movement stretching back millennia and encompassing near-constant interaction, suppression, struggle, and deep suffering. There is no reason, however, to view contemporary Europeans as descended from the victims of these upheavals. If you look at the settlement of Europe as the drama it so often was, then at least 70 percent of its cast are descended from the antiheroes: the migrants who arrived on the continent and subjugated it 8,000 and 5,000 years ago. The genetic makeup of the hunter-gatherers who had previously dominated is now in the minority, although it's still one of the three genetic pillars of Europe.

Genetic data offers us a much more detailed picture of the flow of migrants thousands of years ago, but its gaps leave plenty of room for interpretation. This much is clear: the early history of migration in Europe does not support either romanticization or fatalism. No, migration was rarely entirely peaceful, and yes, without it the continent would not be as advanced as it is today. A prehistoric Europe without migration would have been a Europe devoid of human beings, although there would have been an impressive wealth of flora and fauna.

Archaic Europeans never had deep roots on the continent. Hunter-gatherers were Europe's sole occupants for millennia, but they weren't the first. They displaced earlier populations, as the 2 percent of Neanderthal DNA testifies (and even the Neanderthals probably ousted types of *Homo erectus* when they arrived). Nor were hunter-gatherers a sterling example of a settled, deeply rooted community: no way of life would have been more alien to these early humans than one limited to a specific piece of land. They were instinctively citizens of the world. They went wherever necessity took them, recognizing no such thing as a homeland, only a broad expanse full of opportunity. The notion of owning a plot of land arrived with the first Anatolian farmers. It was they who hammered stakes into the earth and declared possession of it. If opponents of immigration want to make an argument against human mobility based on early history, they must take into account the cultural impact of one of Europe's biggest waves of migration.

LONGING FOR THE FIELDS AND FORESTS

THE ERA OF EUROPEAN HUNTER-GATHERERS, THOUGH it gradually started to disappear 8,000 years ago, remains enduringly fascinating for many people. They associate this lifestyle with a long-lost freedom. Modern hikers trudging around with their tents and backpacks through (tamed) nature, hunters, and anglers testify to a longing for a supposedly "unspoiled" way of life. There's a lot of idealization going on here. Early humans ate not just filleted meat but anything they could get their hands on, including snails, insects, and other creepy-crawlies. Of course, their bodies were perfectly adapted to these food sources, while ours still haven't fully digested the switch to a carbohydrate-heavy diet, which took place during the Neolithic period. To draw the conclusion that the culture migrants brought to Europe during and after the Neolithic era led humans astray from their intended path, however, is to make a quasi-religious error of judgment. Ever since we first began to walk upright and make tools to hunt, we—unlike all other creatures on Earth—shaped our own fate, adapting when necessary or desirable. If an essential part of being human were to live as we have always lived, then we wouldn't have any of the benefits of modern life.

Yet it's precisely this irrational longing for some sort of mythical, unspoiled "roots" that many people in modern societies share. They eat "paleo" diets, purportedly in the manner of Stone Age humans. They favor natural remedies. They produce enormous amounts of particulates warming themselves by open fires. And sometimes they take dangerous risks. When parents refuse to vaccinate their children, for instance, arguing that human beings survived for thousands of years without immunization, they are flying in the face of modern medical orthodoxy: while it's true that our ancestors didn't vaccinate their kids, it's also true that many of them died of illnesses that can easily be treated today. Even the shaman of Bad Dürrenberg, an icon of the hunter-gatherer era, was barely out of her teens before she perished, probably due to an infection. In the Stone Age, nature had a wide variety of ways to end a human life. Heart attacks, diabetes, and strokes generally weren't among them, but this is not only because people ate a more balanced diet. It's also because they usually died too young to suffer them. Similarly, rates of cancer are increasing primarily in wealthy countries because it's a disease typically associated with a ripe old age.

The lives of contemporary Europeans are the most comfortable in human history. This is, in part, thanks to Stone and Bronze Age immigration. Agriculture established early forms of community in Europe: people were no longer dependent on families or small tribes but could rely on the support and cohesion of wider settlements. Though droughts or climate crises continued to pose existential problems, the ability to stockpile food gradually emancipated farmers from the whims of nature. The wave of immigration from the steppes laid the groundwork for a Europe characterized by hierarchies, division of labor, and innovation, and thus for a continent that, in the modern era if not before, would come to shape the whole world with its technology and knowledge.

When migrants left Europe, a continent that had been shaped by immigrants for millennia, and crossed the Atlantic to the New World, they repeated that history all over again—with all its terrible consequences for the indigenous populations. The innovations they contributed were inextricable from their invasion. Of course, it's important to note that early currents of migration and the wave triggered by Christopher Columbus in 1492 are not comparable from a moral perspective. After all, the colonization of the Americas took place in the context of religious and judicial norms and moral restrictions that many European settlers consciously trampled underfoot. In early history, by contrast, these norms were not likely to exist; people seem to have lived in a brutal "state of nature" that was gradually fought back as they developed societies and civilizations.

HAS GENETICS BEEN REHABILITATED?

UNTIL RECENTLY, WE ONLY HAD A VAGUE SENSE OF WHAT constituted the early waves of migration into Europe that contributed to various partially conflicting theories. Although some nooks and crannies of this archaic period remain unexplored, archaeogenetics has done much to shed light on it. Genetic sequencing has enabled us to read archaic and contemporary genomes as if they were journals chronicling personal stories of migration and genetic intermingling. Genetics must therefore become an essential element of historical writing.

To describe this as a challenge of scientific ethics would be a profound understatement, especially in German-speaking countries. After all, it was the Nazis who took the deluded notion that history is nothing more than a battle between "races" and put it into practice in the most horrifically barbaric way. Many archaeologists in the early to mid-twentieth century postulated that the dominance of certain cultures (for "cultures" read "peoples" and for "peoples" read "populations") went hand in hand with their genetic superiority. They undergirded this claim with various arguments, including the thesis that the Bronze Age in Europe began not with the adoption of new tools but with the arrival of "battle-axe warriors" from Scandinavia. These "Nordic" peoples, they thought, were superior to others—they had driven progress forward and brought with them the Germanic languages. The Nazi interpretation of history was frequently contradicted by archaeological discoveries, but it served as ideological justification for designating other "races"—in

Eastern Europe, for example—as genetically inferior. It's hardly surprising, then, that after the Second World War many archaeologists in Germany rebounded to the opposite extreme, rejecting the idea that the spread of cultural technologies and languages was closely bound up with migration. The Neolithic era and the Bronze Age, these archaeologists argued, spread across Europe when people who were already living there learned and adopted these new technologies.

The genetic data now shows the opposite. In fact, both technological and linguistic changes in early history are inseparable from waves of migration in which immigrants largely displaced established populations. The Nazis would hardly have been pleased that progress arrived 8,000 years ago from Anatolia and 5,000 years ago from Eastern Europe, but it's reasonable to argue that recent discoveries have partially rehabilitated archaeological theses from the first half of the twentieth century. Reasonable, but too simplistic. A detailed look at the genetic data reveals how complicated the interplay between migration and cultural exchange really was and makes it impossible to draw sharp lines between the different populations.

Yes, agriculture was brought to Europe from Anatolia, after which the hunter-gatherers of the Fertile Crescent began to farm the land—but this was largely to do with the increasingly warm climate in the region and the wide variety of wild grains that grew there and could be cultivated. Similarly, there's no proof that a superior population migrating from the steppes enabled progress; the inhabitants of the steppes can be traced back to immigrants from the Near East just as easily as to established hunter-gatherers. The steppe people did bring bronze-working skills to the West, but the leap from nomadic to farming lifestyle was accomplished only in Europe. It was primarily in Europe that they adopted a settled way of life, enriching it with technological innovation. Exchange, in addition to migration, has always played a crucial role in cultural innovation. We Europeans are the product of this process; to this day we retain traces of immigration, suppression, and cooperation in our genes.

NATIONAL BORDERS AREN'T GENETIC

NOBODY CARRIES GENES THAT IDENTIFY THEMSELVES as a "pure" member of a particular ethnic group. The old yet still cherished idea that a special set of genes belongs to Teutons, Celts, and Scandinavians, or even to specific nationalities, has been thoroughly debunked. It's true that the frequency of particular gene variants undergoes consistent shifts as we move from the Iberian Peninsula to the Urals, and geneticists can say on this basis where individual people roughly come from. Yet attempting to make genetic variants conform to national borders makes about as much sense as the notion of splitting a color gradient into individual colors. The transitions are too fluid: we can measure a difference between two individuals—or colors—but we cannot assign them to separate neighboring groups, or at least not on a rational basis.

To use an example from my own country: Freiburg and Heidelberg are both in the German state of Baden-Württemberg, but an average person from Freiburg will be more genetically similar to someone from Strasbourg, in France, than to someone from Heidelberg because Heidelberg is farther away. To reach the same degree of genetic difference between someone from Flensburg, in the very north of Germany, and Passau, in the south, you'd have to cross roughly half a dozen borders in southeastern Europe—a region devastated in the 1990s by violent conflicts over real and supposed ethnic differences. In Europe there is a smooth genetic gradient that can be reliably drawn on a map, but it is not consistent with national borders. The only exceptions are islands like Iceland or, clearer still, Sardinia; in places where there has been little genetic exchange over time, the population's DNA is more homogenous than elsewhere.

The gradient principle holds true worldwide. There's no break at the Urals or the Bosphorus, for instance—the geographical borders of Europe. On the other side of the Mediterranean, people don't suddenly have completely different DNA. The gradual genetic shift occurs along the directions in which early modern humans spread out across the planet from sub-Saharan Africa. North Africans are therefore more closely related to Europeans and West Asians in genetic terms, not only because these regions were settled first by migrants leaving Africa, but also because there was plenty of genetic exchange. The differences between these populations and inhabitants of the Pacific region are bigger, then bigger again between them and the original inhabitants of North America, and biggest of all between them and those of South America, the part of the globe that was settled last by human beings. From East Africa to Tierra del Fuego, the general operative rule is that the smaller the geographic distance between two populations, the closer the genetic relationship. For the most part, ethnic minorities are no exception. Sorbs, for example, are genetically indistinguishable from the Saxons, Brandenburgers, and Poles around them, while the

Basques are no different from some of the adjacent Spanish and French groups.

The delineations between these groups, apparent primarily through language, are due largely to cultural and political factors. Their coexistence makes society more diverse, but also occasionally more prone to conflict. Genetic justifications for ethnic conflicts have no scientific basis and should not persist in today's world. It is on the grounds of unscientific claims made during the previous century that the field still has a reputation for smuggling in racist ideologies under the guise of genetic arguments. To the contrary, genetics today is less compatible with race-based thinking than ever before.

AFRICA, THE CRADLE OF HUMANITY

SUB-SAHARAN AFRICA IS HOME TO ALMOST AN EIGHTH of the global population, more than 900 million people, and is host to a significantly greater spectrum of genetic diversity than anywhere else on Earth. This is where the family tree of modern humankind is rooted. Its branches spread right across the planet, but also across the vast continent of Africa, which today is home to the greatest number of humanity's genetic forks and branches. The relationship between geographical and genetic proximity still holds, but there it's on a much bigger scale than anywhere else on Earth. In concrete terms, the difference between the DNA of people in East and West Africa is roughly twice the size of the difference between European and East Asian DNA. From a genetic perspective, therefore, everyone on Earth is part of African diversity. The only thing distinguishing people outside Africa from those on the continent is their connection to the Neanderthals, and in Australia and Oceania the genetic influence of the Denisovans.

Despite these fundamental facts, Africa is wrongly viewed by many non-Africans as a singular, homogenous whole; this ignorance may stem from a global imbalance of power, which gives less voice and visibility to the continent's countries and their diversity in the media, politics, and world economy. This diversity—unlike the diversity that exists in Europe—tends to be almost compulsively oversimplified even today. Though you no longer hear the term "Black Africa," commonly used during the colonial era to refer to the area south of the Sahara, other terms with similar implications have replaced it. Inhabitants of sub-Saharan Africa and their descendants are referred to as "Black" right across the world, often as distinct from "white." When the US census for the year 2000 asked what "race" its citizens belonged to, it classified all people descended from sub-Saharan African ancestors as "Black."

Arguably, this grouping into various types is not racist per se; often it simply expresses the human impulse to classify and delineate. Yet requiring human beings to sort themselves by skin color is a way of showing how pointless the question should be. The average Irish person has obviously paler skin than, say, someone from southern Italy, yet both are considered "white." Similarly, dark-skinned individuals from Sardinia or Anatolia can be difficult to distinguish from South African Khoisan people in terms of their skin color, while it would seem bizarre to a Khoisan to compare their skin tone to that of, say, a Congolese. Yet both of the latter are considered "Black."

It should be obvious to anyone walking up to the makeup

counter of any well-stocked pharmacy and seeing the vast array of shades of foundation available that skin color is impossible to categorize. Yet having visibly "Black" ancestry still has a disproportionate influence on how individuals are perceived. This is the reason that Barack Obama's Kenyan ancestry on his father's side received much more attention than his Irish-Scottish ancestry on his mother's side. We now know that many different genes affect the skin color of a human being, so the distinctions between skin tones are accordingly fluid. Yet, as a culture, we are still far from truly appreciating this insight. It's often convenient to overemphasize skin tone; after all, there are hardly any other physical traits so immediately apparent. Unfortunately, there are still sociopolitical imbalances ascribed and connected to it that lace our skin with meaning.

At first glance there are a few reasonable medical justifications for classifying people by geographical origin, for which skin color is at least one indication. For an oncologist treating a patient from West Africa, for example, it's important to know that a particular gene that causes prostate cancer is more common in that region of origin than elsewhere. This is not, however, a definite medical prognosis by any stretch of the imagination: although illnesses and the effectiveness of medications vary between regions, genetic ancestry does no more than indicate likelihood. Genetic defects that make someone resistant to malaria but increase intolerance to certain medications, for example, appear more commonly in Africa, but only in specific regions and even then only in certain individuals.

It may be true that in previous decades, ancestry offered important clues about medical risks and probabilities and thus had to be taken seriously. Today, however, this model is outdated. Given scientific progress, the genome of an individual patient can be examined with relative ease and a much more reliable medical profile established. Worrying about "race," ethnicity, or genetic origin when treating a patient should have less weight nowadays, because we have the technology to see an individual for what he or she is: a unique mixture of DNA. In the medical sphere, at least, this egalitarian perspective could become standard in as little as ten years, as genetic testing becomes more and more cost-effective. In society more broadly, however, history shows that the impulse to categorize people on the basis of external traits may have altogether more staying power.

ETHNICITY AND RACE: A THING OF THE PAST?

FOR MILLENNIA, AS HUMANS SETTLED ACROSS THE WORLD, the number of forks and differentiations between populations grew, as did genetic disparities. Yet within the past few thousand years, the branches of the human family tree have increasingly become intertwined and our DNA is becoming more similar. One important factor here is significantly greater mobility: these days there is virtually nowhere on Earth human beings from across the world have not set foot and left descendants. The genetic differences between people from Europe and West Asia have reduced over the past 10,000 years by more than half, and the gap worldwide is narrowing. This trend looks set to continue as people become ever more mobile.

This is not good news for anybody keen to classify people

from individual nations according to their genetic profile. As human DNA becomes increasingly similar across the globe, constructs such as ethnicity and "race" should be even harder to justify than before. It may be precisely for this reason that those who are uncomfortable with greater global connectedness are ever more aggressively defending the case to keep these terms and the categories within them distinct and separate; concepts that vanished ages ago from public discourse are rising again like the undead. In Germany, terms associated with the Nazis such as *Umvolkung* (forced assimilation of different ethnic groups into the German *Volk*) and *Überfremdung* (excessive immigration of foreigners) are regaining currency, based on the notion that all migration changes the DNA of a population as well as its culture. There are echoes here of the cultural, linguistic, and ethnic theories of the early twentieth century, according to which culture and society were based primarily on genetic commonalities. Adherents to this point of view simultaneously exaggerate and belittle the role of their own culture: they ascribe to it immense value, yet have no faith in its ability to win over foreigners. This attitude completely fails to recognize the power that successful societies have to integrate immigrants. The United States, as well as many European countries, attests to this. In Germany today, nearly one in four people has a recent migrant background—without the country having gone to rack and ruin. Many individuals who want to protect German or more generally Western society from change—especially changes wrought by immigration—are trying to seal off a supposedly static model of success that in fact would not have been possible without the migration that has already occurred in previous decades.

Calls for national isolation have come back into vogue in recent years, completely independent from or even in inverse proportion to the actual pressures of immigration or the number of foreigners within a population. Nationalist and right-leaning populist parties are increasingly being given a share in government; in the European Parliament they've formed their own faction. Usually their sole points of agreement have to do with rejecting migration and avowing some vague notion of a "Europe of nations," an "ethnopluralistic" community in which individual countries have sharply defined borders. Most object not only to immigration into Europe but also to the idea of mobility—the construct of a separate, clearly delineated "people" functions only if every group accepts that delineation. In this sense, an aversion to individuals who are considered too cosmopolitan is understandable, because such cosmopolitanism is attributed to a lack of fidelity to one's homeland. One politician in the German parliament implied precisely this in 2018, accusing this "globalized class" of controlling information and thereby setting the "cultural and political agenda." Possibly without realizing it, he also made a genetic reference when he called this mobile class of "digital information workers" its own "species."

Such derogatory references to human mobility and internationalism often carry unmistakably anti-Semitic undertones. Hannah Arendt saw this attitude toward "cosmopolitanism" as one of the factors behind the Nazis' relentless hatred of the Jews. Jews, according to Arendt, represented for the Nazis a supranational network, united by genetics and their status as a "chosen people," exercising their power in individual countries without loyalty to any one in particular.

Though the idea of "Jewish genes" has long since been

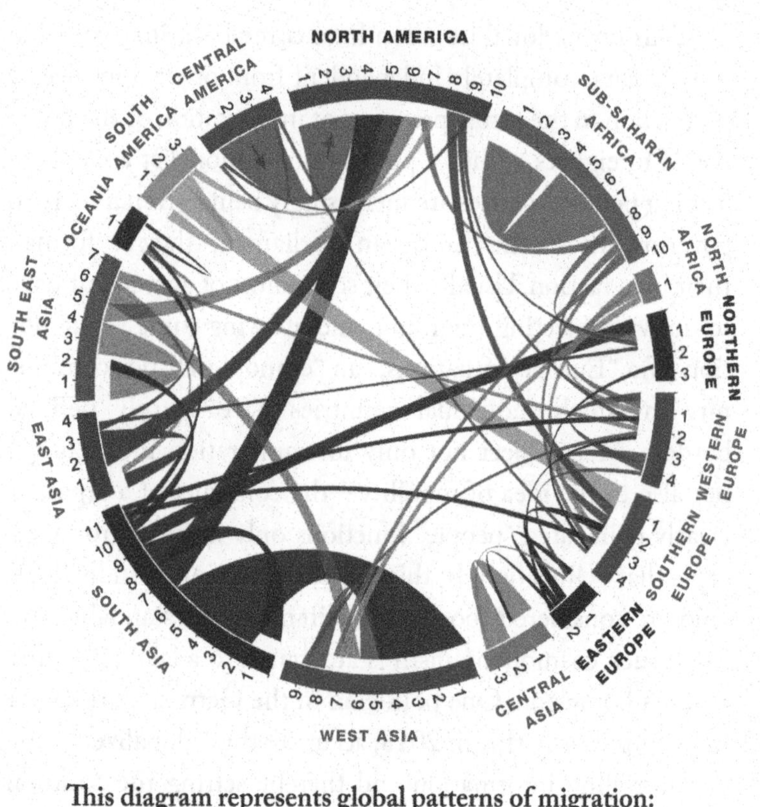

This diagram represents global patterns of migration: the thicker the arrow, the more people are migrating. Compared to West Asia and North America, Europe attracts relatively few migrants.

refuted, it's still widespread. In 2010, for instance, the author Thilo Sarrazin said in a newspaper interview that "all Jews share a specific gene." Sarrazin had misunderstood something fundamental. Many Ashkenazi Jews—those members of the religion whose forebears have lived for centuries in Central and Eastern Europe—do have similar genetic components that can be traced back to their ancestry from the Near East and to genetic mixing with Central and Eastern

Europeans. Strict conventions around marriage meant that for centuries Jewish people usually only had children with other members of their faith, preserving a genetic signature that was distinct from the non-Jewish population. The result, however, was not a specific gene that all Ashkenazi Jews share but a special mixture of genes—the components of which originate from Eastern Europe and the Near East—that tends to appear in Ashkenazi populations more frequently. But the Eastern European components of Ashkenazi DNA are also found in the genomes of people from such regions as Thüringia, Saxony, and Brandenburg in Germany, and even their Near Eastern component is closely linked to the Anatolian farmer component that accounts for more than half of a Central European genome.

THE LIMITED REACH OF THE "INTELLIGENCE GENE"

WHILE NO SERIOUS SCIENTIST THESE DAYS WOULD STILL claim that national, religious, or cultural borders are determined by genetics, there is less consensus when it comes to other issues. One of these is whether there are genetically determined levels of intelligence that vary across diverse parts of the globe. A few years ago one geneticist caused a furor when he made a statement supporting this thesis: James Watson, Nobel Prize–winning codiscoverer of the structure of DNA, said in an interview in 2007 that Africans were less intelligent than Europeans. All the tests that had been conducted to prove the opposite, he claimed, had "not really" shown that. He couldn't point to a demonstrable genetic difference, of course, but seemed convinced that one would soon be identified. After the scandal triggered by these remarks, Watson said he'd been misunderstood. He insisted that he simply wanted to make clear that there were genetic differences between populations and that components would soon be identified in specific populations—not, he suspected, among dark-skinned populations—that contributed to higher levels of intelligence.

Watson's prognosis is still unfulfilled, and will probably remain so. In recent years, tiny portions of the genome whose presence is correlated with higher intelligence have in fact been identified, but these genetic components are only one part of the puzzle. Nor are these components unique to particular geographical areas: the gene variants that support intelligence are evenly distributed all across the world. This doesn't preclude the possibility that a segment of genetic code will eventually be found that gives a higher-than-average number of people from particular regions or descended from particular origins greater intelligence, but this is highly unlikely. Millions of genomes have already been mapped out and countless intelligence tests conducted. If certain groups had higher levels of genetically determined intelligence, we would know by now.

Generally speaking, genetic dispositions should not be overemphasized. New information uncovered in recent years about the impact of genetics on body height testify to this. Roughly a hundred gene segments influencing body height have been identified, many of which vary across regions. Far more important, however, are environmental conditions. In many parts of the world, today's humans are a head taller than their grandparents, and this is due solely to better nutrition. Nobody would suggest that this height difference has emerged as a result of genetic changes within three generations. Similarly, it's not true that more people these days have an "intelligence gene" simply because they would perform better than average on an intelligence test from 1950. Rather, the conditions for nurturing intelligence—such as education—have improved.

This does not mean, of course, that genes supporting intelligence are irrelevant to the development of someone's personality. A person without these favorable prerequisites will probably find it harder to achieve good grades at school or university unless their disadvantage is balanced out by other factors, such as social status. Countless studies have consistently proved a connection between parental income and educational success.

Frankly, it's problematic to conclude from comparisons of genetic traits and the results of intelligence tests that an "intelligence gene" exists at all. Intelligence is what intelligence tests measure. In other words, the current tests primarily reflect whatever society considers important. A correlation between high IQ and certain genetic components in particular populations would only prove that these populations are better on average at taking a particular test. If we were to use a different test as a benchmark, one tailored to the demands of another society, the same population might perform much worse while another did much better. There'd be no point pitting a high jumper against a 100-meter runner in a sprint, for instance, because it would tell you nothing about which one is more athletic.

What we now know about the impact of genes on intelligence contradicts hypotheses about regional or even national discrepancies, but it certainly does not render ethical debates superfluous. If genetic research can identify in a relatively short span of time segments of DNA that influence intelligence, then in the coming years and decades our understanding of this nebulous quality will be significantly expanded and deepened. We can already pick out certain autistic or schizophrenic personality traits in DNA. Nobody can predict what kind of personality profile will be mappable by DNA in the future. What will we do when for a few euros or dollars we can determine not only medical risks but also character traits? As vast sums of money are being poured into genetic research, humanity faces a difficult task in answering this and other highly complex ethical questions, though we are on the verge of being presented with a fait accompli. In 2012, the China National GeneBank was established with the express purpose of decoding not merely the human blueprint but that of the entire biosphere. Meanwhile, a major shareholder in 23andMe, one of the world's largest private genetic-testing firms, is the data company Google.

THE LURE OF THE DESIGNER HUMAN

THE DEVELOPMENT OF GENETIC RESEARCH IS LIKE THE development of supersonic flight—we're fascinated by its extraordinary promise yet have only the vaguest sense of the risks that might be lurking behind the technology. We're just about to break the sound barrier, but we have no idea what kind of sonic boom we're going to hear. Still, there are good grounds to be optimistic. We have a fantastic evolutionary history behind us, in which a combination of happy accidents enabled us to develop incredibly powerful brains. In evolutionary terms, scarcely the blink of an eye has passed since humans developed agriculture and formed settlements. We shaped the planet according to our own needs, explored the natural world, and grasped the laws of physics—and the tiny role humanity plays in its great game. Now we're facing one of the biggest—if not *the* biggest—revolution in human history.

Decoding the human genome is only the beginning of the road: eventually we will become the first creatures on Earth to take evolution into our own hands. The CRISPR/Cas9 system was only developed in 2012, but already these "genetic scissors" are a standard tool in gene technology, allowing us to edit the genome of living beings in a precise and targeted way.[1] The game-changing nature of CRISPR/Cas9 is also reflected by the fact that Jennifer Doudna and Emmanuelle Charpentier, who discovered the basic principle, received the Nobel Prize for their groundbreaking discovery in 2020. The possibilities offered by this technology are obvious, particularly in the medical sphere. Genetic predispositions to cancer and other diseases could, once identified, be removed and repaired with these genetic scissors. In the not-so-distant future, we may be able to modify bacterial and viral strains to fight other strains, while doing no damage to human beings. Humans could be immunized against deadly illnesses. In the best-case scenario, genetic scissors and other technologies could even provide answers to the looming catastrophe of antibiotic-resistant bacteria.

The medical possibilities are innumerable, but there are plenty of unknown variables. Nobody can yet say for sure whether gene editing may not simply eliminate one disease only to replace it with another. We're still some way off from using genetic scissors as a standard form of treatment, although the first experiments on human stem cells are already under way. In late 2018, Chinese scientist He Jiankui announced the birth of the first gene-edited babies using CRISPR/Cas9. According to He's own statements, he switched off the CCR5 receptor in twins Lulu and Nana, editing the genome at the embryonic stage, to protect the children from HIV. It was a relatively simple intervention, because the CCR5 gene is well researched. At the same time, there seems little justification for it, because HIV is relatively rare in China and the virus can be effectively controlled through medication—whereas there is no treatment for the potentially deadly West Nile fever, a virus that may be encouraged by a mutation in the CCR5 receptor. It seems likely that He Jiankui was less interested in protecting Lulu and Nana from HIV, as he claimed, than in conducting pioneering research.

Nobody knows whether He's actions will have unforeseen negative consequences for the twins later in life. The huge medical potential of CRISPR/Cas9 technology is not in dispute—but to proceed without fully weighing up the risks would be to do it a disservice. The response to He's announcement, around the world as well as in China, showed that the vast majority of the medical community is willing to engage with ethical debates and act accordingly. Maybe Lulu and Nana have jolted the world out of its slumber and opened a debate that should have been settled long ago.

In any case, the dark side of these new technologies is readily apparent. If we continue to identify genetic factors associated not merely with disease but with traits such as intelligence, size, or even personality, it's a short hop toward using gene editing to create the infamous "designer baby." Even today, babies revealed by genetic tests to be at risk of Huntington's disease or spinal muscular atrophy are being aborted. Gene editing may even be preferred in this scenario—after all, rather than ending an unborn life, it prevents it being created in the first place. It's understandable that parents want to have a healthy child, and thanks to CRISPR/Cas9 this can be made a reality. Yet isn't it equally understandable that they might want genes that raise their child's level of intelligence? Or genes that contribute to looks many societies find pleasing, perhaps lighter skin and blue eyes? The line between a healthy society and a molded one can get blurry. In most Western countries, such scenarios have, until now, bumped up against countless ethical and legal barriers. Finding a way to deal with the uncertain risks of genetic self-empowerment will, without doubt, be one of the biggest tasks facing us over the coming years and decades.

It certainly won't be comfortable. And we can't ban all new procedures—such a ban wouldn't be enforceable anyway, as illustrated by the case of the Chinese twins. Neglecting to pursue these avenues would also be hard to justify, given that gene editing may be able to save lives or provide desperately needed relief. In most Western countries, wondering whether to protect people from malaria via gene-editing technology is an ethical debate, but in many African countries it's an existential one.

LIMITLESS

SOMEWHERE ALONG OUR GENETIC JOURNEY WE HUMANS have become our own guides. Over the last hundred years the global population has quadrupled, rising from less than 2 billion to almost 8 billion people. Since 1970 it has expanded by roughly the same number as in the 2 million years before that. We have an impressive capacity for evolutionary assertiveness, but our success created most of the existential challenges we face today. More people require more resources, and increased levels of greenhouse gas emissions have accelerated climate change. Large numbers of people are competing for rapidly dwindling opportunities for growth in regions that are rapidly becoming uninhabitable. Yet, as difficult as it may be to believe, humanity is still in the ascendant: year after year, our situation in almost every area of life is improving. Prosperity is on the rise across the globe, while world hunger, rates of deadly diseases, and maternal and infant mortality—to mention only a few factors—are dropping.

This kind of progress will continue, not least because the impulse to move and mingle is part of human nature. As we spread out across the planet, we laid the foundations for the global society that took shape over the past thousand years and has recently developed at breathtaking speed. Almost one in two people worldwide now has access to the internet. The volume of stored data is soaring, as is the amount of information available via any smartphone. In the coming decades, digitalization will reach virtually all areas of society. Even the medical community's great hopes for genetics rely on such new technologies and the ability to process proliferating amounts of data at ever-increasing speed. This data includes the human genome and its billions of base pairs, whose secrets we are slowly uncovering. The goal of science and medicine is always the same: to fully explore ourselves and our nature.

Continuing along the path humanity has trodden since its inception, we will continue to build a networked world, a global society. Where it ends, no one knows. One thing that seems clear is that—pandemic social distancing aside—dogmatically insisting on social, cultural, and physical isolation within our nations is a dead end. The world has never been that way. The journey of humankind will carry on. We will find our limits—and we will not accept them.

Through the journey of our genes, we know that humans are born travelers; we are made to wander.

ACKNOWLEDGMENTS

JOHANNES KRAUSE WOULD LIKE TO THANK WOLFGANG Haak, Alexander Herbig, Henrike Heyne, Svante Pääbo, Kay Prüfer, Stephan Schiffels, and Philipp Stockhammer for casting a critical eye over individual chapters. Special thanks from both the authors are due to Harald Meller, who lent invaluable support, and whose wealth of knowledge and stories about the ancient and early history of Europe were a huge inspiration to us.

The information presented in this book on the evolution of humanity and the genetic history of Europe would not have been possible without the scientific work of countless colleagues. Particular thanks are due to Adrian Briggs, Hernan Burbano, Anatoli Derevjanko, Qiaomei Fu, Richard Edward Green, Janet Kelso, Martin Kircher, Anna-Sapfo Malaspinas, Tomislav Maricic, Matthias Meyer, Svante Pääbo, Nick Patterson, Kay Prüfer, David Reich, Montgomery Slatkin, Udo Stenzel, and all the other members of the Neanderthal Genome Consortium.

Heartfelt thanks go to Mark Achtmann, Kurt Alt, Natasha Arora, Hervé Bocherens, Jane Buikstra, Alexandra Buzhilova, David Caramelli, Stewart Cole, Nicholas Conard,

Isabelle Crevecoeur, Dominique Delsate, Dorothée Drucker, Mateja Hajdinjak, Fredrik Halgren, Svend Hansen, Michaela Harbeck, Katerina Harvati, Jean-Jacques Hublin, Daniel Huson, Corina Knipper, Kristian Kristiansen, Carles Lalueza-Fox, Iosif Lazaridis, Mark Lipson, Sandra Lösch, Frank Maixner, Iain Mathieson, Michael McCormick, Kay Nieselt, Inigo Olalde, Ludovic Orlando, Ernst Pernicka, Sabine Reinhold, Roberto Risch, Hélèn Rougier, Patrick Semal, Pontus Skoglund, Viviane Slon, Anne Stone, Jiri Svoboda, Frédérique Valentin, Joachim Wahl, Albert Zink, and many other colleagues from the fields of archaeology, anthropology, bioinformatics, genetics, and medicine. Without them, we would never have been able to reconstruct all these stories from Europe's past.

Johannes Krause would also like to thank his colleagues and staff at the University of Tübingen, the Max Planck Institute for the Science of Human History in Jena, and the Max Planck Institute for Evolutionary Anthropology in Leipzig. Particular thanks are due to Aida Andrades, Kirsten Bos, Guido Brandt, Michal Feldman, Anja Furtwängler, Wolfgang Haak, Alexander Herbig, Choongwon Jeong, Marcel Keller, Ben Krause-Kyora, Aditya Lankapalli, Alissa Mittnik, Angela Mötsch, Alexander Peltzer, Cosimo Posth, Verena Schünemann, Maria Spyrou, Ashild Vågene, Marieke van der Loosdrecht, Chuanchao Wang, Christina Warinner, and everybody else who made decisive contributions to the projects described in this book.

At Ullstein Verlag, Kristin Rotter gave us particular support in developing the concept for the book, as did Jan Martin Ogiermann in refining it. We would like to thank Peter Palm for his lucid maps. Thanks are also due to Ralf Schmitz,

Frank Vinken, and Bence Viola for providing the images and Johannes Künzel for his support with the authors' photographs.

Johannes Krause would like to thank his wife, Henrike, for their countless discussions about this book, and especially about the future of medical genetics. He would also like to thank his parents, Maria and Dieter, and his sister, Kristin, for their critical eye and constructive commentary on the manuscript as a whole. His coauthor, Thomas Trappe, would like to thank Claudia, Clara, and Leo. For everything.

NOTES

CHAPTER 1: A NEW SCIENCE IS BORN

1. The polymerase chain reaction reproduces a process that takes place in the body millions of times a day: the duplication of the genome as new cells are formed. Enzymes similar to those used by the body are employed in the lab. A single molecule of DNA can be repeatedly doubled to create a billion identical copies within a few hours.

2. This genetic information is inherited via twenty-three chromosomes from each parent. Whether the father passes on a Y or an X chromosome determines whether the child will be a boy or a girl.

3. The job of decoding the human genome was distributed among thousands of scientists around the world, like a much-too-large cake. Their laboratories were almost like factories, with dozens of sequencers worth millions of dollars. Over the years, every laboratory sequenced millions of base pairs in an unbroken research marathon, and at the end the results of each laboratory were added up to form the whole picture.

4. Paradoxically, this new knowledge could actually make people more uncertain. Shortly after a birth, parents would be informed in writing of the potential risks to their child throughout its life. Some people might feel overwhelmed by this knowledge, especially because the data provided by the sequencers has to be considered in the context of statistical probability.

5. Since the nineteenth century, archaeologists have been examining bones and artifacts—crockery, weapons, jewelry—in an attempt to determine how their ancestors lived and when they spread across the world. For a long time, archaeology worked like Sudoku: by combining several finds in conjunction with other indicators, you can slowly piece together the whole puzzle. If a ceramic bowl made in a particular style is found beside a skeleton and a similar

bowl is found next to another, you can assume that they were members of the same culture and epoch. Other nearby finds—inscriptions or tools, for example—can be used to establish a chronology for the various epochs.

Until well into the twentieth century, finds were nearly always dated using rough estimates, and when skeletons were discovered without grave goods, even that wasn't possible. This only changed with the introduction of radiocarbon dating, without which modern archaeology would be inconceivable. The carbon-14 method, developed in 1946, uses a physical constant as a measuring tool: the rate at which radioactive carbon decays. Radiocarbon is a material found in archaeological artifacts made out of organic materials, functioning rather like an inbuilt clock. The decay of carbon-14 takes place at the same rate during all eras and independently of external factors. This is what makes radiocarbon dating useful, because archaeological digs usually find objects that contain carbon, often bones or burnt wood. The ratio of stable to unstable carbon isotopes allows us to calculate when these unstable isotopes stopped being incorporated into the wood or bone—in other words, when the organism died. Since the 1960s, the carbon-14 method has been standard practice in archaeology, and today millions of archaeological objects have been dated on this basis. The data is equally useful to archaeogeneticists. The DNA found in a bone may open a window into that bone's past, but if we don't know when this window opened, the knowledge is much less valuable.

6. Each of us inherits between thirty and sixty such mutations from our parents, most of them from our father, because more mutations appear in sperm cells, which are constantly being produced. Girls, on the other hand, only have a limited stock of egg cells, and do not produce new ones after birth.

7. The notion of DNA as life's blueprint is based on the principle of translation and transcription. DNA is read in the cell's nucleus and transcribed into RNA. RNA then transports the DNA's information out of the nucleus. Ribosomes, small protein factories within the cells, read the information and produce proteins based on what it says. Essential to the production of these proteins is the order of the base pairs, which are read via RNA from the DNA in the nucleus.

8. At 3.3 billion base pairs, the amount of information in nuclear DNA is significantly greater than that of mtDNA, which has only 16,500 positions. However, nuclear DNA has only two copies per cell, inherited from the mother and the father, while mtDNA has several hundred copies, all identical.

9. A woman who gives birth to a daughter and a son passes her mtDNA on to both children. Only the daughter will pass on her mtDNA to the next generation, however, and only the granddaughter will pass it on to her children. In theory, the series could continue indefinitely. If each woman has one daugh-

ter and one son, then in a thousand years—assuming a generational gap of thirty years—that makes thirty-three women with the same mtDNA, as well as thirty-two men, although they do not pass on their mtDNA to their children. If, however, every woman has two daughters, then in the same span of time, astonishingly, we get more than 8 billion women with this mtDNA, plus all those women's sons. If we trace back the mtDNA in our family trees, we will find that at some point each of us shares a common female ancestor with any individual chosen at random. And yet nobody alive today has the original mtDNA belonging to "mitochondrial Eve," even though we are all her descendants. Over the last 160,000 years, so many mutations have accumulated that mtDNA has diverged into various different lines.

10. The greater the difference between the mtDNA of two modern humans, the further back they diverged. Because a mutation will reliably occur in mtDNA about every 3,000 years, a person living today will probably have around thirty-three mutations in their mtDNA that their ancestors did not have 100,000 years ago. When it comes to the split between two types of human—say, Neanderthals and modern humans—the effect is twice as pronounced: one type developed roughly thirty-three mutations in 100,000 years, and so did the other, giving a difference of sixty-six mutations. If we look at the mtDNA of three different types of human—Denisovans, Neanderthals, and modern humans, for example—then we can use the molecular clock to determine who must have split off from whom, and when. Precisely the same thing goes for chimpanzees and humans: using the differences in the mtDNA belonging to present-day individuals of both species, we can calculate that the split occurred roughly 7 million years ago. (It should be noted that the molecular clock is less reliable for these longer spans of time than for more recent splits, such as those that have taken place between Neanderthals and modern humans.) There are significantly more inherited mutations in nuclear DNA than in mtDNA—three per year rather than one every 3,000 years. The molecular clock works for nuclear DNA too, but there are far more measurable mutations involved.

11. The split took place in Africa, but it took some time for them to reach the Iberian Peninsula.

12. Everybody has two parents, four grandparents, eight great-grandparents, and sixteen great-great-grandparents. This spans four generations, approximately 80 to 100 years. If we go back twenty generations, 400 to 500 years, we find more than a million ancestors. Thirty generations, and we find more than a billion—far more people than existed 650 years ago. And in the forty generations (at least) that have passed since Charlemagne, we're looking at more than a trillion. This is admittedly a purely theoretical figure: not everyone had chil-

dren, and some had more than this calculation takes into account. If you follow a family tree back in time, you find that many of the lines cross, concentrating around the ancestors who had an above-average number of children. It follows that all the people who had children 600 to 700 years ago and whose descendants continued to produce offspring up to the present day can very likely be found somewhere in the family trees of all living Europeans.

CHAPTER 2: PERSISTENT IMMIGRANTS

1. This figure comes from another DNA analysis our laboratory conducted on a Neanderthal who lived near Ulm approximately 120,000 years ago. His mtDNA was different from that of previously identified Neanderthals who lived later and had the mtDNA of early modern humans. Using the molecular clock, we were able to calculate that the two Neanderthal populations must have diverged 220,000 years ago at the latest. At some point between the Spanish Neanderthal and this split, early modern humans must have come to Europe and given their mtDNA to the Neanderthals. Where exactly this happened is impossible to say—it may also have been in the Near East.

2. In the whole of Europe and Asia, archaeologists have found bones belonging to 350 Neanderthals at most. In Germany, half a dozen individuals have been discovered thus far, and the Neandertal Valley itself is one of the northernmost sites.

3. There were natural barriers on the African continent too, of course, but far fewer of them, and they weren't so merciless—the Sahara, for example, was much smaller than it is today, and intermittently completely green. There may therefore have been fewer restrictions between early modern humans in Africa, and thus more genetic mixing.

4. Whether the Neanderthals' reclusiveness protected them from threats—from other humans, for instance—is speculation. Neanderthal evolution certainly did not profit from having such a small gene pool. It's likely that disadvantageous genes had a greater chance of being passed on because they had such a limited choice of partners. Since they were closely related, parents in many cases would carry the same unfavorable mutation. And the Denisovans were even worse off than the Neanderthals. Their DNA shows signs of extensive inbreeding. The ancestors of the Denisova girl were closely related many times over, because large parts of Asia were also sealed off during the Ice Age. It's generally assumed that isolated Denisovan areas of settlement covered roughly the area of medium-sized German states, populated by only a few hundred individuals. These archaic humans thus had few options when it came to choosing a partner, resulting in damaging genetic overlap.

5. If this were not the case, if the languages of the modern humans who emigrated developed only after they left Africa, then we would see differing levels of linguistic competence among present-day populations, on a par with the differences between peoples who have long been isolated and those who have remained in constant contact with other groups. Since all modern-day populations have the same level of linguistic competence, we can rule out this scenario.

6. The FOXP2 gene is what's known as a transcription factor. It can switch hundreds of other genes in the genome on and off. Why this function affects the ability to speak has never been explained in detail. The case of the "KE family," a family living in England, has gained particular notoriety in scientific circles. Half its members have severe difficulties articulating words or understanding language. They inherited the mutated FOXP2 gene from one parent. In the course of my doctoral work, in which I examined genes in Neanderthals' nuclear DNA—years before the whole genome was decoded—I discovered that while the FOXP2 genes in chimpanzees and modern humans differ in two key ways, those of Neanderthals and modern humans do not. It follows that FOXP2 changed before modern humans and Neanderthals diverged. Since it's clear that FOXP2 enables speech only indirectly, I've taken to phrasing this rather more cautiously: comparing FOXP2 genes in Neanderthals and humans doesn't lead us to conclude that Neanderthals *couldn't* speak.

7. Shortly before the Second World War, the bones of an individual who died 100,000 years ago, and whose ancestors lived in the southern Sahara, were found in the Skhul Cave in present-day Israel. Since then, hardly a year has gone by without new evidence of modern humans being discovered outside Africa more than 50,000 years ago. One thing they all have in common is that their genes no longer exist in contemporary humans.

8. The person found at Oase, who lived around 40,000 years ago, left no genetic traces in today's Europeans, but the Markina Gora man, who lived after the volcanic eruption around 38,000 years ago, did. The following scenario therefore seems realistic: the eruption could have decimated or even completely annihilated all the groups of modern humans who came to Europe beforehand—then our direct ancestors, the Aurignacians, arrived in a fresh wave of migration via the Danube corridor. There's no definitive proof that this occurred, because the chain of events 40,000 years ago cannot be reconstructed with enough precision. In fact, we have only two pieces of genetic evidence from the Aurignacian period. The second individual sequenced from this era lived approximately 38,000 years ago in Goyet, Belgium, and also shared genes with present-day Europeans.

9. It's possible that the Gravettians were pursuing mammoths, which

were expanding into Europe during this period. One theory is that big game in Europe did not survive the volcanic eruption, and that the Asian species moved in to take their place. It's equally conceivable, however, that they were wiped out by human beings during the Aurignacian period, or even that the newcomers were followed by "their" wildlife and the local species died out. There is genetic evidence that the Aurignacians were cut off. In 2018, we decoded the first Ice-Age genome from North Africa. The bones came from the Grotte des Pigeons in Morocco. DNA sequencing revealed that the people who lived there around 15,000 years ago did not mix genetically with their European neighbors.

CHAPTER 5: SINGLE YOUNG MEN

1. To achieve a similar effect today, one would have to usher 10 billion people into Europe at a single stroke, more people than currently live on this planet. Or, to remain within the realm of possibility, you could achieve this effect by bringing a billion migrants to Germany.

CHAPTER 6: EUROPEANS FIND A LANGUAGE

1. We refer to them as Mycenaens here, even though this term dates from the nineteenth century and we can safely assume they referred to themselves by an entirely different name.

CHAPTER 8: THEY BRING THE PLAGUE

1. "Reservoir" is the term for the mammals in which the pathogen primarily lives, and from which it is transmitted to human beings.

CHAPTER 10: CONCLUSION

1. CRISPR stands for "clustered regularly interspaced short palindromic repeats." "Cas9" stands for "CRISPR-associated protein 9."

SOURCES

In the interests of flow, we have avoided using footnotes to reference sources. The following list includes the publications, books, and other sources we drew on for each chapter. A few details in the book are taken from conversations with scientific colleagues, whose assessments and interpretations found their way into the text if they were shared by the authors. Sources are only mentioned once.

CHAPTER 1: A NEW SCIENCE IS BORN

Mullis, K., et al., Specific enzymatic amplification of DNA in vitro: the polymerase chain reaction. *Cold Spring Harb Symp Quant Biol*, 1986. **51 Pt 1**: 263–73.

Venter, J. C., et al., The sequence of the human genome. *Science*, 2001. **291**(5507): 1304–51.

International Human Genome Sequencing Consortium, Finishing the euchromatic sequence of the human genome. *Nature*, 2004. **431**(7011): 931–45.

Reich, D., *Who We Are and How We Got Here: Ancient DNA Revolution and the New Science of the Human Past.* 2018. Pantheon Books.

Pääbo, S., Über den Nachweis von DNA in altägyptischen Mumien. *Das Altertum*, 1984. **30**: 213–18.

Pääbo, S., *Neanderthal Man: In Search of Lost Genomes.* 2014. Basic Books.

Krause, J., et al., The complete mitochondrial DNA genome of an unknown hominin from southern Siberia. *Nature*, 2010. **464**(7290): 894–97.

Gregory, T. R., *The Evolution of the Genome.* 2005. Elsevier Academic.

Nystedt, B., et al., The Norway spruce genome sequence and conifer genome evolution. *Nature*, 2013. **497**(7451): 579–84.

ENCODE Project Consortium, An integrated encyclopedia of DNA elements in the human genome. *Nature*, 2012. **489**(7414): 57–74.

Kimura, M., Evolutionary rate at the molecular level. *Nature*, 1968. **217**(5129): 624–26.

Posth, C., et al., Deeply divergent archaic mitochondrial genome provides lower time boundary for African gene flow into Neanderthals. *Nat Commun*, 2017. **8**: 16046.

Kuhlwilm, M., et al., Ancient gene flow from early modern humans into Eastern Neanderthals. *Nature*, 2016. **530**(7591): 429–33.

Meyer, M., et al., Nuclear DNA sequences from the Middle Pleistocene Sima de los Huesos hominins. *Nature*, 2016. **531**(7595): 504–7.

Reich, D., et al., Genetic history of an archaic hominin group from Denisova Cave in Siberia. *Nature*, 2010. **468**(7327): 1053–60.

Krings, M., et al., Neandertal DNA sequences and the origin of modern humans. *Cell*, 1997. **90**(1): 19–30.

Krause, J., and S. Paabo, Genetic time travel. *Genetics*, 2016. **203**(1): 9–12.

Krause, J., et al., A complete mtDNA genome of an early modern human from Kostenki, Russia. *Curr Biol*, 2010. **20**(3): 231–36.

Lazaridis, I., et al., Ancient human genomes suggest three ancestral populations for present-day Europeans. *Nature*, 2014. **513**(7518): 409–13.

Haak, W., et al., Massive migration from the steppe was a source for Indo-European languages in Europe. *Nature*, 2015. **522**(7555): 207–11.

Andrades Valtuena, A., et al., The Stone Age plague and its persistence in Eurasia. *Curr Biol*, 2017. **27**(23): 3683–91 e8.

Key, F. M., et al., Mining metagenomic data sets for ancient DNA: recommended protocols for authentication. *Trends Genet*, 2017. **33**(8): 508–20.

Rasmussen, S., et al., Early divergent strains of *Yersinia pestis* in Eurasia 5,000 years ago. *Cell*, 2015. **163**(3): 571–82.

CHAPTER 2: PERSISTENT IMMIGRANTS

Green, R. E., et al., A draft sequence of the Neandertal genome. *Science*, 2010. **328**(5979): 710–22.

Kuhlwilm, M., et al., Ancient gene flow from early modern humans into Eastern Neanderthals. *Nature*, 2016. **530**(7591): 429–33.

Meyer, M., et al., Nuclear DNA sequences from the Middle Pleistocene Sima de los Huesos hominins. *Nature*, 2016. **531**(7595): 504–7.

Posth, C., et al., Deeply divergent archaic mitochondrial genome provides lower time boundary for African gene flow into Neanderthals. *Nat Commun*, 2017. **8**: 16046.

Prufer, K., et al., The complete genome sequence of a Neanderthal from the Altai Mountains. *Nature*, 2014. **505**(7481): 43–49.

Stringer, C., and P. Andrews, *The Complete World of Human Evolution.* Rev. ed. 2011. Thames & Hudson.

Meyer, M., et al., A high-coverage genome sequence from an archaic Denisovan individual. *Science*, 2012. **338**(6104): 222–26.

Faupl, P., W. Richter, and C. Urbanek, Geochronology: dating of the Herto hominin fossils. *Nature*, 2003. **426**(6967): 621–22.

Krause, J., et al., Neanderthals in central Asia and Siberia. *Nature*, 2007. **449**(7164): 902–4.

Enard, W., et al., Intra- and interspecific variation in primate gene expression patterns. *Science*, 2002. **296**(5566): 340–43.

Krause, J., et al., The derived FOXP2 variant of modern humans was shared with Neandertals. *Curr Biol*, 2007. **17**(21): 1908–12.

De Queiroz, K., Species concepts and species delimitation. *Syst Biol*, 2007. **56**(6): 879–86.

Dannemann, M., K. Prufer, and J. Kelso, Functional implications of Neandertal introgression in modern humans. *Genome Biol*, 2017. **18**(1): 61.

Fu, Q., et al., Genome sequence of a 45,000-year-old modern human from western Siberia. *Nature*, 2014. **514**(7523): 445–49.

Fu, Q., et al., An early modern human from Romania with a recent Neanderthal ancestor. *Nature*, 2015. **524**(7564): 216–19.

Fu, Q., et al., The genetic history of Ice Age Europe. *Nature*, 2016. **534**(7606): 200–205.

Kind, N. C. K.-J., *Als der Mensch die Kunst erfand: Eiszeithöhlen der Schwäbischen Alb.* 2017. Konrad Theiss.

Conard, N. J., A female figurine from the basal Aurignacian of Hohle Fels Cave in southwestern Germany. *Nature*, 2009. **459**(7244): 248–52.

Conard, N. J., M. Malina, and S. C. Munzel, New flutes document the earliest musical tradition in southwestern Germany. *Nature*, 2009. **460**(7256): 737–40.

Lieberman, D., *The Story of the Human Body: Evolution, Health, and Disease.* 2013. Pantheon Books.

Grine, F. E., J. G. Fleagle, and R. E. Leakey, eds. *The First Humans: Origin and Early Evolution of the Genus* Homo: *Contributions from the Third Stony Brook Human Evolution Symposium and Workshop, October 3–October 7, 2006.* Vertebrate Paleobiology and Paleoanthropology Series. 2009. Springer.

Giaccio, B., et al., High-precision (14)C and (40)Ar/(39) Ar dating of the Campanian Ignimbrite (Y-5) reconciles the time-scales of climatic-cultural processes at 40 ka. *Sci Rep*, 2017. **7**: 45940.

Marti, A., et al., Reconstructing the plinian and co-ignimbrite sources of large volcanic eruptions: a novel approach for the Campanian Ignimbrite. *Sci Rep*, 2016. **6**: 21220.

Marom, A., et al., Single amino acid radiocarbon dating of Upper Paleolithic modern humans. *Proc Natl Acad Sci USA*, 2012. **109**(18): 6878–81.

Krause, J., et al., A complete mtDNA genome of an early modern human from Kostenki, Russia. *Curr Biol*, 2010. **20**(3): 231–36.

Fellows Yates, J. A., et al., Central European woolly mammoth population dynamics: insights from Late Pleistocene mitochondrial genomes. *Sci Rep*, 2017. **7**(1): 17714.

Mittnik, A., et al., A molecular approach to the sexing of the triple burial at the Upper Paleolithic site of Dolni Vestonice. *PLoS One*, 2016. **11**(10): e0163019.

Forni, F., et al., Long-term magmatic evolution reveals the beginning of a new caldera cycle at Campi Flegrei. *Science Advances*, 2018. **4**(11): eaat9401.

CHAPTER 3: IMMIGRANTS ARE THE FUTURE

Odar, B., A Dufour bladelet from Potočka zijalka (Slovenia). *Arheoloski vestnik*, 2008. **59**: 9–16.

Posth, C., et al., Pleistocene mitochondrial genomes suggest a single major dispersal of non-Africans and a late glacial population turnover in Europe. *Curr Biol*, 2016. **26**: 1–7.

Tallavaara, M., et al., Human population dynamics in Europe over the Last Glacial Maximum. *Proc Natl Acad Sci USA*, 2015. **112**(27): 8232–7.

Alley, R. B., The Younger Dryas cold interval as viewed from central Greenland. *Quaternary Science Reviews*, 2000. **19**(1): 213–26.

Broecker, W. S., Was the Younger Dryas triggered by a flood? *Science*, 2006. **312**(5777): 1146–8.

Walter, K. M., et al., Methane bubbling from Siberian thaw lakes as a positive feedback to climate warming. *Nature*, 2006. **443**(7107): 71–75.

Zimov, S. A., E. A. Schuur, and F. S. Chapin III. Climate change. Permafrost and the global carbon budget. *Science*, 2006. **312**(5780): 1612–3.

Grünberg, J. M., et al., eds. *Mesolithic burials—Rites, symbols and social organisation of early postglacial communities.* 2013. Landesamt für Denkmalpflege und Archäologie Sachsen-Anhalt.

Mannino, M. A., et al., Climate-driven environmental changes around 8,200 years ago favoured increases in cetacean strandings and Mediterranean hunter-gatherers exploited them. *Sci Rep*, 2015. **5**: 16288.

Botigue, L. R., et al., Ancient European dog genomes reveal continuity since the early Neolithic. *Nat Commun*, 2017. **8**: 16082.

Thalmann, O., et al., Complete mitochondrial genomes of ancient canids suggest a European origin of domestic dogs. *Science*, 2013. **342**(6160): 871–74.

Arendt, M., et al., Diet adaptation in dog reflects spread of prehistoric agriculture. *Heredity* (Edinb), 2016. **117**(5): 301–6.

Mascher, M., et al., Genomic analysis of 6,000-year-old cultivated grain illuminates the domestication history of barley. *Nat Genet*, 2016. **48**(9): 1089–93.

Riehl, S., M. Zeidi, and N. J. Conard, Emergence of agriculture in the foothills of the Zagros Mountains of Iran. *Science*, 2013. **341**(6141): 65–67.

Larson, G., The evolution of animal domestication. *Annu Rev Ecol Evol Syst*, 2014. **45**: 115–36.

Gamba, C., et al., Genome flux and stasis in a five millennium transect of European prehistory. *Nat Commun*, 2014. **5**: 5257.

Feldman, M., et al., Late Pleistocene human genome suggests a local origin for the first farmers of central Anatolia. bioRxiv, 2018. DOI: 10.1101/422295.

Lazaridis, I., et al., Genomic insights into the origin of farming in the ancient Near East. *Nature*, 2016. **536**(7617): 419–24.

Lazaridis, I., et al., Ancient human genomes suggest three ancestral populations for present-day Europeans. *Nature*, 2014. **513**(7518): 409–13.

Mathieson, I., et al., Genome-wide patterns of selection in 230 ancient Eurasians. *Nature*, 2015. **528**(7583): 499–503.

Jablonski, N. G., and G. Chaplin, Human skin pigmentation as an adaptation to UV radiation. *Proc Natl Acad Sci USA*, 2010. **107**(Suppl 2): 8962–8.

Gamarra, B., et al., 5000 years of dietary variations of prehistoric farmers in the Great Hungarian Plain. *PLoS One*, 2018. **13**(5): e0197214.

Liem, E. B., et al., Increased sensitivity to thermal pain and reduced subcutaneous lidocaine efficacy in redheads. *Anesthesiology*, 2005. **102**(3): 509–14.

Ryan, C., et al., *Sex at Dawn: The Prehistoric Origins of Modern Sexuality*. 2010. Harper.

Uthmeier, T., Bestens angepasst—Jungpaläolithische Jäger und Sammler in Europa. In: H. Meller and Th. Puttkammer, eds., *Klimagewalten: Treibende Kraft der Evolution*. 2017. Konrad Theiss.

Behringer, W., Das wechselhafte Klima der letzten 1000 Jahre. In: H. Meller and Th. Puttkammer, eds., *Klimagewalten: Treibende Kraft der Evolution*. 2017. Konrad Theiss.

Müller, A., Was passiert, wenn es kälter oder wärmer wird? In: H. Meller and Th. Puttkammer, eds., *Klimagewalten: Treibende Kraft der Evolution*. 2017. Konrad Theiss.

Hallgren, F., et al., Skulls on stakes and in water. Mesolithic mortuary rituals at Kanaljorden, Motala, Sweden 7000 BP. In: J. M. Grünberg et al., eds., *Mesolithic burials—Rites, symbols and social organisation of early post-glacial communities.* 2013. Landesamt für Denkmalpflege und Archäologie Sachsen-Anhalt.

CHAPTER 4: PARALLEL SOCIETIES

Bollongino, R., et al., 2000 years of parallel societies in Stone Age Central Europe. *Science*, 2013. **342**(6157): 479–81.

Bajic, V., et al., Genetic structure and sex-biased gene flow in the history of southern African populations. *Am J Phys Anthropol*, 2018. **167**(3): 656–71.

Mummert, A., et al., Stature and robusticity during the agricultural transition: evidence from the bioarchaeological record. *Econ Hum Biol*, 2011. **9**(3): 284–301.

Cohen, M. N., and G. J. Armelagos, *Paleopathology and the Origins of Agriculture.* 1984. Academic Press.

Mischka, D., Flintbek LA 3, biography of a monument. *J Neolithic Archaeol*, 2010.

Brandt, G., et al., Ancient DNA reveals key stages in the formation of central European mitochondrial genetic diversity. *Science*, 2013. **342**(6155): 257–61.

Haak, W., et al., Massive migration from the steppe was a source for Indo-European languages in Europe. *Nature*, 2015. **522**(7555): 207–11.

Meller, H., M. Schefzik, and P. Ettel, eds., *Krieg—eine archäologische Spurensuche.* 2015. Konrad Theiss.

Meller, H., ed., *3300 BC. Mysteriöse Steinzeittote und ihre Welt.* 2013. Nünnerich-Asmus.

Mittnik, A., et al., The genetic prehistory of the Baltic Sea region. *Nat Commun*, 2018. **9**(1): 442.

Fugazzola Delpino, M. A., and M. Mineo, La piroga neolitica del lago di Bracciano, La Marmotta 1. *Bullettino di Paletnologia Italiana (Rome)*, 1995. **86**: 197–266.

Greenblatt, C., and M. Spigelman, *Emerging Pathogens: Archaeology, Ecology and Evolution of Infectious Disease.* 2003. Oxford University Press.

CHAPTER 5: SINGLE YOUNG MEN

Patterson, N., et al., Ancient admixture in human history. *Genetics*, 2012. **192**(3): 1065–93.

Skoglund, P., and D. Reich, A genomic view of the peopling of the Americas. *Curr Opin Genet Dev*, 2016. **41**: 27–35.

Raghavan, M., et al., Upper Palaeolithic Siberian genome reveals dual ancestry of Native Americans. *Nature*, 2014. **505**(7481): 87–91.

Allentoft, M. E., et al., Population genomics of Bronze Age Eurasia. *Nature*, 2015. **522**(7555): 167–72.

Anthony, D. W., *The Horse, the Wheel, and Language: How Bronze-Age Riders from the Eurasian Steppes Shaped the Modern World*. 2007. Princeton University Press.

Wang, C. C., et al., The genetic prehistory of the Greater Caucasus. bioRxiv, 2018. DOI: 10.1101/322347.

Mathieson, I., et al., The genomic history of southeastern Europe. *Nature*, 2018. **555**(7695): 197–203.

Andrades Valtuena, A., et al., The Stone Age plague and its persistence in Eurasia. *Curr Biol*, 2017. **27**(23): 3683–91 e8.

Olalde, I., et al., The Beaker phenomenon and the genomic transformation of northwest Europe. *Nature*, 2018. **555**(7695): 190–96.

Adler, W., Gustaf Kossinna. In: *Studien zum Kulturbegriff in der Vor- und Frühgeschichtsforschung*. 1987. R. Habelt.

Heyd, V., Kossina's smile. *Antiquity*, 2017. **91**(356): 348–59.

Kristiansen, K., et al., Re-theorizing mobility and the formation of culture and language among the Corded Ware cultures in Europe. *Antiquity*, 2017. **91**: 334–47.

Orlando, L., et al., Recalibrating Equus evolution using the genome sequence of an early Middle Pleistocene horse. *Nature*, 2013. **499**(7456): 74–78.

Gaunitz, C., et al., Ancient genomes revisit the ancestry of domestic and Przewalski's horses. *Science*, 2018. **360**(6384): 111–14.

Goldberg, A., et al., Ancient X chromosomes reveal contrasting sex bias in Neolithic and Bronze Age Eurasian migrations. *Proc Natl Acad Sci USA*, 2017. **114**(10): 2657–62.

Meller, H., A. Muhl, and K. Heckenhahn, *Tatort Eulau: Ein 4500 Jahre altes Verbrechen wird aufgeklärt*. 2010. Konrad Theiss.

Meller, H., and K. Michel, *Die Himmelsscheibe von Nebra: Der Schlüssel zu einer untergegangenen Kultur im Herzen Europas*. 2018. Propyläen Verlag.

Segurel, L., and C. Bon, On the evolution of lactase persistence in humans. *Annu Rev Genomics Hum Genet*, 2017. **18**: 297–319.

CHAPTER 6: EUROPEANS FIND A LANGUAGE

Haspelmath, M., M. S. Dryer, and D. Gil, *The World Atlas of Language Structures*. 2005. Oxford Linguistics.

Gray, R. D., Q. D. Atkinson, and S. J. Greenhill, Language evolution and human history: what a difference a date makes. *Philos Trans R Soc Lond B Biol Sci*, 2011. **366**(1567): 1090–100.

Renfrew, C., *Archaeology and Language: The Puzzle of Indo-European Origins*. 1987. Cambridge University Press.

Gray, R. D., and Q. D. Atkinson, Language-tree divergence times support the Anatolian theory of Indo-European origin. *Nature*, 2003. **426**(6965): 435–39.

Gimbutas, M., Culture change in Europe at the start of the second millennium B.C.: a contribution to the Indo-European problem. In: A. F. C. Wallace, ed., *Men and Cultures: Selected Papers of the Fifth International Congress of Anthropological and Ethnological Sciences*. 1956. University of Pennsylvania Press.

Kontler, L., *Millennium in Central Europe: A History of Hungary*. 1999. Atlantisz.

Narasimhan, V., et al., The genomic formation of South and Central Asia. bioRxiv, 2018. DOI: 10.1101/292581.

Wang, C. C., et al., The genetic prehistory of the Greater Caucasus. bioRxiv 2018. DOI: 10.1101/322347.

Jones, E. R., et al., Upper Palaeolithic genomes reveal deep roots of modern Eurasians. *Nat Commun*, 2015. **6**: 8912.

CHAPTER 7: REFUGEE SHIPS ON THE MEDITERRANEAN

Fokkens, H., and A. Harding, *The Oxford Handbook of the European Bronze Age*. 2013. Oxford University Press.

Anthony, D. W., *The Horse, the Wheel, and Language: How Bronze-Age Riders from the Eurasian Steppes Shaped the Modern World*. 2007. Princeton University Press.

Risch, R., Ein Klimasturz als Ursache für den Zerfall der alten Welt. In: *7. Mitteldeutscher Archäologentag*. 2014. Landesamt f. Denkmalpflege u. Archäologie Sachsen-Anhalt.

Knipper, C., et al., A distinct section of the Early Bronze Age society? Stable isotope investigations of burials in settlement pits and multiple inhumations of the Unetice culture in central Germany. *Am J Phys Anthropol*, 2016. **159**(3): 496–516.

Knipper, C., et al., Female exogamy and gene pool diversification at the transition from the Final Neolithic to the Early Bronze Age in central Europe. *Proc Natl Acad Sci USA*, 2017. **114**(38): 10083–8.

Mittnik, A., et al., Kinship-based social inequality in Bronze Age Europe. Unpublished, 2019.

Maran, J., and P. Stockhammer, *Appropriating Innovations: Entangled Knowledge in Eurasia, 5000–1500 BCE*. 2017. Oxbow Books.

Hofmanova, Z., et al., Early farmers from across Europe directly descended from Neolithic Aegeans. *Proc Natl Acad Sci USA*, 2016. **113**(25): 6886–91.

Meller, H., M. Schefzik, and P. Ettel, eds., *Krieg—eine archäologische Spurensuche*. 2015. Konrad Theiss.

Lidke, G., T. Terberger, and D. Jantzen, Das bronzezeitliche Schlachtfeld im Tollensetal—Krieg, Fehde oder Elitenkonflikt? In Meller, H., M. Schefzik, and P. Ettel, eds., *Krieg—eine archäologische Spurensuche*. 2015. Konrad Theiss.

Schiffels, S., et al., Iron Age and Anglo-Saxon genomes from East England reveal British migration history. *Nat Commun*, 2016. **7**: 10408.

Schrakamp, I., Militär und Kriegsführung in Vorderasien. In: H. Meller, M. Schefzik, and P. Ettel, eds., *Krieg—Eine archäologische Spurensuche*. 2015. Konrad Theiss.

Risch, R., et al., Vorwort der Herausgeber. In: H. Meller et al., eds., *2200 BC—Ein Klimasturz als Ursache für den Zerfall der Alten Welt?* 2015. Landesamt für Denkmalpflege und Archäologie Sachsen-Anhalt.

Weiss, H., Megadrought, collapse, and resilience in late 3rd millennium BC Mesopotamia. In: H. Meller et al., eds., *2200 BC—Ein Klimasturz als Ursache für den Zerfall der Alten Welt?* 2015. Landesamt für Denkmalpflege und Archäologie Sachsen-Anhalt.

CHAPTER 8: THEY BRING THE PLAGUE

Little, L. K., *Plague and the End of Antiquity: The Pandemic of 541–750*. 2007. Cambridge University Press.

Bos, K. I., et al., Eighteenth century *Yersinia pestis* genomes reveal the long-term persistence of an historical plague focus. *Elife*, 2016. **5**: e12994.

Bos, K. I., et al., Parallel detection of ancient pathogens via array-based DNA capture. *Philos Trans R Soc Lond B Biol Sci*, 2015. **370**(1660): 20130375.

Bos, K. I., et al., A draft genome of *Yersinia pestis* from victims of the Black Death. *Nature*, 2011. **478**(7370): 506–10.

Bos, K. I., et al., *Yersinia pestis*: new evidence for an old infection. *PLoS One*, 2012. **7**(11): e49803.

Du Toit, A., Continued risk of Ebola virus outbreak. *Nat Rev Microbiol*, 2018. **16**(9): 521.

Rasmussen, S., et al., Early divergent strains of *Yersinia pestis* in Eurasia 5,000 years ago. *Cell*, 2015. **163**(3): 571–82.

Achtman, M., et al., *Yersinia pestis*, the cause of plague, is a recently emerged clone of *Yersinia pseudotuberculosis*. *Proc Natl Acad Sci USA*, 1999. **96**(24): 14043–8.

Allocati, N., et al., Bat-man disease transmission: zoonotic pathogens from wildlife reservoirs to human populations. *Cell Death Discov*, 2016. **2**: 16048.

Armelagos, G. J., and K. Barnes, The evolution of human disease and the rise of allergy: epidemiological transitions. *Medical Anthropology: Cross Cultural Studies in Health and Illness*, 1999. **18**(2).

Armelagos, G. J., A. H. Goodman, and K. H. Jacobs, The origins of agriculture: population growth during a period of declining health. *Population and Environment*, 1991. **13**: 9–22.

Omran, A. R., The epidemiologic transition: a theory of the epidemiology of population change. *Milbank Mem Fund Q*, 1971. **49**(4): 509–38.

Gage, K. L., and M. Y. Kosoy, Natural history of plague: perspectives from more than a century of research. *Annu Rev Entomol*, 2005. **50**: 505–28.

Benedictow, O. J., *The Black Death, 1346–1353: The Complete History*. 2004. Boydell & Brewer.

Hinnebusch, B. J., C. O. Jarrett, and D. M. Bland, "Flea-ing" the plague: adaptations of *Yersinia pestis* to its insect vector that lead to transmission. *Annu Rev Microbiol*, 2017. **71**: 215–32.

Hinnebusch, B. J., and D. L. Erickson, *Yersinia pestis* biofilm in the flea vector and its role in the transmission of plague. *Curr Top Microbiol Immunol*, 2008. **322**: 229–48.

Wiechmann, I., and G. Grupe, Detection of *Yersinia pestis* DNA in two early medieval skeletal finds from Aschheim (Upper Bavaria, 6th century A.D.). *Am J Phys Anthropol*, 2005. **126**(1): 48–55.

Vagene, A. J., et al., *Salmonella enterica* genomes from victims of a major sixteenth-century epidemic in Mexico. *Nat Ecol Evol*, 2018. **2**(3): 520–28.

Andrades Valtuena, A., et al., The Stone Age plague and its persistence in Eurasia. *Curr Biol*, 2017. **27**(23): 3683–91 e8.

Rascovan, N., et al., Emergence and spread of basal lineages of *Yersinia pestis* during the Neolithic decline. *Cell*, 2018.

Hymes, R., Epilogue: a hypothesis on the East Asian beginnings of the *Yersinia pestis* polytomy. *Medieval Globe*, 2016. **1**(12).

Yersin, A., Sur la peste bubonique (sérothérapie). *Ann Inst Pasteur*, 1897. **11**: 81–93.

Bergdolt, K., *Über die Pest. Geschichte des Schwarzen Tods*. 2006. C. H. Beck.

Keller, M., et al., Ancient Yersinia pestis genomes from across Western Europe reveal early diversification during the first pandemic (541–750). bioRxiv. 2018. DOI: 10.1101/481226.

Wheelis, M., Biological warfare at the 1346 siege of Caffa. *Emerg Infect Dis*, 2002. **8**(9): 971–75.

Schulte-van Pol, K., D-Day 1347: Die Invasion des schwarzen Todes. *Die Zeit*, 1997. December 5.
Buntgen, U., et al., Digitizing historical plague. *Clin Infect Dis*, 2012. **55**(11): 1586–8.
Spyrou, M. A., et al., Historical *Y. pestis* genomes reveal the European Black Death as the source of ancient and modern plague pandemics. *Cell Host Microbe*, 2016. **19**(6): 874–81.
Spyrou, M. A., et al., A phylogeography of the second plague pandemic revealed through the analysis of historical *Y. pestis* genomes. bioRxiv. DOI: 10.1101/481242.

CHAPTER 9: NEW WORLD, NEW PANDEMICS

World Health Organization, *Wkly Epidemiol Rec*, 2011. **86**(389).
Brody, S. N., *The Disease of the Soul: Leprosy in Medieval Literature.* 1974. Cornell University Press.
Cole, S. T., et al., Massive gene decay in the leprosy bacillus. *Nature,* 2001. **409**(6823): 1007–11.
Daffé, M., and J.-M. Reyrat, eds. *The Mycobacterial Cell Envelope.* 2008. ASM Press.
World Health Organization, Fact sheet leprosy. 2015.
Robbins, G., et al., Ancient skeletal evidence for leprosy in India (2000 B.C.). *PLoS One*, 2009. **4**(5): e5669.
Schuenemann, V. J., et al., Ancient genomes reveal a high diversity of Mycobacterium leprae in medieval Europe. *PLoS Pathog*, 2018. **14**(5): e1006997.
Schuenemann, V. J., et al., Genome-wide comparison of medieval and modern *Mycobacterium leprae. Science*, 2013. **341**(6142): 179–83.
Truman, R. W., et al., Probable zoonotic leprosy in the southern United States. *N Engl J Med*, 2011. **364**(17): 1626–33.
Singh, P., et al., Insight into the evolution and origin of leprosy bacilli from the genome sequence of *Mycobacterium lepromatosis. Proc Natl Acad Sci USA*, 2015. **112**(14): 4459–64.
Avanzi, C., et al., Red squirrels in the British Isles are infected with leprosy bacilli. *Science*, 2016. **354**(6313): 744–47.
Irgens, L. M., [The discovery of the leprosy bacillus]. *Tidsskr Nor Laegeforen*, 2002. **122**(7): 708–9.
Cao, A., et al., Thalassaemia types and their incidence in Sardinia. *J Med Genet*, 1978. **15**(6): 443–47.
Wambua, S., et al., The effect of alpha+-thalassaemia on the incidence of ma-

laria and other diseases in children living on the coast of Kenya. *PLoS Med*, 2006. **3**(5): e158.

Luzzatto, L., Sickle cell anaemia and malaria. *Mediterr J Hematol Infect Dis*, 2012. **4**(1): e2012065.

O'Brien, S. J., and J. P. Moore, The effect of genetic variation in chemokines and their receptors on HIV transmission and progression to AIDS. *Immunol Rev*, 2000. **177**: 99–111.

Wirth, T., et al., Origin, spread and demography of the Mycobacterium tuberculosis complex. *PLoS Pathog*, 2008. **4**(9): e1000160.

World Health Organization, Tuberculosis (TB). 2018.

Brosch, R., et al., A new evolutionary scenario for the *Mycobacterium tuberculosis* complex. *Proc Natl Acad Sci USA*, 2002. **99**(6): 3684–9.

Comas, I., et al., Out-of-Africa migration and Neolithic coexpansion of Mycobacterium tuberculosis with modern humans. *Nat Genet*, 2013. **45**(10): 1176–82.

Bos, K. I., et al., Pre-Columbian mycobacterial genomes reveal seals as a source of New World human tuberculosis. *Nature*, 2014. **514**(7523): 494–97.

Vagene, A. J., et al., *Salmonella enterica* genomes from victims of a major sixteenth-century epidemic in Mexico. *Nat Ecol Evol*, 2018. **2**(3): 520–28.

Dobyns, H. F., Disease transfer at contact. *Annu Rev Anthropol*, 1993. **22**: 273–91.

Farhi, D., and N. Dupin, Origins of syphilis and management in the immunocompetent patient: facts and controversies. *Clin Dermatol*, 2010. **28**(5): 533–38.

Crosby, A. W., *The Columbian Exchange: Biological and Cultural Consequences of 1492*. 2003. Praeger.

Diamond, J. G., *Guns, Germs and Steel*. 1997. W. W. Norton.

Winau, R., *Seuchen und Plagen: Seit Armors Köcher vergiftete Pfeile führt*. 2002. Fundiert.

Schuenemann, V. J., et al., Historic *Treponema pallidum* genomes from Colonial Mexico retrieved from archaeological remains. *PLoS Negl Trop Dis*, 2018. **12**(6): e0006447.

Knauf, S., et al., Nonhuman primates across sub-Saharan Africa are infected with the yaws bacterium *Treponema pallidum* subsp. *pertenue*. *Emerg Microbes Infect*, 2018. **7**(1): 157.

Taubenberger, J. K., and D. M. Morens, 1918 influenza: the mother of all pandemics. *Emerg Infect Dis*, 2006. **12**(1): 15–22.

Gygli, S. M., et al., Antimicrobial resistance in *Mycobacterium tuberculosis*: mechanistic and evolutionary perspectives. *FEMS Microbiol Rev*, 2017. **41**(3): 354–73.

Findlater, A., and Bogoch, I. I., Human mobility and the global spread of infectious diseases: a focus on air travel. *Trends Parasitol*, 2018. **34**(9): 772–83.

CHAPTER 10: CONCLUSION

Findlater, A., and Bogoch, I. I., Human mobility and the global spread of infectious diseases: a focus on air travel. *Trends Parasitol*, 2018. **34**(9): 772–83.

Klein, L., Gustaf Kossinna: 1858–1931. In: T. Murray, ed., *Encyclopedia of Archaeology: The Great Archaeologists.* 1999. ABC-CLIO.

Kossinna, G., *Die Herkunft der Germanen. Zur Methode der Siedlungsarchäologie.* 1911. Kabitzsch.

Grünert, H., Gustaf Kossinna. Ein Wegbereiter der nationalsozialistischen Ideologie. In: A. Leube, ed., *Prähistorie und Nationalsozialismus: Die mittel-und osteuropäische Ur-und Früh geschichtsforschung in den Jahren 1933–1945*, 2002. Synchron Wissenschaftsverlag der Autoren.

Eggers, H. J., *Einführung in die Vorgeschichte.* 1959. Piper.

Eggert, M. K. H., *Archäologie. Grundzüge einer historischen Kulturwissenschaft.* 2006. A. Francke.

Schulz, M., Neolithic immigration: how Middle Eastern milk drinkers conquered Europe. *Spiegel*, 2010. October 15.

Martin, A. R., et al., An unexpectedly complex architecture for skin pigmentation in Africans. *Cell*, 2017. **171**(6): 1340–53 e14.

Jinek, M., et al., A programmable dual-RNA-guided DNA endonuclease in adaptive bacterial immunity. *Science*, 2012. **337**(6096): 816–21.

Wade, N., Researchers say intelligence and diseases may be linked in Ashkenazic genes. *New York Times*, 2005. June 6.

Gauland, A., Warum muss es Populismus sein? *Frankfurter Allgemeine Zeitung*, 2018. October 6.

Rosling, H., *Factfulness: Wie wir lernen, die Welt so zu sehen, wie sie wirklich ist.* 2018. Ullstein.

Ahrendt, H., *Elemente und Ursprünge totaler Herrschaft: Antisemitismus. Imperialismus. Totale Herrschaft.* 1955. Piper.

Seibel, A., et al., Mögen Sie keine Türken, Herr Sarrazin? *Welt am Sonntag*, 2010. August 29.

Hunt-Grubbe, C. The elementary DNA of Dr Watson. *Sunday Times*, 2007. October 14.

IMAGE CREDITS

Annette Günzel, Berlin: p. 200

Archäologisches Landesmuseum Baden-Württemberg, M. Schreiner, Z. Konstanz [Ausstellungsort Urgeschichtliches Museum Blaubeuren]: pp. 42–44

Deutsches Archäologisches Institut, Göbekli Tepe Project: p. 69

Herzog August Bibliothek, Wolfenbüttel: p. 161

Kunstmuseum Basel, Martin P. Bühler: p. 173

Landesamt für Denkmalpflege und Archäologie Sachsen-Anhalt, Juraj Lipták: p. 147

Landesamt für Denkmalpflege und Archäologie Sachsen-Anhalt, Karol Schauer: pp. 63, 86, 94, 111

Museum Ulm, Oleg Kuchar: p. 43

The American Association for the Advancement of Science: p. 228

The Trustees of the British Museum: p. 179

Thomas T., https://www.flickr.com/photos/theadventurouseye/5602930382/: p. 49

Vandenhoeck & Ruprecht Verlage: p. 150

Private: pp. 9, 16, 17, 102, 132

INDEX

Notes: Page numbers in *italics* refer to maps and illustrations. Page numbers after 242 refer to Notes section.

PHOTO: © JOHANNES KÜNZEL

JOHANNES KRAUSE was a founding director of the Max Planck Institute for the Science of Human History in Jena, Germany, and is now heading the department of archaeogenetics at the Max Planck Institute for Evolutionary Anthropology in Leipzig, Germany, and the Max Planck–Harvard Research Center for the Archaeoscience of the Ancient Mediterranean. His research has been featured in numerous television, radio, print, and online media sources, including *The New York Times, The Washington Post,* BBC, Discovery Channel, *National Geographic,* and more.

THOMAS TRAPPE is one of Germany's leading health journalists. He is an editor in chief at Berlin's *Tagesspiegel,* where he covers politics, health policy, and science. Before coauthoring *A Short History of Humanity,* Trappe had reported on Johannes Krause's research numerous times, having followed his work for many years.